Feminist Fandom

Feminist Fandom

Media Fandom, Digital Feminisms, and Tumblr

Briony Hannell

BLOOMSBURY ACADEMIC
NEW YORK • LONDON • OXFORD • NEW DELHI • SYDNEY

BLOOMSBURY ACADEMIC
Bloomsbury Publishing Inc
1385 Broadway, New York, NY 10018, USA
50 Bedford Square, London, WC1B 3DP, UK
29 Earlsfort Terrace, Dublin 2, Ireland

BLOOMSBURY, BLOOMSBURY ACADEMIC and the Diana logo are
trademarks of Bloomsbury Publishing Plc

First published in the United States of America 2024

Cover design by Annabel Hewitson | Images © iStock

Bloomsbury Publishing Inc does not have any control over, or responsibility for, any
third-party websites referred to or in this book. All internet addresses given in this
book were correct at the time of going to press. The author and publisher regret
any inconvenience caused if addresses have changed or sites have ceased
to exist, but can accept no responsibility for any such changes.

A catalog record for this book is available from the Library of Congress.

ISBN: HB: 979-8-7651-0180-3
ePDF: 979-8-7651-0178-0
eBook: 979-8-7651-0177-3

Typeset by Integra Software Services Pvt. Ltd.

To find out more about our authors and books visit www.bloomsbury.com
and sign up for our newsletters.

For the feminist fans whose words, insights and experiences populate Feminist Fandom. *I hope I have done them justice. This research would not, and could not, exist without them.*

Contents

List of illustrations

Acknowledgements

Thank you to my brilliant friends, mentors, and colleagues at the University of East Anglia (UEA) and the University of Sheffield for making this research possible. Thank you to Helen Warner, John Street, and Tom Phillips for their intellectual and personal mentorship, for their endless patience and good humour, and for their accidentally coordinated knitwear. Thank you to Debra Ferreday and Alison Winch for an insightful and all-round enjoyable viva examination. Thank you to the members of the Feminist Media Studies Research Group and the Cultural Politics, Communications, and Media Research Group at UEA for providing a lively and engaging research culture. Thank you to Sarah Ralph and the late Martin Barker for cultivating my initial interest in fan studies, to Tori Cann for providing invaluable feedback during the early stages of this project and remaining an advocate since, to Fi Roxburgh for being a pillar of support throughout my formative years, and to Ysabel Gerrard for her mentorship as I navigate early career academia. Thank you to my editor, Katie Gallof, and to Stephanie Grace-Petinos at Bloomsbury Academic for their advice and encouragement throughout the writing process. Thank you also to the anonymous reviewers who commented on my proposal and manuscript so generously and constructively. *Feminist Fandom* is all the better for it.

I am unconditionally thankful for my friends, family, and loved ones who have supported me throughout this long process. There are more than I can possibly thank here. A heartfelt thank you to Faayza for her endless love and generosity of spirit. Thank you to Andrea, Charlotte E., Charlotte H., Floor, and Gemma for their all-round good vibes and their mutual love for handicrafts, errands, and soup season. Thank you to The Canoe for more than a decade of shared fandom and feels, for supporting my ventures into aca-fandom, and for so skilfully finding ways to hang out across six time zones. Thank you to my postgraduate researcher friends, writing companions, and trade union comrades for providing a sense of community and belonging at UEA – even during a global pandemic! Thank you to my parents: my mother, Karen, for so generously giving me the benefit of the doubt while I was glued to my laptop as an internet-obsessed teen, and my late father, Chris, for instilling in me a lifelong fannishness. Thank you to my beloved sister, Becky, for being a wonderful sister and an even better friend. Finally, an enormous thank you to my partner and best friend, Josh, for everything and so much more.

Introduction

Over the past decade, contemporary popular culture has been marked by the resurgence of feminist politics. From the selection of high-profile celebrities declaring their identification with feminism, to popular feminist books dominating the bestseller charts, to the coverage of 'feminist' issues in popular magazines including *Elle* and *Teen Vogue*, to the #MeToo movement against rape culture and sexual violence, popular culture has itself rendered feminism 'popular' (Banet-Weiser 2018, 156). These visibilities and popularity have been heightened by the affordances of participatory digital media technologies, which have enabled feminists to share dialogue, exchange information, network, organize, and mobilize in vast and varied ways. The relationship between digital media technologies, popular culture, and feminism has subsequently been examined, for example, with regard to school- and university-based feminisms (Lewis, Marine, and Kenney 2016; Kim and Ringrose 2018); testimonial projects such as Hollaback!, Everyday Sexism, and #MeToo (Wånggren 2016; Mendes, Keller, and Ringrose 2019; Durham 2021); and the circulation and reception of celebrity feminisms (Tennent and Jackson 2017; Chidgey 2021).

Additionally, the visibility of popular feminism within participatory digital media spaces, particularly on social media, has been described as instrumental to the increasing numbers of girls and young women identifying themselves as feminists (Keller 2016a; Jackson 2018). This marks a shift away from an earlier sociocultural context in which feminism was largely repudiated by girls and young women. In fact, contemporary feminism is increasingly signified as a 'popular' (Banet-Weiser 2018), 'cool' (Valenti 2014), 'stylish' (Gill 2016a, b), and ultimately desirable identity in complex, and often contradictory, ways that call for the continuing need to critically re-evaluate and re-examine the contours of young people's engagements with contemporary feminisms.

However, one under-theorized site of young people's engagement with feminism is media fandom. While recent accounts have noted the increasing slippage between feminism, digital cultures, and popular culture, few have located media fandom at this juncture. As communities formed around a shared and sustained interest in specific media texts or media cultures, media fans are deeply invested in critiquing and celebrating popular culture in ways that resonate throughout discussions of the messy entanglement of feminism, digital cultures, and the politics of popular culture. Moreover, many online fan communities are located at the very sites associated with particularly high levels of digital feminist activism, such as Tumblr and Twitter, where the networked nature of these platforms brings fannish and feminist communities together.

Forging a sustained dialogue between feminist cultural studies and fan studies, this book examines the nature of the relationship between media fandom and young people's engagements with digital feminisms. Throughout this book, I address three key and interrelated research questions: Firstly, what is the role of fandom in the development of young people's feminist identities? Secondly, how do feminist fan communities bring together both fannish and feminist discourses, practices, and positionalities? Finally, what is the role of the micro-blogging and social networking platform Tumblr in facilitating these connections between media fandom and digital feminisms?

Drawing upon a range of interdisciplinary frameworks rooted in an anti-foundationalist and constructivist feminist epistemology, my research is based on a digital ethnography of what I term 'feminist fandom' on Tumblr. Tumblr emerged as my primary research site for several reasons. Firstly, the site has, since its conception in 2007, developed a reputation as a platform that is largely populated by marginalized groups, including LGBT youth, girls and young women, and people of colour (McCracken et al. 2020; Tiidenberg, Hendry, and Abidin 2021). It is also an important site where fan communities, many members of whom belong to the aforementioned groups, convene. This reputation circulates in both academic and popular discussions of the site. For example, mainstream journalistic coverage of Tumblr describes its users as having 'a strong interest in social justice issues' (Safronova 2014), as 'help[ing] to queer an entire generation' (Madden 2019), and as committed to 'open, self-governing exchange of ideas' (Watercutter 2019).

Secondly, the technological affordances of Tumblr differentiate it from other popular social media platforms such as Facebook. Unlike Facebook, where explicit 'identity cues' (Baym 2015), including one's real name, age, location, occupation, relationship status, etc., are required for meaningful participation, the only identity information Tumblr requires a user to provide is their age,[1] email address, and a username. Tumblr affords users a high level of control over their self-presentation, visibility, and disclosure of identity information that many social networking sites do not. The platform therefore invites engagements from users for whom a sense of privacy, if not full anonymity, may be preferred, lending itself to participation from those seeking to explore identities, issues, and interests that may be unwelcome elsewhere. These technological affordances make the site particularly conducive to 'counterpublic' (Fraser 1990) modes of address that are of great importance to the digital circulation, and contestation, of contemporary feminisms.

Finally, my insider position as an acafan (see Cristofari and Guitton 2017), an academic *and* fan, immersed in the feminist fan community on Tumblr before undertaking this research, provided invaluable access to the feminist fans whose voices and experiences I detail throughout *Feminist Fandom*. My personal engagement not only provided a point of reciprocity, accountability, and transparency between myself and participants but was also key to producing a complex understanding of feminist fandom grounded in prolonged deep immersion within the feminist fan community. While the digital environment is slippery, and fannish and feminist practices on Tumblr can be located within a networked and multi-sited digital ecology, my work focuses primarily on a single research site, Tumblr, for the above reasons yet nevertheless reveals fannish and feminist discourses, practices, and positionalities that resonate beyond it.

Feminist Fandom subsequently draws upon ethnographic data gathered over a four-year period through narrative survey, follow-up interviews, and participant observation to unpack the experiences of young people who are engaging with feminist discourses, practices, and positionalities in a routine, informal and everyday way through their ties to media fandom on Tumblr during the 2010s. In doing so, I foreground the close relationship between feminist cultural studies and fan studies methodologically, theoretically, and empirically. Moreover, I argue that, just as feminist cultural studies and fan studies are connected (Hannell 2020b), so too are digital feminisms and media fandom. Examining the nature of this connection is important because it grants us insight into an overlooked site of young people's engagement with digital feminism. My analysis locates media fandom as a space in which meanings of feminism are produced, negotiated, and contested in a routine, informal, and everyday way. Throughout *Feminist Fandom*, I emphasize the intimate relationship between popular culture, media fandom, and feminist pedagogy and position fandom as an important and accessible space for bringing feminism to a wider audience and providing space for 'the multiplicity of voices therein' (Harvey 2020, 57).

In what follows I will outline the intellectual and cultural context in which *Feminist Fandom* is located. Firstly, I offer an overview of debates about contemporary feminisms with regard to the supposed move away from postfeminism. I then discuss the circularity between fourth-wave feminisms, popular culture, and digital cultures, while also highlighting various points of continuity and change between fourth-wave feminisms and their predecessors. Finally, I locate media fandom at the juncture between fourth-wave feminisms, popular culture, and digital cultures before presenting an overview of my methodology and the subsequent chapters of the book.

Emergent feminisms: From post to popular

Since the 1990s, the concept of postfeminism has become central to feminist cultural analysis. The concept is contentious and has been characterized in numerous ways: as a regressive backlash against feminism; to refer to a time after (second-wave) feminism; to signify an epistemological break with second-wave feminism and alignment with other 'post-' anti-foundationalist movements, such as postmodernism, poststructuralism, and postcolonialism; and to propose a historical shift towards third-wave feminism. The term, as Diane Negra (2004) highlights, 'exhibits a plasticity that enables it to be used in contradictory ways'.

Rosalind Gill (2007c) encourages us to move beyond understandings of postfeminism as an epistemological break, as a historical shift, or simply as backlash. Instead, she conceives of postfeminism as a distinctive 'sensibility' deeply enmeshed within neoliberalism. Gill highlights several relatively stable features and interrelated themes that comprise or constitute a postfeminist discourse: the shift from sexual objectification to sexual subjectification; the notion of femininity as a bodily property; the emphasis upon self-surveillance, monitoring, and self-discipline; the emphasis on individualism, choice, agency, and empowerment; the dominance of the makeover paradigm; and the sexualization of culture. Gill argues that the patterned articulation of these ideas constitutes a postfeminist sensibility. Moreover, she argues that these themes coexist with, and are structured by, continuing inequalities and exclusions that relate to ethnicity, class, age, sexuality, and disability – as well as gender. Postfeminism, she argues, is part of a neoliberal political economy (see Rottenberg 2018) that produces specifically gendered subjects that reaffirm normative gender, race, class, and sexual identities (see Gill and Scharff 2011; Scharff 2016). Postfeminist discourses are thus implicated in the 'undoing' of feminism (McRobbie 2009), and postfeminism is often adopted as a theoretical framework to explore girls' and young women's dis-identification with feminism and feminist politics in the contemporary era.

However, the analytic purchase of postfeminism has more recently been called into question by feminist scholars who have challenged the dominant logic that feminism is 'in retreat' (McRobbie 2009). For these scholars, feminism's increased visibility, embrace, and circulation within popular media cultures over the past decade have made visible a shift in the relationship between feminism, identity politics, and popular media cultures that calls for a re-evaluation of the utility of postfeminism as a critical-analytic framework to make sense of our cultural landscape. Negra (2014, 275), for example, questions whether 'accounts of gender developed in an earlier and distinctly different economic era still apply'. Similarly, Keller and Ryan (2015) argue that postfeminism is potentially redundant in the light of emergent fourth-wave feminisms which harbour the potential to rupture or displace the postfeminist sensibility Gill describes. However, while Gill (2016a) acknowledges that the position of feminism within the contemporary era has several novel features, she cautions that it may be premature to claim we have moved 'beyond' postfeminism entirely.

Nevertheless, over the past decade, feminism has become increasingly visible across popular media culture, centred across popular television programmes and films, popular music, fashion media, advertising campaigns, digital cultures, celebrity culture, and popular literature. As a result, the renewed visibility of feminism has produced a cultural formation in which feminism is increasingly positioned as 'cool' (Valenti 2014), 'popular' (Banet-Weiser 2015b, 2018), 'trending' (Guillard 2016), and 'stylish' (Gill 2016a, b) to such an extent that it has become, as Sarah Banet-Weiser (2018, 7) writes, 'both hypervisible and normative within popular media'. This moves us away from an earlier context in which feminism was largely repudiated by girls and young women (McRobbie 2009; Scharff 2012). While popular manifestations of feminism are not unique to the twenty-first century (see, e.g. Dow 1996), they remain an important space for a *new* generation of feminist theorizing.

Crucially, I want to emphasize that the current moment in feminism does not represent a unified, singular popular feminism. Instead, it consists of a messy, often fraught, entanglement of different feminisms competing within what

Sarah Banet-Weiser (2018) describes as an 'economy of visibility'. As she notes, precisely because feminism is now located in the 'popular', which is, as cultural theorist Stuart Hall ([1981] 2016) argues, 'a terrain of struggle', it is a space where

> competing demands for power battle it out. This means that there are many different feminisms that circulate in popular culture in the current moment, and some of these feminisms become more visible than others.
>
> (Banet-Weiser 2018, 1)

Feminist scholars have subsequently used a variety of terms, often critically, to describe contemporary feminisms: 'celebrity' (Prins 2017), 'popular' or 'pop' (Smith-Prei and Stehle 2016; Banet-Weiser 2018), 'mainstream' (Olufemi 2020; Phipps 2020), 'intersectional' (Villesèche, Muhr, and Śliwa 2018), 'queer' (Marinucci 2010), 'public' (Keller 2020), 'emergent' (Harris 2010; Keller and Ryan 2018), and 'neoliberal' (Rottenberg 2018). For Banet-Weiser (2018), contemporary popular feminisms exist along a continuum, where spectacular, media-friendly feminisms achieve more visibility, and thus popularity, while more critical expressions of feminism rooted in structural critique are obscured. An understanding of contemporary feminism as slippery and multiplicitous, as *feminisms*, is therefore necessary. This context shapes my deliberate use of the plural term 'feminisms' in this book's title. When I refer to the singular form 'feminism', I do so while recognizing that feminism is itself inherently plural.

However, there is no 'authentic' feminism that exists beyond its popular manifestations, and the popular itself remains a site of struggle over the meanings of feminism. Rather than dismissing popular feminisms in favour of some 'real' or 'authentic' feminism which is 'elsewhere' (Brunsdon 1997, 101), I take up Scharff's (2012) insistence that feminism must be approached 'flexibly' in recognition of the multiple iterations of the word. Writing of the need to observe the range of perspectives and positionalities that fall under the rubric of feminism, Kaplan (2003) reminds us:

> That there is no monolithic feminism is a good, if at times uncomfortable, fact: positions, actions and knowledge – constantly being contested, questioned, and debated – mean that feminism is alive and well, and always changing in accord with larger social, historical and political changes.
>
> (47)

Moreover, Budgeon (2001) highlights that popular feminisms provide interpretative frameworks for young feminists to understand and engage with feminism. While popular feminism is not without critique, it remains crucial in making feminist discourses and identities accessible and intelligible to those outside of academia. As Skeggs (1997, 144) notes, 'fragmentation, dispersal and the marketability and notoriety of certain aspects of feminism' means that many have a 'limited and partial knowledge about feminism'. Additionally, one of the most accessible types of feminist discourse available to girls and young women within their everyday lives is popular feminism. For example, while research suggests that teen girls feel scepticism towards celebrity feminism (Keller and Ringrose 2015; Jackson 2020), they also recognize their desire for a 'visible feminist presence' (Zaslow 2009, 128) within popular media culture. Thus, the cultural work of these popular manifestations of feminism enables many girls and young women to more 'confidently perform a once scorned feminist identity' (Keller 2016a, 183). In turn, while feminist scholars express ambivalence towards 'popular feminism', they also note that 'the overlaps and intersections of affect, desire, critique, and ambivalence that characterise popular feminism are potentially opening spaces for, and connections to, mobilising feminist practice' (Banet-Weiser 2018, xi). Given this, over the past decade we have witnessed rapid transformations in both the way feminist politics and identities circulate and are taken up within the contemporary moment, as well in our understandings of girls and young women's engagements with feminism.

Mapping fourth-wave feminisms

The renewed interest in feminisms within the public sphere has led many to describe the contemporary feminist zeitgeist as ushering in a 'fourth wave' of feminism. While the wave metaphor is contentious, and some have argued that we are in fact 'beyond the waves' (Smith-Prei and Stehle 2016, 49), many feminists continue to define themselves through the wave metaphor and produce academic evaluations of certain identities and practices within this framework. The metaphor subsequently persists, and the term 'fourth wave' appears in both academic (Rivers 2017; Lawrence and Ringrose 2018) and popular (Solomon 2009; Cochrane 2013) discussions of contemporary feminism. Given its persistence, we should engage critically with the wave metaphor and consider the role of feminist continuity and feminist change as part of this critical engagement. As Keller and Ryan (2018) note, contemporary feminisms are emerging 'in ways that both converge with, and diverge from, the feminisms of previous decades' (2).

Given the multiplicity of feminisms circulating in the contemporary era, there is no singular understanding of the 'fourth wave'. However, it can be broadly characterized by two key features: firstly, the increasing take-up of digital media technologies for feminist activism and debate and, secondly, an increased public and media engagement with, and interest in, feminism(s), particularly within popular media cultures. The wave metaphor is primarily used within accounts of fourth-wave feminism as a way of thinking through feminist practice chronologically, wherein the 'newness' of the fourth wave is signified by the hypervisibility of feminism with popular media cultures, as well as the recent explosion in the number of websites, blogs, and online networked communities that facilitate feminist community building, practice, and activism.

Digital cultures

For many feminist scholars, the conceptual distinction between third-wave and fourth-wave feminisms rests largely on the 'new model for feminism being built online' (Valenti 2009), particularly on social media platforms. Proponents of the fourth wave argue that the proliferation of feminist discourse and activism online, initially through blogging platforms and later through networked social media, has had a profound impact on contemporary feminisms. Social media platforms such as Twitter, Facebook, and Tumblr have been identified as shaping feminist pedagogy and contemporary feminist activism, resulting in the cultivation of new modes of feminist cultural critique and 'models of political agency for practising feminism' (Rentschler and Thrift 2015, 329).

For example, 'hashtag feminism' is now a popular form of digital feminist activism, providing opportunities for feminists to connect, share information and resources, and establish solidarities. Hashtags, denoted by the # symbol that precedes them, are shared terms used to make social media posts, particularly on platform such as Twitter, both searchable and collectable. Hashtags specifically related to feminist causes have made an indelible mark on feminist activism over the past decade, and researchers have examined a range of feminist hashtags tackling issues such as rape culture, sexual violence, intersectionality, popular culture, gendered harassment, border violence, trans rights, racialized police brutality, and violence against women (Thrift 2014; Jiménez 2016; Keller, Mendes, and Ringrose 2016; Durham 2021). Feminist hashtags have been positioned as a new form of collective 'discursive activism' (Clark 2016) that, through their visibility, generates a wider feminist consciousness. Moreover, the reach of hashtag feminism is not restricted to Anglophone countries in the Global North, and feminist researchers have subsequently examined feminist hashtag activism across the Global South (e.g. see Akyel 2014; Jun 2021).

Similarly, the feminist 'blogosphere', which Jessalynn Keller (2012a, 137) defines as 'a loose affiliation of blogs dedicated to discussing feminism and gender inequality', has also been described in terms of its ability to generate a wider feminist consciousness and broaden the scope of public feminist dialogue. While methodologically difficult to measure, researchers have claimed that girls and young women are the largest group of creators and readers of blogs and social networking websites (boyd 2007; Lenhart 2015). Blogs and social networking sites have been described as 'a virtual room of one's own' for girls (Mitchell and Reid-Walsh 2004) and as 'safe spaces' (Mazzarella and Pecora 2007) from which young women speak out. They therefore harbour enormous potential in terms of consciousness-raising, campaigning, organizing, and feminist activism and pedagogy.

The analysis of digital feminist spaces often draws upon Nancy Fraser's (1990) popular concept of subaltern 'counterpublics', which Fraser defines as 'parallel discursive arenas' (67) that, historically, have 'contested the exclusionary norms of the bourgeois public, elaborating alternative styles of political behaviour and alternative norms of public speech' (61). Fraser's concept of counterpublics has been widely used within feminist scholarship to build a compelling case for the emergence of online feminist counterpublics (Salter 2013; Keller, Mendes, and Ringrose 2016; Sills et al. 2016; Clark-Parsons 2018) and to emphasize the importance of girls' and young women's use of new media technologies (Harris 2008b; Keller 2016a). Increasing numbers of girls and young women are developing online 'networks of affinity' (Rentschler 2014, 79) and producing their own media and online counterpublics to express, enact, and network around their feminist politics. Online spaces, in this respect, can make it easier for subaltern voices to find their way into popular consciousness.

While the modality of these forms of online feminist practice and activism may well be new, the issues that feminists are addressing through these digital practices have a rich and established history that precedes fourth-wave feminism. The practice of hashtag feminist activism can, therefore, be conceptualized as developing continuities between fourth-wave feminism and earlier feminist practices designed to generate a wider feminist consciousness. Moreover, the modes of community building and consciousness-raising situated within the digital landscape of fourth-wave feminism can be understood as a continuation of established feminist practice. For example, both Keller (2016a) and Smith-Prei and Stehle (2016) situate feminist blogging as a continuation of earlier feminist forms through their interest in dialogue, community building, consciousness-raising, and information sharing. This interrupts the markedly 'linear' (Hemmings 2011) understanding of fourth-wave feminism as an entirely 'new' and decontextualized phenomena. However, the affordances of networked digital technologies have nevertheless made these feminisms highly visible in unprecedented ways through their collapsing of temporal and spatial constraints. We thus cannot abandon the notion of 'newness' entirely.

Popular culture

Another key feature of fourth-wave feminism is its complicated entanglement with popular culture. This entanglement, the 'push and pull of feminism and pop' (Smith-Prei and Stehle 2016, 171), has been conceptualized in two distinct yet interrelated ways. The first involves an understanding of fourth-wave feminism *in/as popular culture*, drawing largely upon feminisms' hypervisibility and circulation within popular media cultures. This perspective recognizes the potential for feminist critique that resides within popular culture and highlights popular culture's position as a site at which meanings of feminism are contested, co-opted, and produced. The second focuses on fourth-wave feminism as *popular critique of popular culture*. This refers to the incorporation of feminism into popular culture, as well as the increased accessibility, and popularization, of feminist analyses and critiques of popular culture that manifest through cultural consumption and production. Reflecting on the slippage between these two understandings of the relationship between fourth-wave feminism and popular culture, Banet-Weiser and Portwood-Stacer (2017, 884; original emphasis) write:

> Feminism has always been a useful lens through which to *understand* popular culture. However, we now are living in a moment when feminism has undeniably *become* popular culture.

For example, Cattien (2019) encourages us to consider the potential of feminist critique to reside within popular culture, as well as the potential of popular culture to adopt 'feminism' as an object of critique. Likewise, Hollows and Moseley (2006) encourage feminists not only to examine what feminism might reveal about popular culture but also to 'examine what popular culture can tell us about feminism' (1). Taking this further, Smith-Prei and Stehle (2016, 56) draw attention to the circularity between fourth-wave feminisms and popular culture. They emphasize that fourth-wave feminisms

> [use] feminism to recode pop culture and pop [culture] to rewrite feminism ... [fourth-wave feminism] provides a feminist approach to pop culture, but it also critiques and redefines both feminism and pop culture.

Crucially, they add, the critique of popular culture by popular feminisms reproduces the popularization and visibility of feminism in the very act of critique. It is in this sense that the mutually constitutive relationship between fourth-wave feminism *in/as popular culture* and as *popular critique of popular culture* comes into being. While popular culture is often the target of popular fourth-wave feminist critique, it also produces the conditions that bring this popular feminist critique into being. It 'mirrors (and messes with) the politics of pop culture' (Smith-Prei and Stehle 2016, 172).

Subsequently, analysing and critiquing social and cultural phenomena through a feminist lens, particularly within the context of popular culture, is one of the core practices of fourth-wave feminisms. Feminist critiques of popular culture have become so pervasive that they have come to constitute popular culture. For example, this is made visible by the proliferation of websites and blogs, both major and minor, devoted to 'the analysis of popular culture and media through a feminist lens' (Naylor 2016, 43). Additionally, Cattien (2019) points to the recent 'genre-fication of feminism' (329) within popular media culture. This, she argues, refers to the number of sociocultural phenomena becoming paratextually tied to the term 'feminist' in ways that facilitate or encourage particular modes of cultural consumption, production, and critique in line with the emergence of popular feminism. According to Ferreday and Harris (2017, 2), popular feminist politics

> [p]ay attention not only to the new representational contexts of popular culture and the effects of their modes of communication and dissemination, but also to the ethics of valuing and recognising gendered and racialised forms of cultural production.

Contemporary feminisms' preoccupation with popular cultural consumption, production, and critique can be contextualized in relation to earlier forms of feminist critique governed by a politics of recognition that situates feminist politics within the realm of the cultural and the symbolic. According to Fraser (1997), recognition feminism positions the cultural and the symbolic as sites of social change and is marked by the belief that 'injustice is rooted in social patterns of representation, interpretation, and communication' (14). Recognition feminism is therefore primarily concerned with issues of 'representation, identity, and difference' (Fraser 2013, 160). Feminist scholars' preoccupation with the relationship between gender, cultural narratives and representations, and structures of power and domination is produced by a politics of recognition (see van Zoonen 1994; Thornham 2007; Gill 2007b; Harvey 2020). This politic resonates throughout feminist histories. For example, feminist research on cultural representations, particularly in film and television, gained momentum during the second wave in the 1970s (Butcher et al. 1974; Mulvey 1975; Tuchman 1979). Similarly, third-wave feminisms were particularly invested in recognition feminism through their attention to representations, communication, fluid-shifting identities, and cultural production (hooks 1996; Harris 2008a; Piepmeier 2009; Zaslow 2009). While second-wave popular cultural critique was governed more by a politics of refusal or rejection, third-wave critique often invested itself in the subversion and remixing of popular culture for feminist ends, resulting in the development of a DIY-feminist ethos captured most saliently, perhaps, within feminist zine culture. Fourth-wave feminisms have somewhat moved away from the third wave's withdrawal to alternative feminist spaces and cultures and can instead be largely located, as discussed, within the terrain of the popular through their heightened visibility and circulation within popular media cultures. The proliferation of contemporary fourth-wave campaigns that are 'themselves *about cultural representation*' (Gill 2016a, 616; my emphasis) speaks to the continued importance of a politics of recognition to these new feminist visibilities of the twenty-first century. Fourth-wave feminism embraces modes of popular cultural critique that are not grounded in refusal or rejection but in close and passionate engagement with popular media cultures that are both critical and embracing. As Piepmeier (2009, 172–3) notes, contemporary feminists 'critique the media and also consume it hungrily, but in both modes they take it seriously, recognising that the symbolic realm is an important site for democratic struggle'.

Fourth-wave feminisms' entanglement with popular culture is also intimately connected to its digital formations precisely because digital cultures are integral to the circulation of both popular culture *and* popular feminisms. The affordances of digital media technologies allow for the immediate popularization of feminist discourses across both national and cultural borders, as well as the transnational (albeit uneven) flow, or 'spread' (Jenkins, Ford, and Green 2013), of popular media culture. Fourth-wave feminisms, digital cultures, and popular culture subsequently exist in a co-constitutive and multidirectional relationship. As Smith-Prei and Stehle (2016, 59) argue,

> [d]igital culture is an integral part of pop cultural circulation. If digital culture distinctly drives popular culture today, then … feminist activisms not only use but also productively disturb the digital economy; however, this means that the digital economy disturbs and reconfigures feminisms.

The entanglement of feminist activism, digital culture, and popular culture is symptomatic of a broader shift during the late-modern era towards modes of cultural citizenship that correspond with cultural identities and practices and address questions of social inclusion and exclusion (Zobl and Drüeke 2012; Hannell 2021). Contemporary feminisms have taken on more cultural and decollectivized forms consistent with broader shifts in protest politics away from hierarchical, vertically organized institutions and organizations. Instead, contemporary feminisms are often marked by their focus on popular media and culture, personal action and voice, and digital media and communication technologies. It is at this juncture, I argue, that we may turn our attention towards media fandom.

Tumblr, media fandom, and social justice

The entanglement of fourth-wave feminisms, digital culture, and popular culture signify feminisms' deeply invested relationship with popular culture, through acts of cultural consumption, production, and critique, in a manner that is not dissimilar from the mixtures of celebration and critique, fascination and frustration, that characterize media fandom (Jenkins 2006b). While fans are often characterized by the depth of their textual and affective immersion in a *specific* set of popular culture texts, feminist and fannish modes of cultural critique are marked both by their creativity and critical engagement and by a combination of 'frustration and fascination' (Jenkins 2006a, 247), or of 'outrage and delight' (Piepmeier 2009, 174), with popular culture texts and media representation. Johnson (2003, 11) describes this combination of outrage and delight as the feminist embrace of 'the conflict. And the glee'. Similarly, Ferreday (2015, 23) draws attention to the connections between feminism and fandom, noting that both are marked by 'an intense engagement with media'. Fandom, she argues, brings together feminist practices of media critique as well as DIY media production.[2]

Moreover, the digital contours of fourth-wave feminisms also resemble those of contemporary media fandom. Like the renewed visibility of feminism, the 'mainstreaming' of fandom and its practices (Jenner 2017) has also been mediated by popular culture and digital culture. With advancements in digital media technologies encouraging audiences to cultivate a traditionally fannish close audience-text relationship subsequently reducing barriers to entry into fandom, media fandom has become increasingly visible in recent years.[3] Crucially, Louisa Stein (2017) suggests that the popularization of feminism and the mainstreaming of fandom are connected, highlighting that 'social activism is in this moment become *mainstreamed* in a way that parallels the mainstreaming of fandom over the last decade'. Scholars have subsequently examined the increased visibility of fannish identities and practices within contemporary social justice movements (Jenkins et al. 2016; Hinck 2019).

The relationship between fourth-wave feminisms and fandom is particularly visible on the micro-blogging and social networking website Tumblr, where the networked nature of the site brings together popular culture, popular feminisms, and media fandom. Created by David Karp in 2007, Tumblr allows users to produce and share multimedia content in the form of text, photos, hyperlinks, audio, and video, on their individually curated blogs.[4] As a platform, Tumblr's public image, in turn, emphasizes its 'simplicity, customisability, interest-driven community, and creative-expression' (Tiidenberg, Hendry, and Abidin 2021, 5). In terms of functions and features, Tumblr combines the traditional features of a blogging platform, with user 'blogs' serving as profiles, alongside interactional features associated with social media. Users post under a (more often than not pseudonymous) username, which also forms the URL through which their Tumblr profile or 'blog' can be viewed and accessed by other users. When sharing a Tumblr post, or a 'blog post', users can attribute user-generated tags to their posts so that they can be more easily catalogued, organized, and retrieved within Tumblr's folksonomic (Vander Wal 2007) multi-user tagging system. Tumblr tags are multifunctional and are used to classify themes and categories and add commentary or other attributes of the multimedia content posted to a user's blog. Other users can use a site-wide search function to navigate these custom tagging systems to locate other users to 'follow' and share ('reblog') content onto their own blog. Tumblr's interface is built around a central reverse chronological timeline (the 'dashboard') featuring the most recent posts from the blogs a user follows interspersed with algorithmic recommendations of blogs and tags. The dashboard allows a user to comment, like, and share ('reblog') posts on their own blog. The reblogging system allows users to add commentary and their own user-generated tags to posts. 'Reblogs' and 'likes' are then truncated in the 'notes' of a Tumblr post, which are used as an indicator of popularity. Several social networking functions are also integrated into the website, including a comment ('reply') system, a question submission system ('inbox' or 'asks'), and a text-based instant messaging system for both individuals and groups.

Over the past decade, Tumblr's reputation and public image, user base and engagement, governance, revenue, and ownership within the social media landscape have undergone rapid change. In 2013, when Tumblr had over 73 million user accounts, Yahoo acquired it for US $1.1 billion. Bronstein (2020) highlights that, at its peak in 2014, Tumblr boasted more users than both Instagram and Pinterest. In 2017, Tumblr formed part of Verizon's $4.8 billion acquisition of Yahoo's internet business. While Tumblr's initially lax approach to content moderation was highly appealing to its substantial userbase (Gillespie 2018), in an attempt to make the platform more appealing to advertisers, Verizon enhanced Tumblr's filtering and moderation of sexual content in 2017. This was followed by an all-out ban on adult content in December 2018. The timing of the ban corresponded with a series of corporate, commercial, and legislative challenges for the platform. For example, changes to federal legislation in early 2018 in the United States, making website operators criminally and civilly liable for sex work and sex trafficking aided and abetted by communication on their platforms, made the proliferation of adult material on the platform legally problematic. This was compounded by Apple's November 2018 removal of the Tumblr application from their App Store in response to the detection of child pornography on the platform. In response to these challenges, Tumblr responded with an all-out ban on adult content through the (imperfect – as Pilipets and Paasonen (2022) note) use of automated hashtag filtering and algorithmic content recognition and content moderation. For many commentators, Tumblr's sudden and poorly executed move to ban adult content cemented the platform's 'demise' (Bronstein 2020). Tumblr reportedly lost between 20 and 40 per cent of its users in response (Romano 2018; Liao 2019; Bronstein 2020), and it was later sold to Automattic, owner of the blogging platform WordPress, in August 2019 for less than $3 million.

Crucially, many of the accounts featured throughout this book centre Tumblr users' experiences on and of the platform in the early 2010s before its acquisition by Verizon and the adult content ban controversy. It subsequently captures a transient moment in time before the platform's 'demise'. However, Tiidenberg,

Hendry, and Abidin (2021) note that the supposed demise of Tumblr is often over-emphasized, and more recent journalistic accounts, such as Kyle Chayka (2022) for *The New Yorker*, instead highlight the platform's enduring appeal to veteran and new users alike despite its tumultuous history. Chayka attributes this, in part, to Tumblr's largely unchanged form and function given its maintenance of the chronological timeline alongside, for example, its core aesthetic, simplicity, and multimodal format.

Unlike other popular social networking sites characterized by a rapidly changing user interface, Tumblr has maintained its core aesthetic and functionality and has consistently afforded users a high level of control over their self-presentation and the identity information they disclose on the platform. It therefore invites engagements from users for whom a sense of privacy, if not anonymity, is preferred, which lends itself to participation from those seeking to explore identities, issues, and interests that may be unwelcome elsewhere. As a result, Tumblr, at its peak in the 2010s prior to the adult content ban, was largely populated by marginalized groups, including LGBT youth, girls and young women, and people of colour. These technological affordances, combined with its popularity among marginalized groups, made the platform particularly conducive to counterpublic modes of address that are of great importance to the digital circulation, popularization, and contestation of contemporary feminisms. Thelandersson (2013) subsequently described Tumblr as a platform for feminist 'worldbuilding' (Berlant and Warner 1995) that provides a safe space for feminist consciousness-raising. For many young feminists, digital platforms like Tumblr are key to discovering feminism, gaining a feminist consciousness, and establishing feminist solidarities online. Harris (2012, 215) positions young people's blogging and social networking practices on platforms like Tumblr as an 'online DIY culture', writing that these spaces can facilitate

> [i]mportant practices of counterpublic construction in that they are forums for debate and exchange of politically and socially engaged ideas by those who are marginalised within mainstream political debate ... They tend to operate for information sharing, dialogue, consciousness-raising and community building, but can also be playful, leisure-oriented and mix up personal and political material.

Thus, while Tumblr was, and is, not fundamentally feminist in orientation, 'feminist interventions there claimed [it] as such' (Rentschler and Thrift 2015, 332). Feminist modes of cultural consumption, production, and critique subsequently proliferate on the platform (Keller 2012b).[5] In turn, Tumblr users have, in the public imaginary, become discursively associated with progressive politics and the term 'social justice'. As Daphne Patai (2014) notes, while the term 'social justice' is usually treated as self-explanatory, when invoked it is often associated with the 'familiar feminist focus on the "intersections" of, or "specialisation in," race, ethnicity, gender, nationality, class, and so on'. Similarly, Massanari and Chess (2018, 528) highlight that the term 'social justice' has long been used by feminists, anti-racists, and other progressives interested in 'ensuring both economic justice and recognition for marginalised identities'. Popular usage of the term has increased in recent years in recognition of a broader emancipatory and progressive politics. This is concurrent with the increasing popularity of intersectionality as a critical-analytic framework for contemporary feminist analysis. The lack of rigidity with regard to contemporary 'feminist' parameters can subsequently be read as an engagement with a feminist politics of intersectionality. I thus take the terms 'feminism' and 'social justice' to be largely interchangeable, and they are employed synonymously by self-identified feminist fans throughout this work. As Tiidenberg, Hendry, and Abidin (2021, 129–30) write,

> [s]ocial justice underpins tumblr's shared sensibility ... Social justice on tumblr is connected to issues related to racism, feminism, sexual and gender diversity, body politics, ableism, and, importantly, the intersection of these.

While Tumblr makes visible the multidirectional relationship between popular feminisms, popular culture, and digital culture, media fandom is rarely located at this juncture (Figure 1), despite the similarities, and increasing slippage, between contemporary feminist and fannish modes of cultural consumption, production, and critique. Over the past decade, Tumblr has cemented its reputation as a popular platform where media fandoms convene, to such an extent that Tiidenberg, Hendry, and Abidin (2021) chart the emergence of 'tumblr meta-fandom' – that is, the fandom that has emerged around the platform itself. The platform is thus immensely popular with both feminists and fans, and the networked nature of the site brought these communities together in varied ways that warrant sustained ethnographic analysis. As Paul Booth (2017, 233) writes in *Digital Fandom 2.0*,

> Tumblr offers a site of ever-changing dynamics wherein fan audiences can be encountered but also where the multi-vocality of the audiences on the site means multiple discourses can be followed at once. There is no one 'ethos' of Tumblr.

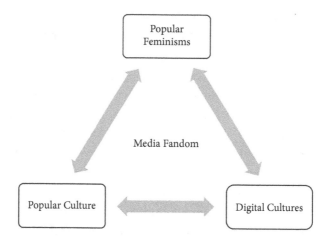

Figure 1 Locating media fandom in the co-constitutive and multidirectional relationship between popular feminisms, digital cultures, and popular culture. Image by author.

The multimodality and multivocality of Tumblr blur the lines between feminist and fannish communities on the site, producing a cultural formation in which feminist, or 'social justice', politics are increasingly, although not exclusively, central to the operation of media fandom on Tumblr. For instance, Hillman, Procyk, and Neustaedter's (2014a, b, c) research suggests that one of the key motivations for participation in fandom on Tumblr is the site's affinity with social justice discourses. Similarly, Kohnen (2018) emphasizes that 'fandom on Tumblr often includes discussions of diversity in media representation and the intersections of fandom and social justice' (465), and McCracken (2017, 157) highlights that 'media representation is a chief concern' to Tumblr users, forming 'the subject of much of their sophisticated criticism, creative production, and pleasure'. Here, we can see how a feminist politics of recognition governs media fandom's passionate relationship with popular culture on Tumblr. Media fandom on Tumblr is therefore implicated in the circularity between fourth-wave feminisms, digital culture, and popular culture. In a Tumblr blog post for *The Daily Dot*, journalist Aja Romano (2014) emphasizes that feminist and counterpublic discourses proliferate on Tumblr precisely because the fans populating the site are also governed by a feminist politics of recognition:

> Feminism thrives on Tumblr because fandom thrives on Tumblr; because they were always hand-in-hand as ways to actively engage with and deconstruct the narratives you've been given, whether that narrative is 'See this dude? He's so totally straight' or whether it's 'The patriarchy works.'

This is central to the formation of what I call 'feminist fandom', and Tumblr has subsequently secured a reputation for its users' in-depth analysis of representational politics and social issues. This has enormous pedagogical potential for young people:

> Young people's experience of media on Tumblr is one of acculturation; their engagement is inevitably affected, to varying degrees, by socially critical users – often self-identified as both progressives *and* fans – speaking from their own lived experience and through shared popular discourses of feminism, anti-racism, queer or gender studies, and postcolonialism. For many youth, Tumblr has become an alternative, tuition-free classroom, a powerful site of youth media literacy, identity formation, and political awareness that often reproduces cultural studies methods of analysis.
>
> (McCracken 2017, 152)

It is here, then, that we can situate media fandom on Tumblr at the juncture between popular feminism, popular culture, and digital culture. Ferreday (2015) subsequently argues, 'fan and feminist identities are not separate, *they coexist and intertwine*' (23; my emphasis). Throughout this book, I use the term 'feminist fandom' to describe the messy entanglement of fannish and feminist identities, discourses, and practices. Admittedly, while several scholars examining the feminist impetus of media fandom on Tumblr have highlighted a trend of fans engaging with social issues in concentrated ways, they often neglect to embed these fannish engagements with feminist politics within a broader historical movement, instead emphasizing the supposed novelty of feminist fandom. However, fandoms have long been characterized as subversive and transformational, challenging norms and existing power structures (Bacon-Smith 1992; Jenkins 1992; Lewis 1992; Penley 1997). From this, a substantial amount of research examines a wide range of fan practices which, as Duffett (2013, 73) writes, offer 'a tool for social criticism' (Bury 2005; Hellekson and Busse 2006, 2014; Merrick 2009; Wills 2013; Coppa 2014; Warner 2015; Jenkins et al. 2016; Busse 2017). Yet, despite fandom's established history of engaging with a cultural politics of recognition, as well as the number of accounts detailing the entanglement of popular feminisms, popular culture, and digital cultures, few have located media fandom at this juncture.

This is of chief concern because it means we risk losing sight of the significance of media fandom in introducing young people to feminism. While media fandom is a central feature of contemporary youth culture (Bennett 2004; Stein 2015; Hannell 2020a), its relationship to contemporary, and especially fourth-wave, feminism remains largely unaccounted for within our understandings of young people's engagements with feminism. Existing accounts of the development of young people's feminist identities and practices overwhelmingly focus not only on (cis-gendered) girls and young women but also on more episodic and ephemeral engagements with feminism – for example through the kinds of 'hashtag feminisms' I detailed earlier – rather than the more routine, everyday, informal engagements with feminism taking place, for example, within fannish digital spaces. Notably, here I refer to girls and young women, rather than the assumedly gender neutral 'youth', in recognition of the dominance of gender (and often, those who are cis-gendered) as an analytic category when exploring young people's engagements and identifications with feminism. As I will discuss shortly, I opened my own research to self-identified feminists (and 'feminist fans') regardless of gender identity, which produced a much more diverse and multivalent sample of participants in terms of gender identity.

Additionally, while critical and celebratory modes of popular culture consumption, production, and critique are central to fourth-wave feminisms *and* media fandom, both feminist and fan studies scholarship is yet to *substantially* account for how media fandom and fourth-wave feminisms are deeply connected in practice, as well as how fannish and feminist communities are converging within the digital landscape. Furthermore, fan studies scholarship often reproduces a normative assumption that media fandom is inherently progressive, emancipatory, or resistant due to its willingness to explore gender and queer sexualities in accordance with the feminist project, yet this assumption is seldom examined or interrogated at an ethnographic level of lived experience. Instead, these studies often focus their analysis of fandom's relationship to feminism at the level of textual productivity, for example with regard to fanfiction (Hellekson and Busse 2014; Busse 2017), or with reference to fandoms formed around specific media texts (Anselmo 2018).

This context subsequently frames my analysis of feminist fandom as I grapple with the complex nature of the relationship between media fandom and young people's engagements with digital feminisms.

Researching feminist fandom

Feminist Fandom forges sustained dialogue between feminist cultural studies and fan studies, emphasizing the close relationship between the two methodologically, theoretically, and empirically. As I have argued elsewhere, fan studies is deeply indebted to the insights of feminist methodologies, especially those emerging from within feminist cultural studies (Hannell 2020b). My experience of fan culture and my conception of fan studies as a discipline, as my own identity as a researcher, are intimately bound up with feminism. To this research, I bring my own fannish and feminist histories. I have been deeply fannish since childhood, although my formal entry into fandom was in my early teens when I discovered fan-video editing or 'vidding' on YouTube in 2007. I gradually began to engage with fandom on Twitter, having joined the website in early 2009, and occasionally used LiveJournal.[6] I began using Tumblr in early 2010 as my fannish friends migrated to the platform, driven by the appeal of its multi-modal, multi-vocal, and 'silosocial' (Tiidenberg, Hendry, and Abidin 2021) affinity – and interest-based nature. This reflects a wider shift within media fandom during this period, as Tumblr began to replace LiveJournal as the main hub of online fandom activity around 2011 (Bury 2016; De Kosnik 2016; Kohnen 2018). Like many of my participants, my first explicit encounters with feminism, or 'social justice', took place on Tumblr, where the lines between fandom and feminist media critique were becoming increasingly blurred.

My memories of these early encounters with feminism through fandom are undoubtedly inflected by what Tiidenberg, Hendry, and Abidin (2021) call 'Tumblr nostalgia'. Tumblr nostalgia is one example of what Bolin (2016) terms 'technostalgia', as a collective and technologically oriented form of nostalgia oriented towards media technologies, platforms, labour investment, habits, and content that evoke social relations and situations from a formative period of one's youth (also see Miltner and Gerrard 2022). Nevertheless, my encounters with feminism on Tumblr during my mid- to late-teens helped me to cultivate a critical language that I could use to name and critique my 'orientation' (Ahmed 2006) to the spaces I inhabited. In researching a selection of the fans who populate(d) feminist fandom on Tumblr, I have reflected on the experiences and life histories of the feminist fans who participated in my research in dialogue with my own. The data I examine throughout this book was collected not as an outsider but as an active member of the feminist fan community on Tumblr. This book is necessarily partial as a result.

As an interdisciplinary scholar, throughout this book I draw from a range of disciplines across the social sciences and arts and humanities. These include media and communications, cultural studies, sociology, philosophy, feminist theory, internet studies, and critical race theory. This book also draws upon four years of digital ethnographic fieldwork on Tumblr conducted between

2016 and 2020. Notably, I completed most of my formal data collection before Tumblr introduced its adult content ban in 2018. My findings and analysis, as I noted earlier, subsequently capture a transient moment in feminist and fannish histories on the platform during the early to mid-2010s. Additionally, while what I term 'feminist fandom' can be located within a networked and multi-sited digital ecology, I am interested in the specificity of Tumblr, of its vernacular and affordances, within the feminist fannish imaginary – something I will examine in more depth in Chapter 2. My empirical data collection subsequently focuses exclusively on Tumblr, where I collected my data using a variety of ethnographic methods and techniques. My analysis draws upon participant observation on Tumblr, online interviews, my personal archive of field notes and screenshots, and a qualitative narrative survey.

My narrative survey produced the largest amount of data, totalling more than half a million words of data produced by 342 respondents. Shkedi (2004) notes that while detailed individual narratives are often gathered during in-depth interviews, surveys allow qualitative researchers to gather the qualitative narratives of larger populations using techniques that are not dissimilar to interviewing. It is in this sense that Hine (2015, 80) positions surveys as a useful method for ethnographers who hope to use their data to characterize larger populations. My survey was designed to elicit in-depth reflective narratives from self-identified 'feminist fans' on their engagements with both feminism and fandom throughout their life course, with broad, open-ended questions designed to invite rich, storied responses. I subsequently focus primarily on my survey data throughout this book, although my interpretation of this data is very much grounded in my ethnographic fieldwork and immersion within Tumblr subcultures and feminist fandom beyond this.

The 342 feminist fans who completed my narrative survey were located in 39 countries, although Anglophone countries in the Global North predominated. Their ages ranged from 13 to 60, yet their average age was 25, and their modal age was 21. While I followed Schilt and Bratter's (2015) method of allowing respondents to describe their social identities in their own words, the majority of my 342 respondents positioned themselves as girls and women, 43 positioned themselves as gender diverse and non-conforming, and 9 as men. Twenty-eight participants specified that they were cisgender. They used a wide range of terms to describe their sexualities, with the majority (157) describing themselves as bisexual. Meanwhile, 247 of the 342 respondents referred to themselves as white, 32 did not specify, and the remaining 63 offered heterogeneous descriptions of their non-white racial and ethnic identities. Where appropriate, I refer to my research participants' verbatim descriptions of their social identities when discussing their contributions to this research. I also extend this logic to my analysis and make extensive use of verbatim quotations from my participants throughout this book. This is in line with a feminist research ethic that seeks to centre research participants' voices and experiences.

When designing my narrative survey, I invited my research participants to choose their own pseudonyms, or 'Public Identifier', for use in my analysis. This provided an opportunity to invite my participants to choose *how* they wished to be represented within the research. Many of my participants provided a pseudonym for public use distinct from their name provided for private and confidential use. Several permitted me to refer to them by their given name in my write-up, and many requested that I refer to them using their Tumblr usernames. While some argue that online pseudonyms and usernames should *always* be anonymized by the researcher, I adopted a more contextual approach to this process and instead abided by requests to be identified by their Tumblr usernames in recognition of their desire for their contributions to my research to remain embedded within the context of their role within the feminist fan community. This adheres to Nissenbaum's (2010) description of 'contextual integrity' as a relationally established research ethic embedded in the norms and values of local research contexts.

My contextually determined approach to participant anonymity and pseudonymity produced a wide range of naming conventions used throughout this book. Whenever I quote my research participants, I do so according to the 'Public Identifier' they provided during our informed consent negotiations and, where relevant, an accompanying number corresponding to the completion rate of my narrative survey. When reproducing or citing fanworks – that is, creative works produced by and for fans – I follow multiple strategies. My citational practice has always centred an openness with the fans whose work I discus, and I view contacting fans to ask for permission to quote or feature their fanworks as an ethical duty. When contacting Tumblr users in this capacity, I used my personal account to do so, providing them with information about the research, offering the chance to ask further questions, and then asking them how they would like to be cited should permission be granted.[7] However, there are several exceptions to this throughout the book. For example, several of the blog posts I feature throughout *Feminist Fandom* were authored by Tumblr accounts which have since been deactivated or are now inactive. Obtaining consent from these sources was thus not possible despite my efforts.

Book overview

Given my interest in my research participants' narrative, or storied, understandings of their experiences of, in, and with feminist fandom, my analysis itself unfolds in a storied form throughout *Feminist Fandom*, growing 'thicker' (Geertz 1973) chapter by chapter. This book subsequently has the most insight to offer when read in its entirety, as its chapters work in close relation to one another to form a more dynamic portrait of feminist fandom. However, I have made a concerted effort throughout the book to chart the connections across and through its chapters to better allow a reader to read chapters separately if necessary. In introducing *Feminist Fandom*, I have located (feminist) media fandom at the juncture between popular feminisms, popular culture, and digital cultures and discussed the methods I used to collect my data. To conclude this introduction, I offer an overview of its chapters.

Chapter 1 focuses on media fandom as a pathway for feminist becoming during youth, moving away from popular narratives within feminist cultural studies which position formal educational contexts and participation in largely ephemeral and episodic acts of digital feminism as dominant pathways towards feminist becoming. Instead, I examine the processes of feminist becoming which are unique to the cultural, social, and spatial specificities of media fandom on Tumblr. Here, three key modes of feminist becoming emerge. The first highlights the significance of fandom as an interpretative tool to *make sense of* feminism and subsequently *make feminist sense* of media texts. The second emphasizes the transference of pre-existing feminisms into everyday fannish practices, demonstrating the importance of an individual's social location in shaping their approach to fannish media consumption and production. The third mode foregrounds the processual and ongoing nature of feminist becoming, emphasizing the fluidity in narratives of fannish and feminist becoming. The self-narratives captured within Chapter 1 vary according to participants' material conditions, cultural contexts, positionalities, and personal histories in ways that highlight the pertinence of identity markers, such as race, class, nationality, sexuality, and gender identity, in the process of becoming a feminist fan. Additionally, in this chapter, I introduce an argument that resonates throughout the book – that fandom is a site where fans collectively construct, negotiate, and contest meanings of feminism and engage in a dynamic and ongoing process of group feminist identity work that corresponds to broader discursive shifts in feminism taking place within both the academy and popular domain.

Chapter 2 examines the interrelated affective, spatial, and relational dimensions of belonging within feminist fandom on Tumblr. It explores my participants' dominant constructions of belonging to feminist fandom that (re)produce an inherently progressive vision of media fandom that reflects the popular imaginary surrounding Tumblr. These dominant articulations of belonging position fandom as an imagined community built upon intensely affective modes of belonging. They also centre the importance of spatial belonging and the specificity of Tumblr's platform vernacular, technological affordances, and sensibility in producing a sense of both safety and privacy for members of feminist fandom.

However, Chapter 3 troubles this normative framing of feminist fandom. Drawing upon the responses of my participants of colour, who detail the structuring force of whiteness within feminist fandom, I question the extent to which the performance of 'intersectional' feminist identities within feminist fandom on Tumblr does the anti-racist and intersectional work that it purports to. Reflecting on articulations of non-belonging and feminist theorizations of more precarious modes of differential belonging, I interrogate normative assumptions within both fan studies scholarship and fandom itself that frame fandom as inherently progressive or resistant, revealing how these narratives flatten difference and obscure how online spaces extend and (re)produce inequalities and power imbalances.

Throughout Chapters 1–3, the pedagogical function of feminist fandom emerges as central to my participants' feminist becoming, as well as their sense of (non-)belonging to feminist fandom. In Chapter 4, I attend to the complex relationship between fandom and feminist pedagogy on Tumblr in more detail. Firstly, I explore the role of feminist fandom as an informal learning culture that fosters the development of critical feminist media literacy, providing access to information and knowledge many participants would otherwise seldom access. Secondly, I explore how these critical feminist media literacies are carried forwards into the communal production of the fantext (Hellekson and Busse 2006), positioning this as a mode of feminist knowledge sharing. Finally, I return to my participants' accounts of ongoing feminist becoming to explore their commitment to a lifelong process of learning and unlearning. To do so, I position *learning through listening* as central to the relational work required of maintaining participants' understandings of feminist fandom as a safe space. I also consider the implications of this commitment to an ongoing process of learning and unlearning with regard to the accounts of racism and non-belonging detailed in Chapter 3. *Feminist Fandom* concludes with a summary of my key findings and draws out the implications of these findings for our understandings of both media fandom and young people's engagements with digital feminisms. In this chapter, I also reflect on Tumblr's changing reputation and public image since I formally began this research in 2016 and consider its implications for the imagined past and anticipated future of the platform.

Becoming feminist: Fandom and feminist identity work

Feminist becoming has been a lively subject of inquiry over the last three decades. Much of the research on young women's feminist becoming focuses on the significance of formal educational contexts as fertile ground for feminist identity development. A great deal of this research examines university contexts (Hercus 2005; Aikau, Erickson, and Pierce 2007; Marine and Lewis 2014), while more recent perspectives focus on high school (Retallack, Ringrose, and Lawrence 2016; Ringrose and Renold 2016; Kim and Ringrose 2018). Furthermore, over the past decade, in response to the increasing visibility of feminism within the mediated public sphere, feminist researchers have explored the significance of the internet and digital cultures (Keller 2016a; Mendes, Keller, and Ringrose 2019), as well as popular culture (Keller 2015; Taylor 2016), as a pathway towards feminist becoming for young people. Digital perspectives have, for instance, focused on the significance of the everyday reach and visibility of online DIY cultures, in addition to networked social media–based feminisms, to feminist awakenings and consciousness-raising (Keller 2012b; Rentschler 2014), while popular culture perspectives have examined feminist becoming through the lens of the concepts including 'celebrity feminism' (Hamad and Taylor 2015; Keller and Ringrose 2015; Jackson 2020) and 'popular feminism' (Banet-Weiser 2018).

In turn, much has been written about the importance of popular culture to identity development for young people. Williams and Zenger (2012, 3), for instance, argue that popular culture provides the 'rhetorical, linguistic and semiotic building blocks' through which young people 'perform identities and make meaning in their own lives', while Gray (2014, 170) notes that many young people 'weave media-generated source materials into their identity work'. Popular culture has been described as a tool for navigating and deciphering everyday life (Lincoln 2014), as comprising the 'primary sites, practices and frames through which people make sense of the world' (Rowley 2010, 14). Feminist research into the interactions between feminism, popular culture, and feminist identity formation is thus the logical extension of this work.

And yet these understandings of the interactions between contemporary feminisms, networked digital cultures, and popular culture have seldom been brought together to examine how digital feminist cultural critique might draw young people towards feminist consciousness and involvement. This means that media fandom, as a space situated at the intersection of digital cultures, digital feminisms, and popular culture, is largely unaccounted for in our understandings of young people's pathways to feminist becoming – with the early exceptions of Alex Naylor's (2016) research on a group of *Game of Thrones* fans on Tumblr and more recently Neta Yodovich's (2022) work on feminist science-fiction fans. When introducing her research, Alex Naylor briefly alludes to evidence that many fans 'see pop culture critique *as a gateway drug* to networked feminist counterpublic discussion' (Naylor 2016, 44; my emphasis).[1] However, beyond Naylor's brief suggestion that media fandom might operate as a pathway, or 'gateway', towards feminist 'counterpublic discussion', the potential connections between media fandom and the development of a feminist identity remain undertheorized.

More recently, sociologist Neta Yodovich (2022), in her study of feminist science-fiction fans, locates fandom as one of three distinct sites where her research participants first encountered feminism. She subsequently describes fandom as a space for feminist 'consciousness raising' (58). While Yodovich's account of the relationship between (science fiction) fandom and feminist becoming is more detailed than Naylor's, Naylor's offers insights into the importance of Tumblr to this process. In my own work, I bring these perspectives and interests together. Through my analysis of feminist fans' self-narratives of feminist becoming detailed throughout this chapter, I explore how contemporary internet-based media fandom can operate as a pathway for 'feminist becoming' during youth. Building upon theorizations of continuity and change in self-narratives and the discursive construction of identity (Bamberg, Fina, and Schiffrin 2011), I examine feminist fans' self-narratives of fannish-feminist becoming to explore how media fandom can, under certain circumstances, offer a social and cultural context conducive to drawing young people towards engagement with myriad feminisms. This troubles the dominant narrative within feminist accounts of young people's feminist becoming as rooted primarily in more formal educational contexts, during high school or university, or through episodic and ephemeral engagement with digital feminisms rooted, for example, in hashtag feminism or single-issue-based online movements. Instead, my participants' self-narratives of feminist becoming offer insight into the significance of ubiquitous and everyday engagements with feminism through interest-based online DIY cultures in the formation and development of young people's feminist identities. Many of the more typical narratives of feminist becoming do not account for the complexity of this process within the context of fandom, within which feminist becoming is bound up with affect, textuality, and shared cultural consumption and production in complex ways.

Narrative identity and identity development

Many sociologists have argued that our sense of self is formed between our internal world and external world and that the process of identity development involves degrees of both self-observation and reflection. The construction of our sense of self often relies upon what McAdams (2011) describes as 'narrative identity'. Narrative identity, he argues, refers to the internalized story of the self that a person constructs, both for the self and for others, to make sense of their life. According to Bamberg, Fina, and Schiffrin (2011), narrative frames are central to identity development and performance, as they work to ensure that the identities we discursively construct align with both our internal and external worlds. Self-narratives allow us to perform, manage, and, in some cases, disavow our identities through social interaction (Fenstermaker and West 2002; Bettie 2014). They become the means by which we come to recognize ourselves, 'the stories we live by' (McAdams, Josselson, and Lieblich 2006, 4). Self-narratives have a *defining* character and can be understood as 'discursive practices' that 'form the locus of identities as continuously practised and tested out' (Bamberg, Fina, and Schiffrin 2011, 186). Self-narratives thus offer insight into how people *construct, perform,* and *make sense of* who they are. It is in this sense that they can grant us insight into the development of young people's feminist identities.

According to Bamberg, Fina, and Schiffrin (2011), self-narratives often draw on prevailing cultural norms about discontinuity and continuity in the process of identity formation. They argue that these themes of discontinuity and continuity permeate discursive constructions of identity formation, wherein

[s]ubjects [position] their sense of self in terms of some form of continuity, i.e., constructing their identities in terms of some change against the background

of some constancy (and vice versa). The choice of particular discursive devices, taken from the range of temporality and aspectual markers, contributes to the construction of events as indexing (potentially radical) transformations from one sense of self to another and constitutes change as discontinuous or qualitative leaps. In contrast, other devices are typically employed to construe change as gradual and somewhat consistent over time.

(Bamberg, Fina, and Schiffrin 2011, 188–9)

These themes of *discontinuity* and *continuity* are well documented in the literature from feminist cultural studies on self-narratives of identity formation and development in relation to becoming a feminist. In recent years, scholars working within fan studies have also begun to explore the process of becoming a fan in more depth (Hills 2014; Riddel 2021; Yodovich 2022). Hills (2014), for instance, draws upon psychoanalytic perspectives to identify two narratives of becoming a fan: fandom as *transformational*[2] and fandom as *transference*. The first mode, which he describes as a kind of transformative and emergent fandom, tends to involve the first subjective appearance of a fan identity, often during childhood or adolescence. I understand this mode of fandom entry as a kind of *change* or *discontinuity*, wherein encountering fandom (and later, as my data suggests, feminism) is discursively constructed as a transformative break from the past. This is a common trope in self-narratives of becoming a fan (Harrington and Bielby 2010; Riddel 2021). The second mode of becoming a fan, Hills (2014) argues, is marked by gradual mediations, pre-configurations, and transfers of fandom from one fan object to the next. These narratives operate as a form of *continuity* or *extension*, where entry into fandom is framed as the natural consequence of a learned fannish predisposition or as the continuation of 'narratives of the self' (Giddens 1991, 76) already at work. This presupposes an established familiarity with fan culture, marking a reorientation or re-articulation of pre-existing fannish attachments and competencies rather than the 'pure discovery' (Hills 2014, 16) of their initial appearance. Fannish becomings articulated through this discursive repertoire are therefore framed as a form of continuity.

Similarly, feminist scholars often examine feminist becomings through self-narratives of transformative *change*, on the one hand, and *continuity* on the other (Skeggs 1997; Taft 2017). For example, Bartky (1975, 425) describes the process of becoming a feminist as a 'profound personal transformation', while Downing and Roush (1985) refer to a transformative 'revelation' stage in the process of becoming a feminist. Alternatively, Hercus (2005) identifies the figure of the 'always feminist', who positions herself as having always held views and had feelings 'consistent with feminism' (37). In becoming feminist, the women Hercus interviewed did not report experiencing dramatic changes in values, beliefs, or their sense of self. Their self-narratives did not include reference to a process of personal transformation or conversion, but rather

> [i]n becoming feminists, these women did not report experiencing dramatic changes in values, beliefs, or their sense of self. The process they described was not so much one of personal transformation, but of becoming aware of the language or discourse of feminism as a vehicle for expression already held beliefs about the world and about themselves, and of linking up with other women who shared their outlook.
>
> (Hercus 2005, 38)

Hercus's description of women coming together to connect and collectively express and name already held beliefs about the world and themselves echoes Friedan's (1963, 15) canonical notion of 'the problem with no name'. The feminist becoming of the 'always feminist', therefore, marks the continuity or extension of pre-existing values and beliefs into the language and discourses of feminism. However, Hercus offers an additional narrative of the 'evolving feminist', which can be positioned at the intersection of both *change* and *continuity*. Many of Hercus's research participants emphasized the fluid and evolving nature of their feminist identity development, framing their feminist identities as 'something that had to be worked at as an *ongoing* project' (Hercus 2005, 56; my emphasis).

Given the operation of both continuity *and* change in self-narratives of identity development, it is not surprising that many sociologists, working from a poststructuralist and anti-foundationalist perspective, understand identity in processual terms. Contemporary feminist theories, for example, have generally embraced the idea that subjects and identities are always in-process or always becoming, doing, or performing, rather than fixed or essential ontological beings (Grosz 1999; Rattansi and Phoenix 2005; Braidotti 2011). As Currie, Kelly, and Pomerantz (2007, 2009) highlight, becoming a feminist is a much more complex and ongoing process than typically acknowledged: one is not positioned simply 'inside' or 'outside' feminism by taking up a subject position within feminist discourse. Feminist identities remain emergent and in-process, much like the 'evolving feminist' that Hercus (2005) describes.

The notion of the evolving feminist as a subject that remains *in process* emphasizes that self-narratives of becoming are often processual, fluid, and non-linear. This speaks to the operation of *some* continuity and *some* change that

Bamberg, Fina, and Schiffrin (2011) refer to in their description of discursive constructions of identity formation. Self-narratives of identity development thus often operationalize discursive themes of both change and continuity. Indeed, many of my participants' self-narratives can be positioned at the intersection of these discursive themes. A dichotomous understanding of my participants' self-narratives, such as those which have been operationalized within both fan studies and feminist cultural studies, does not allow for the nuance and complexity of my participants' personal biographies. Throughout this chapter, I argue that feminist fans' narratives of becoming as *change* or *continuity* are not necessarily mutually exclusive and in many cases can be understood as change *and/or* continuity. Many of the feminist fans who participated in my research used discourses of both change and continuity in their narratives of becoming a feminist fan, assigning varying levels of emphasis to moments of transformation in their narratives of the self.

Fandom and feminist becoming

Building primarily upon feminist fans' responses to Q2 ('Fannish History') and Q3 ('Feminist History') of my qualitative narrative survey, I will now explore their self-narratives of feminist becoming to examine the relationship between digital media fandom and feminist identity development. In doing so, I move away from earlier feminist research examining young women's ambivalence towards and dis-identification with feminism. Instead, I align my findings with contemporary accounts which centre young people's emergent feminisms. Building upon this, I explore 342 feminist fans' self-narratives of feminist becoming to examine the significance of media fandom and popular cultural critique to their feminist becoming. In doing so, I consider how the process of feminist becoming is organized and structured by and through the discourses, practices, and subject positions of media fandom – that is, through engaging with the multitude of social and cultural practices associated with fandom. This is distinct from other perspectives on fandom and feminist becoming, which emphasize a 'significant difference between feminism and fandom' (Yodovich 2022, 55) in biographical narratives of becoming. Additionally, I also consider how my participants' self-narratives of feminist becoming vary according to their material conditions, cultural contexts, social positionalities, and personal histories. These negotiations highlight the pertinence of identity markers, such as race, nationality, sexuality, and gender identity, in the process of becoming a feminist fan.

Because my research consists of a purposefully self-selecting sample of participants who identify as feminists *and* fans, or 'feminist fans', it is not surprising that their self-narratives emphasize that feminism is a significant part of their lives and sense of self. Three dominant discursive themes emerged across their narratives of feminist becoming: fandom and feminist sense-making, translating feminism to fandom, and fans' emergent feminisms. I examine the first and second theme through the lens of Gray's (2010) theorization of paratexts to reveal how the totality of the texts both consumed and produced by fans – the *fantext* (Hellekson and Busse 2006) – contributes to the process of feminist becoming. The first theme, *fandom and feminist sense-making*, examines self-narratives which emphasized the significance of fandom as an interpretative tool to *make sense of* feminism. In these self-narratives, fandom is positioned as providing the language, social structures, shared interests, and shared cultural signs, frameworks, and symbols through which participants come to understand and make sense of feminism. In these accounts, fandom renders feminism intelligible, prompting the transformative re-direction and re-evaluation of the frameworks fans use to interpret texts. Within the second theme, *translating feminism to fandom*, participants' self-narratives focus less on processes of feminist becoming within fandom and more so on how pre-existing feminisms are integrated and taken 'into' everyday fannish practices and interpretative strategies. These narratives thus emphasize processes of feminist continuity, particularly through engaging in fannish cultural production instilled with a feminist 'ethos'. Additionally, the self-narratives which adhered to this theme revealed how different social positions and standpoints, particularly surrounding race, can mediate this process of continuity. In the final theme, *fans' emergent feminisms*, I explore self-narratives which emphasized the processual and emergent nature of feminist becoming. In these narratives, respondents positioned feminism as an active and ongoing form of group identity work which takes place within and through fandom, fan culture, and fan communities. These accounts positioned fannish feminisms as the starting point in an ongoing process of feminist becoming.

Fandom and feminist sense-making

Feminists have long been interested in how popular cultural texts offer interpretative frameworks for how feminism is understood and interpreted by the wider public. They have long examined textual representations of feminism within mass media, with particular emphasis on both print and broadcast news media coverage (van Zoonen 1992; Dean 2010; Mendes 2015). Elsewhere, Dow (1996), Taylor (2016), and Cattien (2019) have examined the significance of popular culture in mediating understandings of feminism, exploring prime-time television and celebrity feminism respectively, while more recent perspectives have explored advertising (Varghese and Kumar 2020) and teen film (Monaghan 2022). Many of these accounts seek to examine how these texts offer visions of what feminism *means*, in order to reveal what they can 'tell us about feminism' (Hollows and Moseley 2006, 1). Popular cultural texts not only shape our understandings of feminism itself, they also inform whether, how, and to what extent many audience members come to engage and identify with feminism. Yet what many of these perspectives do not account for is the way that these popular cultural texts circulate more widely within popular media cultures. What about the very readers and viewers who populate the text? To what extent do these perspectives account for the participatory nature of the process of constructing and circulating textual meaning? And how might this participatory and social process of constructing and circulating meaning impact understandings of and identifications with feminism itself? In many feminist fans' narratives of feminist becoming, they emphasized that popular cultural texts helped them to make sense of feminism, its practices, identities, and discourses, in ways which were unique to the specificity of their identities and practices as fans. That is, their sustained and communal fannish engagement with popular cultural texts helped them to cultivate an interpretative framework for understanding feminism on not only a *textual* level of the fan object but also a *paratextual* level of the wider fan community.

Paratexts and media reception

Jonathan Gray (2010) argues that paratexts structure and guide the reception of media texts, forming an extensive part of our contemporary mediated environment. Building upon French literary theorist Gérard Genette's (1997) work, Gray defines paratexts as 'semi-textual fragments that surround and position' (2003, 72) a primary text. Within the context of television, for example, Gray lists 'introductory sequences, spoilers and ads, newspaper, magazine or web article, merchandise and the very buzz or … talk that surrounds any given programme' (2003, 72) as important examples of paratexts. They structure the consumption of media, surrounding texts, audiences, and industry, filling the spaces between them. To study paratexts, then, is to study 'how meaning is created' (2010, 26). Gray highlights that fan-created paratexts operate as important additions to a text, forming a 'paratextual assemblage' (2003, 73), and are a fruitful site at which we can examine how meanings are created, constructed, and contested. Paratexts, he argues, govern expectations of 'what a text should be like, of what is a waste of media time and space, of what morality or aesthetics texts should adopt, and of what we would like to see others watch or read' (2003, 73). The paratextual assemblage surrounding a given text subsequently grants insight into what expectations and values structure media consumption.

The cultural practices and social formations of fandom, ranging from fannish commentary, debate, and analysis to the cultural production of a wide range of fanworks, have been framed as paratextual in line with this framework (Castleberry 2015; Fathallah 2015; Leavenworth 2015; Geraghty 2015b; Ng 2017). Hellekson and Busse (2006), for example, offer the concept of the 'fantext' to encapsulate the totality, or assemblage, of fan-created paratexts.[3] The *fantext* refers to the entirety of fan additions to a text (in addition to the original source text itself) so that the multitude of fan-created texts, discussions, analyses, and interpretations, as an assemblage of paratexts, therein becomes

[a] work in progress insofar as it remains open and is constantly increasing; every new addition changes the entirety of interpretations. By looking at the combined fantext, it becomes obvious how fans' understanding of the source is always already filtered through the interpretations and characterisations existing in the fantext. In other words, the community of fans creates a communal (albeit contentious and contradictory) interpretation in which a large number of potential meanings, directions, and outcomes co-reside.

(Hellekson and Busse 2006, 7)

An understanding of the cultural practices and social formations of fandom as paratextual, then, accounts for how fandom operates as a site of communal and reciprocal meaning-making. Gray differentiates between *entryway paratexts* and *in medias res paratexts*. *Entryway paratexts* preface a work and guide us *into* it. They shape the reading strategies that we take forwards 'into' a text and provide the interpretative frameworks which we use to examine, react to, and evaluate textual consumption. *In medias res paratexts* interrupt, inflect, or possibly redirect a reading in the middle of a text. They shape and inflect our 're-entry' into a text, offering frames through which we can interpret and make sense of the text at hand. They can thus subtly or radically alter our reading of texts accordingly. A single paratext can operate as both an entryway and an *in medias res* paratext, depending upon the reception context and reader of the paratext. For instance, for one reader at a specific moment in time, a paratext might operate as an entryway paratext, whereas for another it may later operate as an *in medias res* paratext. This, as I will shortly argue, is especially important to consider within the context of feminist fandom.

Gray (2010, 146) argues that the fantext can work as 'a powerful *in medias res* paratext' in its ability to redirect a reading in the middle of a text, 'directing its path elsewhere'. Fannish commentary, debate, creativity, and analysis can, he writes, call for subtle changes in interpretation and open up new 'paths of understanding' (147). Indeed, many fan studies scholars have mapped such lines of textual resistance, particularly with regard to issues surrounding fannish creativity and gender and sexuality (Hellekson and Busse 2006; Busse 2017). It is in this sense that, as I discussed in the introduction, the fantext has been described as a tool for social criticism that can carve out 'alternative pathways through texts' (Gray 2010, 143).

Within this schema, I consider fandom as an important site at which meanings of feminism are paratextually constructed, negotiated, and contested. Rather than attributing the process of feminist becoming solely to the myriad ways in which feminism has been incorporated into popular culture over the past decade, as discussed in the introduction, I am interested in how the paratextual circulation of popular cultural texts offers interpretative frameworks for young people to make sense of feminism. Building upon my participant's self-narratives of becoming feminist fans, I argue that fan-created *in medias res* paratexts can operate as an important pathway towards feminist becoming, wherein the paratextual framing and reframing of texts within feminist fandom are important to the transformative process of *making feminist meaning* of texts, as well as *making meaning of feminism* itself.

Making meaning of feminism, making feminist meaning

Many of my research participants' self-narratives of feminist becoming emphasized the processes by which fandom helped them to cultivate the shared language, cultural signs, symbols, and frameworks through which they came to understand feminism. In one response, 25-year-old Isolde-thelady described this process of feminist becoming in length:

> I think being on Tumblr and having the amazing big sister that I have was the catalyst to my feminism … It started small, reading posts and articles about how the world works and microaggressions and studies about stereotypes … And it

just snowballed until I was the annoying girl who always had to talk about the patriarchy and systematic racism and ableism and every other ism that people around me could give a fuck less about.

(Isolde-thelady, #315)

Having been involved in fandom since her mid-teens, Isolde-thelady explains that her process of feminist becoming began initially as a more gradual, drawn-out process closely tied to her participation in fandom on Tumblr. She explained that fan-created paratexts circulating on Tumblr introduced her to feminist interpretative frameworks, concepts, and discourses through the lens of the popular cultural texts she was interested in as a fan. Isolde-thelady's self-narrative implies that the Tumblr posts she encountered during this period functioned in a consciousness-raising capacity that allowed her to begin to make sense of feminism through the familiarity of her interests as a fan. Isolde-thelady's self-narrative subsequently supports feminist researchers' claim that blogging platforms such as Tumblr may generate a wider feminist consciousness (Kennedy 2007; Larson 2016; Keller 2016a). Once this consciousness-raising process had been initiated, Isolde-thelady explained that it soon 'snowballed' into a much more rapid and transformative process of feminist becoming.

Later, when elaborating further on the fan-created paratexts that initiated her process of feminist becoming, Isolde-thelady listed fan meta analysis, a form of fan-created self-reflexive critical writing and analysis that is stylistically unique to fandom, as particularly conducive to this process. Describing meta as a 'conduit' for feminist becoming, she explained:

Long text posts that get really involved in a specific character or scene or arc and talk about them in the context of the media, but as though they were happening in real life. I think it's so interesting the way people are able to get into a character's head and talk about what they were going through or thinking about that made them make this specific decision or give another character a specific look. And I think that's super important for female characters especially. It gets people to engage with the idea that women have multi-dimensional thoughts, feelings, ideas, or personalities that exist outside of a plot or, in the case of real life, outside of the men around them.

(Isolde-thelady, #315)

Here, Isolde-thelady's positions meta as a fan-created paratext that can interrupt and redirect interpretations of a text. Such fan-created paratexts enable fans to construct and negotiate frames through which they can re-read and re-interpret texts from a feminist perspective, devoting renewed attention to the 'multi-dimensional thoughts, feelings, ideas' of the characters who populate the text. Isolde-thelady's description of the snowballing effect of this process, wherein her interpretation of media texts is 'always' mindful of 'the patriarchy and systematic racism and ableism and every other ism', implies permanence in the shift in the interpretative process prompted by the fan-created paratexts which circulate throughout feminist fandom. Josie (#227) similarly described the benefits of fan-created paratexts using similar discursive themes:

> People spend so much time thinking and writing and engaging in discussions about reasons behind/implications of so many things (and not just in source material, but also within the fandom). I appreciate reading so much of this, even when it's uncomfortable for me because … I come from a really privileged background and I approach a lot of material from a very different perspective. Reading about what other people have to say deepens my understanding not only of the source material, but also of other people.

As Gray (2010, 43) notes, *in medias res* paratexts often 'build themselves into the text, becoming inseparable from it'. Self-narratives of feminist becoming highlight how paratexts can prompt powerful processes of transformation in fans' development of a feminist identity. Fan-created paratexts can provide a framework through which they make sense of feminism. The role of such *in medias res* paratexts in shaping the process of feminist becoming subsequently points to the pedagogical value of fandom as a space to 'engage in a variety of issues and real-world problems' (Booth 2015) through the lens of fannish engagement with texts. I will explore this in more depth in Chapter 4. Additionally, Isolde-thelady's self-narrative notably highlights the significance of being embedded within a social context that is conducive to feminist becoming. In this case, Isolde-thelady's close relationship with her 'amazing big sister' was also an important aspect of her trajectory towards feminist becoming. This indicates that, while fandom (and the fan-created paratexts it encompasses) can provide a pathway towards feminist becoming, this process does not take place in a vacuum and is often dependent on other contingencies within the individual biographies and positionalities of fans. This is something that I will explore in more depth shortly.

However, other feminist fans similarly described a gradual process of feminist transformation through fandom, much like Isolde-thelady's account. Sugarcoatish (#304), an 18-year-old from the Netherlands, for example, also emphasized the significance of fannish analysis, commentary, and critique to her process of feminist becoming. While she admits that she was aware of feminism before encountering it in fandom, she emphasized that she only became more deeply invested in feminist issues after engaging with them within the context of 'the internet and fandom'. She explained that it was through encountering 'feminist discussions and the analysis of (problematic) representation' in fannish spaces that she began to re-evaluate her interpretation of popular cultural texts. These feminist discussions within fannish spaces opened new paths of understanding and were central to her trajectory of feminist becoming. This, she later emphasized, involved a gradual 'process' of transformation that is still ongoing. Similarly, zeppelinfish (#255) also wrote that it wasn't until she became involved with fandom that she began to identify strongly with feminism. She subsequently positioned 'feminist takes on fandom' as central to her meaning-making process as a fan, as well as more broadly:

> It wasn't until after I got heavily into fandom and the internet that I was properly 'woke' as a feminist and realised how important it was to me. I spend a lot of time reading feminist takes on fandom and feminist blogs, and I view the world through a heavily feminist lens.

Many of these self-narratives emphasized that the process of feminist becoming, initiated by *in medias res* paratexts circulated within fandom, subsequently inflected the kinds of fannish content they consumed after coming to recognize themselves as feminist fans. Sara (#333), for instance, explained that her process of feminist becoming had a transformative impact on the way she approaches cultural consumption. 'The way I consume content has changed a lot ever since I started taking my participation in the feminist movement seriously,' Sara explained. Marie (#37) similarly noted, 'I've learnt about abuse and unequal power dynamics from fandom and it's shaped what fannish content I consume.'

Many of the narratives of feminist becoming centred specific fantexts in this process of making sense of feminism and in turn making feminist sense of texts. These included, for example, those surrounding Anglophonic franchises such as *Harry Potter* and *The Hunger Games*, television series such as *Glee*, *Game of Thrones*, and *Orange Is the New Black*, boybands such as *One Direction*, and celebrity feminist stars such as Emma Watson. In these narratives, the specific fantexts surrounding these popular cultural texts are positioned as offering a shared cultural framework through which fans come to understand and make sense of feminism, wherein the familiarity of the fantext makes feminist interpretative frameworks more accessible and intelligible. As 17-year-old Tuva

(#231) wrote, 'I find these discussions or threads are more engaging when they are about things I already have a connection to.'

In these accounts, the specificity of the fantext is significant, as the fan's pre-existing affective investment in, and engagement with, the text operates as the foundation for feminist becoming. These narratives of feminist becoming emphasized how the paratextual commentary circulating surrounding the object of fandom interrupted and redirected their readings of specific texts, subsequently initiating the process of a transformative feminist awakening. As fan studies scholar Busse (2017, 3) notes, fannish commentary and debates are often 'enmeshed with larger social issues'. Thus, if we are to understand feminist becoming as deliberative (see Marine and Lewis 2014), it is important to consider how the deliberative nature of fandom might be conducive to the development of young people's feminist identities. For example, one respondent named spelertoneel (#36), reflecting upon her process of own feminist awakening, wrote that the commentary circulating around the US teen musical comedy-drama television series *Glee* (2009–15) was especially important:

> I can't quite remember when it all started but my feminism did sprout from discourse on Tumblr, and I'm quite certain it was around one of the latter seasons of *Glee* which had such controversial moments that Tumblr did discuss them in detail and, looking back on it, used much of feminist language to strengthen their points. It was around that time that I started to identify as a feminist too; although it was a gradual process before I actually realised that I was.
>
> (#36)

Having been embedded within a community of *Glee* fans for several years, and thus having developed a certain level of affective investment in and attachment to the text, as well as meaningful relationships with other fans, spelertoneel was particularly receptive to the in-depth discussion circulating around the fantext during this period (see Stein 2019). This discussion, she notes, often used feminist language, discourses, and frameworks to interpret the text. In a follow-up email exchange, she explained that she routinely encountered blog posts discussing and critiquing *Glee*, and its fandom accordingly, from a feminist perspective, focusing on a wide range of issues relating to gender, sexuality, race, and disability. Fans' use of feminist discourses to collectively make sense of the text (see Bury 2005) within the fandom subsequently enabled spelertoneel to make sense of these very discourses, as well as make sense of the text in relation to them, subsequently initiating her gradual process of feminist becoming. Likewise, Alejandra (#16) also reported a similar experience within the *Glee* fandom, noting that many of the fan blogs she followed on Tumblr 'were bringing up all these issues that I hadn't questioned before, so I started doing research about it and after seeing all the inequality and injustice I began sympathising with the cause'.

Twenty-four-year-old Emily (#71), who has used Tumblr since mid-2011, described a similar process of feminist becoming rooted in fan-created paratexts. Emily's feminist awakening was closely tied to her favourite character in the US fantasy-drama television series *Game of Thrones* (2011–19, adapted from George R. R. Martin's *A Song of Ice and Fire* fantasy novels), a teen girl named Sansa Stark. Her self-narrative is linked to an intensely affective and identificatory engagement with the text and is thus distinctly fannish in its mode of feminist becoming. She explained, 'I don't think I really identified as a feminist until I joined the *ASOIAF* fandom and decided to stan for Sansa Stark.' As I have explored elsewhere (Hannell 2017a), many fans use Sansa's storyline as a framework to discuss issues surrounding sexual violence, trauma, abuse, victim blaming, and internalized misogyny, moving outwards from textual analysis towards wider social and political commentary (also see Naylor 2016; Barker, Smith, and Attwood 2021). This is something that Emily affirmed throughout our interactions, and these themes appear frequently throughout her blog posts over the years. In her survey responses, Emily explained how her participation in debates and discussions about these issues during her late teens introduced her to a community of feminist fans who 'were older and gave me a lot of words and pedagogy and theory'.

Notably, a number of my research participants also discussed the significance of multi-generational dialogue about feminism within fandom to their feminist becoming. Sabrina (#25), for example, wrote that older fans helped her to re-examine her positionality and work through her internalized misogyny. She told me that older fans were subsequently integral to her feminist becoming. They 'helped me realise how to be a better person/feminist regarding women in fandom,' she wrote. Several of my older research participants, such as 40-year-old Willow (#75), emphasized their awareness of their role in this capacity. Willow explained that she felt it was important to engage 'in conversation with other women, especially young women' about feminist issues in fandom. She emphasized that she viewed it as a moral 'responsibility' to do so. It is in this sense that my participants' narratives adhere to Stein's (2015, 175) understanding of contemporary media fandom as a 'safe but multi-generational environment', wherein multi-generational dialogue can offer 'an empowering route to knowledge within a supportive community'. Moreover, these accounts mark a divergence from popular narratives within the feminist imaginary about inter-generational conflict, of feminist loss and feminist progress, where 'the intellectual convictions and political will of young, old, or in between are assumed to be radically different and our lives fully differentiated from one another's' (Hemmings 2011, 148).

For Emily, her feminist becoming was driven, in part, by her intense identification with Sansa, as well as in her sense of belonging to a multi-generational community of like-minded Sansa fans with whom she felt a sense of solidarity and mutual recognition. 'For me,' she explained, 'at age 18/19/20 defending Sansa felt a lot like finally defending myself, and was when I really had my feminist awakening'. For Emily, the fan-created paratexts circulating around Sansa not only served a pedagogical consciousness-raising function, equipping her with the 'words and pedagogy and theory' through which she came to make sense of feminism, they also had a powerful impact on her sense of self that was central to her feminist awakening. As Gray (2010, 38) notes, 'paratexts can amplify and/or clarify many of a text's meanings and uses, establishing the role that a text and its characters play outside the boundaries of the show, in the everyday realities of viewers' and non-viewers' lives'. The paratextual circulation of texts creates spaces in which fans can create 'meaning *from* and *within* the text' (Geraghty 2015a, 2; my emphasis). Emily explained that, while fandom provided her with the language to describe 'things I had felt and experienced but didn't have the verbiage to explain', thus allowing her to make sense of feminism, it more importantly provided her with a space in which she was able to make sense of her own experiences of trauma and abuse as a child:

> For me, feminism was about finally having the tools to understand my abuse, and how it was perpetrated and why and how my abuser got away with it – and having the tools to try to protect other little girls and other vulnerable women and know I'm fighting a battle alongside many others and feeling less alone.
>
> (#71)

Through Emily's experience as recounted in her self-narrative, then, we can see how powerful and transformative the impact of feminist becoming can be to feminist fans' sense of self. The use of fandom as a space to evaluate, negotiate, and make sense of feminist discourses, practices, and identities can have far-reaching consequences for one's biographical sense of self. Emily's interactions with feminist fan-created paratexts enabled her to make feminist meaning of the text, and make meaning of feminism itself, while also facilitating a broader shift in Emily's understanding of her life narrative and the conditions and experiences which have shaped it. Crucially, for Emily, this process of feminist transformation was tied to the feminist solidarities that she established with other fans with whom she is 'fighting a battle alongside'. This points to the significance of media fandom as a space that can be both socially and culturally conducive to feminist becoming.

Like Emily, who emphasized that fandom provided her with the language and frameworks to describe things she 'had felt and experienced but didn't have the verbiage to explain', many other feminist fans also emphasized that they had long held views and had feelings and experiences consistent with feminism but did not have the appropriate means to name them as such until they encountered them in fandom. As 18-year-old Natalie (#52) reflected, media fandom often operates as 'a place where a lot of people find solidarity and even the language to describe themselves'. The role of fandom in helping participants to develop the language and frameworks through which they could come to express pre-existing sentiments, thoughts, and feelings was a common theme across the responses. Mirime, for example, explained:

> I was always the can-do-anything-be-anything type of a person. I looked up to women who excelled at things, who did things to impact and change the world. My favourite characters in fiction were always women who were strong and confident and took no shit from anybody. ... Then, as I was getting more exposure to various viewpoints ... I began to have vocabulary to express these feelings, to express why it was so important to me to see women have a place in my favourite stories and be treated with respect.
>
> (Mirime, #257)

Mirime explained how her immersion in fandom helped her to make sense of not only her orientation towards cultural texts but also her sense of self more broadly. Her engagement with, and creation of, fan-created paratexts helped her to develop the appropriate language and vocabulary to describe and express feelings she had long held. In doing so, it helped her make sense of the ways in which she had always been drawn to stories that centred women. These moments of transformative self-recognition in the feminist discourses and frameworks that circulate within fandom are subsequently common across the responses to my narrative survey. In becoming feminist fans, my participants did not necessarily report experiencing dramatic and transformative *changes* in values, beliefs, or sense of self. As Sedgwick (1990) reminds us, the act of 'coming out' does not necessarily require the revelation of new information or actions but the discursive articulation of a subject position that may or may not be previously known. Rather, the processes of transformation they describe centre the process of becoming aware of the language or discourse of feminism as a framework for making sense of and expressing pre-existing sentiments and feelings, as well as connecting with other like-minded fans. As Budgeon (2001, 24) observed in her research with young women in England, even though her interviewees did not initially recognize themselves as the subject of feminism, she discovered that a subtle affinity with feminism was often already at play. She noted that many of her interviewees practised 'identities informed by feminist ideals', adding that identification with feminism does not necessarily depend on recognizing oneself as a feminist. Likewise, many of my participants emphasized that, while they often had an implicit long-term affinity with feminism, it was not until they encountered feminist concepts, practices, and discourses in fandom that they began to recognize themselves as such. Their narratives subsequently draw upon discursive frameworks of both *transformation* and *revelation* and *recognition*. This suggests that, while fandom can operate as a pathway towards feminist becoming, to do so may also mark the continuation of narratives of the self already at work, if not yet recognized as such.

In some cases, participants explained that, while they were already aware of the language and discourse of feminism through more formal educational settings, particularly with regard to university, it was not until they encountered 'queer, feminist, and intersectional readings of pop culture' (Peyton, #213) in the informal and everyday fannish spaces they inhabit that these concepts began to resonate with them on a much more immediate level. Such accounts echo earlier research on feminist identification which emphasize the tendency of many young women to regard feminism as a largely academic and middle-class domain (hooks 1994a; Skeggs 1997). One participant named Peyton (#213), for example, explained that while she had studied feminism in a formal capacity at university, feminist discourses, practices, and positionalities did not truly resonate with her until she encountered them in relation to texts and storyworlds she was deeply invested in as a fan. She explained, 'Tumblr really put those frameworks in a more direct context. It went from theoretical to applicable to the world.' Similarly, Willow (#75) noted that the familiarity of the fantext to fans offers a productive space to work through feminist issues, often for the first time. She explained,

'I do think that the issues of relevance to feminism in canon/source material can be a safer platform for discussion than making people expose themselves and their lives.' Joslynnyc (#157) also echoed this understanding of fandom as a safer and more contained space to engage with these issues, highlighting that 'we use the things we love as a jumping off point to examine feminist issues'. In doing so, these discussions that invite alternative feminist reframings of popular cultural texts can be integral to the process of feminist becoming. Jenkins (2006a) notably positions popular culture as mattering politically for this very reason. He argues that 'popular culture allows us to entertain *alternative framings* in part because the stakes a low ... this is in the end another reason why popular culture matters politically – because it doesn't *seem* to be about politics at all' (238–9; my emphasis). Popular culture, he later adds, can offer shared references, resources, and frameworks that fans can use to articulate their hopes and fears about the world (Jenkins et al. 2016; Jenkins, Peters-Lazaro, and Shresthova 2020). Jenkins's understanding of popular culture as a space in which people can entertain alternative political framings in a more informal sense thus resonates with my participants' narratives of feminist becoming.

While these narratives do not necessarily pinpoint a sudden, life-changing transformation in one's sense of self, self-narratives such as 18-year-old Ingrid's, featured below, nevertheless demonstrate how important this process of coming to name these aspects of the self can be and the powerful feelings of belonging that it can produce:

> I believe it was fandom that introduced me to feminism ... I identified as a feminist the moment I learned what the word really meant. I never really studied it formally, but since then I've been educating myself constantly. Feminism is an important part of my identity. It gave me words and explanations for gut feelings that I had never really been able to understand before. It helped me with self-esteem, it gave me power, it made me kinder and more aware.
>
> (Ingrid, #313)

Throughout these self-narratives, fandom operates as a space conducive to feminist sense-making and meaning-making in two distinct yet interrelated ways. Firstly, fandom emerges as an important space in which young people, and particularly young women, come to make sense of feminism, marking the beginning of an ongoing process of feminist becoming. In some cases, this marks feminist fans' first sustained encounter with feminist discourses, concepts, and frameworks, wherein *in medias res* fan-created paratexts circulated within feminist-fannish spaces gradually interrupt and redirect readings of a text, subsequently initiating the process of feminist becoming as one begins to re-evaluate their interpretative frameworks. *In medias res* paratexts, in this sense, can be understood as operating in a consciousness-raising capacity that makes feminism more accessible to younger fans. These accounts tend to frame this broader process of feminist becoming through discursive themes of transformation and change.

Secondly, in other narratives which adhered to this broader theme, feminist fans' self-narratives of feminist becoming emphasize that, while fandom might mark their first *explicit* encounter with feminist discourses, concepts, and frameworks, they had long had feelings, beliefs, and experiences consistent with feminism. In these narratives, feminist fans emphasize that their engagement with feminist fandom helped them to cultivate the shared language, concepts, and frameworks through which they came to recognize, evaluate, and make sense of *pre-existing* feminist narratives of the self already at work. In these accounts, the multi-generational community of like-minded fans and the *in medias res* paratexts they produce are framed as an important part of this process of feminist becoming and coming to recognize oneself as a feminist fan. Additionally, these narratives subsequently frame the process of feminist becoming through discursive themes of transformation, revelation, and self-recognition.

In the next section, I will explore how pre-existing and self-identified feminisms can guide fans' entries into texts, functioning as a kind of entryway paratext in narratives of feminist becoming. Notably, the two paratextual narratives of feminist becoming that I explore here are not necessarily mutually exclusive. Once fans have had their reading of a text interrupted and often redirected by *in medias res* paratexts, they take these interpretative strategies forwards into the texts they encounter hereafter. The fluidity and non-linearity of this process of paratextual feminist becoming are thus important to consider.

Translating feminism to fandom

While many of my research participants emphasized that their feminist becoming was initiated both within and through fandom, a significant number positioned themselves as having *always-already* been feminists. In these self-narratives, fans' pre-existing feminisms were positioned as the result of particular social and cultural prerequisites. Like in many other accounts of feminist becoming (see Hercus 2005; Marine and Lewis 2014), the feminist fans in my research discussed the importance of other feminist role models in their lives to their increased feminist consciousness. Many of the responses discussed the impact of mothers, sisters, and other female relatives to their feminist becoming, as well as the impact of sympathetic friends, teachers, and colleagues. Guilia (#3), for example, told me, 'I was raised by a single working mother which has always relied on her strength and resources to achieve success through her life ... she was my first point of reference for understanding feminism.' Other respondents, particularly from North American and Western European countries, additionally discussed the significance of being raised in middle-class 'liberal' households and educational environments to their feminist identities. As Emily X (#328), a 25-year-old from the United States, explained, for example,

> My parents both consider themselves feminists, and I think my grandparents do as well, so it's something I've always been around ... I grew up in a family that talked about it a lot, and went to a liberal arts college where discussions of feminism were frequent in most of my classes, regardless of what the official topic of the course was.

For these respondents, a long-term awareness of issues surrounding feminism, social justice, and progressive politics inflected their approach to cultural consumption, production, and critique, both in a fannish context and more broadly. These self-narratives thus frame participation in feminist fandom as the extension or continuity of a feminist predisposition. In doing so, they focus less so on the process of becoming feminist and more so on how they integrated their feminisms into their fannish practices and their orientation towards fandom more broadly.

Throughout these self-narratives, fans' pre-existing understanding of, and affiliation with, feminism operates as a kind of entryway paratext, wherein one's pre-existing feminist identity structures and guides entry into a text, as well as fandom more broadly. As I discussed earlier, entryway paratexts preface a work and guide us *into* it. They shape the reading strategies that we take forwards into a text and provide the interpretative frameworks which we use to examine, react to, and evaluate cultural consumption. Entryway paratexts, Gray (2010, 36) argues, provide 'an initial context and reading strategy for the text ... they control our interactions with and interpretations of texts'. In these self-narratives, feminism structures fans' relationship to fandom. As Shea (#246) explained:

> When analysing media or creating fandom-related works feminism is always in the front of my mind. It is very interesting to me how different identities

are presented and how interactions between people of different identities are depicted. I think my interactions with fandom itself are also significantly influenced by feminism.

Here, 23-year-old Shea, who noted that they have always considered themselves a feminist, explains that their feminist subject position has a significant influence on the way they interact with fandom and the fantext. Feminism, they write, 'is always in the front of my mind'. Similarly, tiny-steve (#232) tells me that 'my feminism has always been linked to how women are portrayed and perceived through film and television', and April (#94) explains that 'feminism shapes everything I do'. Similarly, C (#187; their emphasis) writes that 'feminism has shaped my view of the world, so it affects the kind of content I consume and how … I feel that I engage in fandom *through* feminism, rather than the other way around'. Thus, Gray's understanding of entryway paratexts as establishing the parameters that surround media consumption, deflecting readers from certain texts or inflecting their reading when it occurs, offers a valuable framework for analysing self-narratives of feminist-fans who position themselves, first and foremost, as feminists who take their feminism forwards into their encounters with fandom. Averita's (#177) self-narrative offers a good example of this. Averita, a 26-year-old, who emphasized that 'I don't remember ever *not* identifying as a feminist', explained that her pre-existing feminism often governs the popular cultural texts (and, in turn, fantexts) she engages with:

> A lot of my interaction with fans and with fan communities is around what I'd like to see canon doing better, and seeing fans take matters into their own hands when it fails to. Whether that's just in terms of female characters and female-driven storylines, or if it's a matter of diversity in other areas, I'm finding that the older and more aware I become, the more I seek out media that works to promote diversity and particularly well-written female characters. If a show doesn't do that, I'm not going to be interested.

While Gray's focus on paratexts centres *texts*, and I am more broadly exploring narratives about feminist fan subject positions and identities, the impact of a feminist predisposition on one's fannish identity often manifests *textually* through acts of cultural consumption and production in ways that suggest a similar function to entryway paratexts. Thus, I am adopting Gray's theorization of entryway paratexts more loosely as a way to interpret fans' self-narratives which position their pre-existing feminisms through discursive themes which resemble Gray's description of entryway paratexts. Many self-narratives under this theme, for example, emphasized how their pre-existing feminist subjectivities inflected their approach to the fantext and the kinds of pleasures they want it to produce (also see Hannell 2017b). Consider 25-year-old centrumlumina's (#298) narrative, for instance, which explained how her feminism inflects her reciprocal consumption and production of the fantext:

> I've always seen feminism and fandom as entwined. I'm a huge fan of female characters and I support (stan) them in every fandom I contribute to. I like to highlight the characters who don't get enough focus or who have very stereotyped roles by fleshing them out in fic.

Noting that she has always understood her feminism and fandom as intertwined, centrumlumina explains how it structures how she enacts her feminist fan identity. She notes, for example, how she centres 'female characters' in all of the fandoms she contributes to. Building on this, she explains that she enjoys writing about female characters in the fanfiction she creates in order to further develop their narratives and characterizations. Centrumlumina's description of this process is reminiscent of fan studies perspectives which emphasize the role of fannish cultural production as a means for fans to 'fill the gaps' (Fiske 1992, 33) in a text according to their needs and desires (see Hellekson and Busse 2006, 2014; Busse 2017; Hannell 2017b). Additionally, centrumlumina's conscious production of female-centred fanfiction adheres to Narai's (2017) concept of 'homoaffection fic' – that is, a genre of fanwork that 'centres and revalues' women's experiences.

Cultural production

Many of my respondents similarly emphasized that they actively sought to centre girls and women, and other intersecting marginalized identity positions, in the fanworks they produced. Cultural production thus emerges as an important site at which my participants carried their feminism forwards into their fandom. Elsie (#247), for example, wrote that she always makes sure that 'female and non-binary characters in my fics are empowered', and emphasized that she always seeks out other fanworks which demonstrate 'an awareness of feminist issues and gender representation'. Bomberqueen7 (#142) similarly told me that 'I make choices in the stories I tell, which characters I give agency, what kind of emotion I want to prioritise', and Rowan (#306) emphasized that they are 'very big on writing fanfiction that focuses on women and their relationships'. In many of my participants' accounts, both producing and consuming such fanworks were positioned as a form of feminist DIY media praxis (see Ferreday 2015). Similarly, Neta Yodovich (2022, 154) noted that the feminist science-fiction fans she interviewed adopted a similar understanding of their creation of fan-created works, infusing 'their content with feminist perspectives and values'.

Trans respondent Jack (#137), for example, explained that one of the most significant ways in which he carries his feminism forwards into is fandom 'is simply by creating'. For Jack, writing slash fanfiction 'in a safe and accepting space' offers an important space for him to 'share my ideas and develop them even further'. He relates this more broadly to his orientation towards fandom, explaining that on his Tumblr blog 'there's also a lot of sharing posts that express feminist beliefs and outrage at the status quo'. Here, through Jack's responses, we can see how Tumblr users bring together popular culture, popular feminisms, and media fandom. Additionally, while my participants may have produced such fanworks as a result of their pre-existing feminisms structuring their entry into the text, operating as a kind of entryway paratext, it is also important to consider how these fanworks might operate for other fans within the community as *in medias res* paratexts.

For centrumlumina (#298), such processes of feminist and fannish cultural production are just one of the ways she understands her feminism and her fandom as intertwined and indistinct. Additionally, as she explains, the reciprocal relationship between her feminism and her approach to fandom is also inflected by her other salient identity categories. Namely, she told me, it is inflected by her position as a bisexual woman. She later explained:

> I've always shipped F/F more than any other kind of pairing, and my femslash blog tries to support queer women in fandom to relate their experiences to the characters onscreen, whether or not the character is canonically queer. We also run events to boost the representation of minorities within F/F, such as Femslash Diversity Bingo, a tongue-in-cheek way for writers to create 5 fics featuring diverse women and NB [(non-binary)] people along axes such as race, gender identity, sexual orientation, disability, body type and class.

Reflecting on her broader orientation to the fantext, she explains that she has always been more drawn to female/female (also known as 'femslash' or 'wlw') pairings than any others, and she co-created a secondary blog alongside a friend to focus on these pairings specifically. As Hellekson and Busse (2014, 11) note, fandom has often been positioned as a space in which fans can 'explore feminist and/or queer identity issues'. Centrumlumina co-runs this blog, she explains, as an attempt to offer support to other queer women in fandom, and runs 'events' to encourage other fans to produce fanworks that centre femslash pairings through an intersectional lens. This is something I will discuss in more detail in Chapter 4. Centrumlumina's positionality as a queer woman and a feminist thus inflects her entry into, and production of, the fantext in line with a feminist politics of recognition, as well as her interaction with the community of fans surrounding it. Jokesandgays (#163), like centrumlumina, also explained that 'because my network on Tumblr is so extremely wlw-heavy, feminism is just sort of an intrinsic part of that experience'.

Difference

Many narratives of feminist continuity, like centrumlumina's, positioned fandom as a space in which their identities as feminist fans are continually constructed, negotiated, and experienced alongside other salient aspects of their identities. The process of transferring one's feminism into fandom was thus often codified in different ways according to one's pre-existing feminisms, social positionalities, and identity categories. For instance, 17-year-old Grace (#264) framed her self-narrative of feminist becoming, and the transference of her feminism into fandom, as being inextricably linked to her position as a half-Taiwanese, half-Singaporean Asian American girl. As she explained, 'feminism and race are so intertwined for being me that I can't separate them into separate experiences ... feminism is tied strongly to my race and how, I, as an East Asian girl, am seen'. Grace explained that her sense of self as a racialized girl has always structured her understanding of fandom and how she encounters and reproduces the fantext. When discussing the reasons she created her Tumblr blog, she explained, 'I only made a Tumblr last year ... for writing and following the community of kpop and a specific KDrama after anonymously following a lot of blogs, including Diverse High Fantasy and others like East Asians on Western Screens'. Thus, her entry into the fantext was mediated by the inseparability of her feminism and her anti-racism, and her subsequent desire to seek out fannish texts and spaces which centre people of colour. As Grace explains, she initially created her blog to engage with fans of musical and televisual Korean genres and to follow fan blogs which examine the representation of East Asians in Western media cultures. She cites two Tumblr blogs in particular, *diversehighfantasy* ('Diverse High Fantasy') and *eastasiansonwesternscreen* ('East Asians on Western Screen'), as examples of this.

Figure 2 Author screenshot of *eastasiansonwesternscreen* Tumblr blog.

Blogs such as *eastasiansonwesternscreen*, which position themselves as multifannish blogs offering intersectional analyses of race, representation, and fandom (Figure 2), operate in this sense as a form of 'critical paratextuality' (Gray 2010) and can play a key role in constructing interpretative communities of fans. For Grace, such blogs provided an important space for her to learn more about 'social injustices and how they can translate to shows and fandom, even'. In Grace's self-narrative, she emphasizes that this was particularly important to her in terms of engaging in discussions about race, fandom, and representation. Grace's experiences demonstrate how salient identity categories can inform and structure the process of migrating one's pre-existing feminisms across to fandom, as well as govern one's engagement with a feminist politics of recognition. For Grace, her anti-racism and feminism influence the fandoms she engages in, the blogs she follows, and how she interprets the fantext. This movement of her feminism into her fannishness thus relates to the specificity of her experience and identity as a fan of colour and specifically as an Asian American girl.

For many fans of colour, like Grace, fandom does not operate as a moment of feminist awakening or becoming precisely because they have long been aware of difference and otherness, and this has subsequently inflected their approach to fandom. As one feminist fan told me, 'I engage in fandom to create media where I see people like me. I am a woman of colour. *I don't know how to engage with anything in my life in a way that isn't feminist or diverse*' (Cara, #334; my emphasis).

Thus, throughout the self-narratives which adhere to this discursive theme fandom operates as a space not for feminist becoming per say but for the continuity between a pre-existing feminism and one's fannish practices and activities. These pre-existing feminisms thus establish the parameters that shape fannish media consumption, operating as a kind of entryway paratext. Their narratives reveal that this continuity varies according to one's social location and position DIY cultural production as a particularly fruitful site for the unification of pre-existing feminisms with fandom.

Fans' emergent feminisms

The final theme of feminist fans' self-narratives moves us away from the important role of (para)textuality. Within this theme, feminist fans emphasized that their process of feminist becoming was still *ongoing*. These self-narratives highlight that to be a feminist fan is not to occupy a static, fixed, and uncomplicated identity position. Rather, to be a feminist fan is to engage in a *continuous* and *ongoing* process of feminist becoming. These self-narratives utilize an understanding of the self as open, flexible, creative, emergent, and in process. April (#95), for instance, told me that 'I feel like I'm having feminist awakenings all the time'. As Currie, Kelly, and Pomerantz (2007, 2009) highlight, becoming a feminist is a much more complex and ongoing process than typically acknowledged: one is not positioned simply 'inside' or 'outside' feminism by taking up a subject position within feminist discourse. Feminisms, and feminist identities, are often complex and emergent. They are imbued with 'becomings, processes, and thresholds' (Smith-Prei and Stehle 2016, 150).

The continual process of feminist becoming is framed throughout these narratives as deliberative, social, and communal, positioning fandom as a site at which fans collectively struggle over meanings of feminism. They emphasize how fandom has provided them with opportunities to discuss and refine their understandings of multiple feminisms, both in theory and in practice, and position themselves as open to new concepts, discourses, and practices. Many of my participants explained, for instance, how they first learned about issues such as intersectionality and privilege through their engagement with one another within fandom, and they subsequently highlight that they are constantly in the process of reconsidering and reworking their identities and practices as feminist fans in relation to the new knowledge they develop. Like Taft's (2011) girl activist interviewees, they tend not to think they have found the definitive 'answer' to a given political problem but instead strive to create opportunities for feminist fans to discuss issues, learn from one another, and develop responses together.

Youth

Throughout these narratives, my participants position the process of becoming a feminist fan as a form of group 'identity work' (Wexler 1992; Best 2011). For them, feminist fandom can be understood as a work in progress marked by continuous growth and change. As I discussed earlier in relation to the *fantext*, fan studies scholars argue that the notion of 'a work in progress' is central to both fandom and the study of fandom (Hellekson and Busse 2006). This understanding of fandom as a work in progress can be carried over to my participants' understandings of *feminist fandom* as a work in progress. Several of the feminist fan self-narratives I gathered, which positioned feminist fandom as a work in progress, as a form of group identity work, did so through discursive themes of youth and adolescence. For instance, a 14-year-old respondent, Starshine2375 (#311), explained, 'I'm young, I'm sometimes under-informed on issues that I should be more aware of and then I try to fix that, it was only recently that I made my own account to be more active and able to engage with these issues.' Similarly, a 16-year-old respondent, Vakyrath (#310), explained, 'I'm a child. I'm unaware and am still developing my opinions. I'm sure I'll be a louder advocate as I grow older, but for now I'll cheer for those who are doing what I believe in when I can't.' In these narratives, my teen participants position their feminist becoming using discourses about adolescence as a time of formation and exploration of the self (Lesko 1996; Wyn and White 1997). Additionally, as Smith-Prei and Stehle (2016, 150) highlight, fourth-wave feminisms' focus on 'becomings, processes, and thresholds' aligns them with an inherently adolescent aesthetic. However, while these teen participants emphasize their desire to develop their understandings of feminism, how they do so, positioning themselves as 'unaware' and 'under-informed', unwittingly reproduces the long-standing idea that youth experiences are primarily relevant for how they impact the supposedly more 'real' and 'legitimate' world of adulthood (James, Jenks, and Prout 1998; Gordon 2010).

From white feminism to intersectional feminism

Alternatively, many of my research participants positioned this group identity work as corresponding to broader shifts within feminist theory and popular feminist discourse that inform the social and cultural practices of feminist fandom. Many narratives, for instance, emphasize how their feminist fan identities have evolved alongside a broader shift from 'mainstream feminism' or 'white feminism' towards a more 'intersectional feminism' over the past decade. Dace's (#21) self-narrative offers an insight into this process. Dace, a 24-year-old from Latvia, explained that, while she grew up in a sheltered environment and was ignorant of social issues for much of her childhood, she began to identify as a feminist after being exposed to more perspectives and current affairs from 'around the world' after joining Tumblr. For Dace, being exposed to transnational feminisms was an important part of her feminist awakening. The fandom blogs she followed, she explains, introduced her to commentary about social justice issues such as race, sexuality, and gender for the first time and thus initiated her feminist becoming. 'I thought that', she told me, 'of course I am a feminist because I care about these issues'. Tumblr was important to this process, Dace explains, 'because I could easily access a million different sources and blogs that focused on specific topics'. For Dace, a particularly transformative moment in her feminist becoming took place during the aftermath of events in Ferguson, Missouri, USA, in August 2014. Following the fatal shooting of Michael Brown, an unarmed African American teenager, by police officer Darren Wilson in August 2014, and the subsequent emergence of the Black Lives Matter movement, Dace explained:

> After Ferguson in the USA, Tumblr completely changed and almost everyone I followed changed their blogging style and started talking more about topics of race, feminism and other issues … Back then it was much simpler to identify as a feminist because it meant you supported equality. Now feminism has so many different layers, and you have to actively work on it so that your feminism would be intersectional, etc.

For Dace, what she felt to be a marked shift in the kinds of feminisms circulating within fandom on Tumblr prompted her to re-evaluate and re-negotiate her understanding of feminism and her own identity as a feminist. In doing so, she explains that she moved away from a relatively singular understanding of feminism as supporting 'equality' towards a more multiplicitous and multivalent understanding of feminism. Wendy (#295) similarly explained, 'I started to get really involved after Michael Brown's death.' Dace and Wendy's accounts of their emergent fannish feminisms align with recent feminist accounts which examine an 'intersectional turn' (Carbin and Edenheim 2013) in feminist discourses over the past decade (Rivers 2017; Villesèche, Muhr, and Śliwa 2018; Kanai 2020a). This is something I will return to, and critique, in Chapter 4. For Dace, her emergent understanding of feminism accounts for 'so many different layers', and she emphasizes that she understands that her feminism is something she must actively work on. Dace's account demonstrates how feminisms articulated by fans correspond to broader discursive shifts taking place within feminism. These modes of fannish feminist becoming do not take place in a vacuum but are contingent upon the specificities, and constraints, of the broader social, cultural, and political context of these becomings.

Many of these self-narratives mobilize discourses about regulating, disciplining, and improving the feminist (and fannish) self, where feminist identity work is incorporated 'into a disciplinary mechanism of self-perfection' (Kanai 2020a, 26). In many cases, these are bound up with anxiety about whiteness, white privilege, and the spectre of 'white feminism'. Within critical whiteness studies, whiteness refers to a racialized social location of power, privilege, and prestige (Yancy 2012). By virtue of its dominance, whiteness often remains invisible, or *unmarked,* to those who inhabit it, and it is instead a taken-for-granted 'normative and universal condition' (Moon 1999, 178). White privilege refers to a structural 'metaprivilege' (Flagg 2005) that confers white people (and those who can successfully proximate whiteness) with unearned advantages across all domains of social, political, economic, and cultural life (McIntosh 1989). The term 'white feminism' brings together this understanding of whiteness and white privilege, denoting 'any feminism which comes from a white perspective, *and* universalises it' (Aziz 1992, 296). 'White feminism', as a critical-descriptive term, has recently been revitalized within feminist discourse. Concurrently, feminist fans frequently reference the term in their self-narratives, often doing so through discourses of anxiety, guilt, shame, and embarrassment. MsSunflower (#24), for example, told me that her feminism initially

> [e]volved into a level of (now cringe-worthy) White Feminism in high school when I got involved in gay rights groups. I now consider myself an intersectional feminist who is constantly trying to educate herself and trying to shut up and let people speak for themselves, promoting platforms for voices rather than being on it myself.

In this narrative, MsSunflower describes her earlier 'white feminism' through discourses of embarrassment, regret, and shame and emphasizes that she has since become an 'intersectional feminist' who consciously engages in an ongoing process of self-education. Likewise, rileybl00 (#106) lamented, '[F]or a few years, I was unfortunately only exposed to white feminism,' and Maaike (#35) reflected:

> Over time, I realised that I was practicing a very simple form of feminism, with just some mainstream facts and anger. White feminism, if you will. Some of my mutuals started getting more into intersectional feminism and I realised that this was the way to go.

For Maaike, the process of reflexively developing her understanding of feminism was prompted by the social context of fandom, wherein her fandom friends' ('mutuals') burgeoning understanding of more 'intersectional' feminist frameworks motivated her to re-evaluate her own perspective. She described this process as 'very enlightening', and later explained, '[N]ow I try to focus my social activism on a broad range of feminist issues, not just the classic wage gap things.'

Throughout these accounts, white feminist fans mobilize anxiety-laden discourses about (white) privilege and self-awareness of their normative identity positions. For example, Willow (#75) reflected that the first time they became aware of the concept of privilege was 'a lightbulb moment' in their feminist becoming and has prompted the re-evaluation of their frameworks and practices since. As they explained, '[t]he dawning understanding that I was far too comfortable in cis white feminism while trans and non-white sisters had things so much worse got me back into actually thinking about things instead of congratulating myself on being so progressive'. My participants' articulation of privilege corresponds to recent discursive shifts within feminism regarding the intersectional turn and subsequently counters earlier perspectives such as Keller's (2016a, 34–5), who noted that her young feminist research participants rarely recognized their privileged identities. Many of my participants emphasized that recognizing their privilege was an important part of their ongoing process of feminist becoming. The articulation of privilege and the performative disavowal of 'white feminism' thus formed the core work of becoming, wherein feminist becoming is entangled with practices of disciplining the feminist self. This identity work, they emphasized, was often undertaken through their engagements with fandom, and they position fandom as a productive site for it.

Feminist fans' disavowal of 'white feminism' aligns with Akane Kanai's (2020a) research, which positions 'interrogations of whiteness' (32) as central to contemporary feminist identity work. Crucially, she emphasizes, white feminists' pursuit of a supposedly intersectional feminist identity often obscures the reinvigoration of practices of middle-class whiteness centred on individual self-monitoring and self-discipline (see Winch 2012, 2013). These disavowals of white feminism, which focus on white guilt, shame, and embarrassment, risk being mobilized as solipsistic 'gesture[s] toward white purity' (Yancy 2012, 156) that affirm and protect 'white moral integrity' (Applebaum 2010, 27) instead of undertaking more meaningful anti-racist work. It is in this sense that disavowing, as well as distancing oneself from, one's complicity in white feminism risks obfuscating it. This is something I will return to in Chapter 3. For many white feminist fans, then, feminist identity work is tangled up in complex racialized discourses surrounding the desire to be perceived as a 'good' or 'perfect' feminist (McRobbie 2015; Kanai 2020a) and a 'nice' or 'good' white person (Moon 1999; Applebaum 2010; Yancy 2012; DiAngelo 2021).

Marginality and emergent feminisms

However, the interrogation of whiteness was also important within the self-narratives of the non-white feminist fans who engaged with my research. Several participants emphasized that their ongoing process of feminist becoming is entangled with their burgeoning awareness and understanding of their marginalized identities, particularly surrounding their race and ethnicity, as well as gender and sexuality. For example, Izzy (#269), a 21-year-old African American, explained that her emergent feminism is tied to moments of disconnect between her identity as an African American woman and the types of feminism she initially embraced during high school:

> I'd initially begun identifying myself as a feminist in high school and it took the form of 'girl power' ra-ra 'girls can be just as strong as boys' sort of deal. I didn't really begin to critically think about feminism and my relationship to it until my freshman year of high school when I began to read more works by the likes of bell hooks and people like her. When I began to think, or rather more readily reflect on the intersection between my race and my status as a woman was when I realised that a significant amount of mainstream feminist rhetoric (or rather feminist rhetoric that had begun to be popularised or even discussed) quite often left out race and I couldn't truly connect with it in a way that I had wanted to.

For Izzy, her ongoing feminist becoming was not tied up in the burgeoning awareness of her *privileged* identity position or social location but rather her increasing self-awareness of her *marginality*, 'the intersection between my race and my status as a woman'. Izzy explained that fandom has since operated as a useful conduit for her to further explore intersectional feminism as well as the work of radical Black feminists like bell hooks. She told me that she enjoys engaging in discussions 'of race and the intersection between race and sexuality or race and gender' in fandom, for instance.

Likewise, 24-year-old Canadian Josie (#227) explains that, while she occupies some privileged identity positions, her feminism has evolved as she has become increasingly aware of her positionality as a Métis[4] person and 'as a product of colonisation':

> When I first got started, it was pretty basic stuff. I didn't think about the interplay between all these other paradigms. Racism? Homophobia? Ableism? Islamophobia? I was very much a White Feminist Woman and didn't see beyond how sexism impacted me. I think the few political things I cared about was white feminism and the environment. By the end of high school, I started reading more about Indigenous issues (mostly because it started to hit home that as a Métis person, I was a product of colonisation) ... At this point, I'm not sure if I can articulate what feminism means to me. It ... encompasses more than before. For me, it involves a lot of listening. Caring about other people. Lot of empathy. But also action.

Josie described her process of feminist becoming as a transformative 'journey' and, like many of my other participants, positioned her earlier understanding of feminism through discourses of shame, describing it as 'embarrassing'. She emphasized that engaging with a community of feminist fans on Tumblr was an important conduit for her feminist becoming and for expanding her understanding of feminism to incorporate intersectional and indigenous frameworks. She explained, 'Tumblr has been pretty important for me. It helped me realised I'm not straight. Helped me get the confidence to actually learn about my Métis heritage and get involved in my community.'

Elsewhere, the process of feminist becoming was framed alongside other processes of identity development and reflexive self-awareness. Sonseulsoleil (#74), a non-binary and trans 21-year-old, for example frames their process of feminist becoming through the lens of their gradual acceptance of their identity as a trans and non-binary person and their increasing immersion in 'social justice communities' on Tumblr:

My [definition] of feminism has certainly changed. I used to be a lot less intersectional. But now that I've come to terms with being trans and nonbinary, not to mention my attraction to women, and the more I've immersed myself in the social justice communities on Tumblr and educated myself, I see feminism as about so much more than just white women. It's about racial equality, it's about fighting transphobia and homophobia and ableism and honestly fighting oppressive capitalism. I want to fucking dismantle everything at this point.

This, they explain, has subsequently led to the expansion and re-evaluation of their understanding of feminism, and themselves as a feminist, to incorporate a much broader range of progressive and emancipatory politics.

Many of these narratives of ongoing identity work are underpinned by an understanding of feminist fandom as a pedagogical space. While I will explore the pedagogical function of feminist fandom on Tumblr in more depth in Chapter 4, it is worth briefly examining here with regard to the process of feminist becoming that my participants describe. Narratives of becoming a feminist fan that emphasize the processual nature of the identity also emphasize a commitment to an ongoing process of learning and self-improvement, of feminist reflexivity. Josie (#227), for example, emphasized, 'I fully expect I will constantly have to check myself and learn/unlearn new ways of thinking'. This, she explained, was motivated by her intention 'to not become complacent'. Similarly, sugarcoatish (#304) explained that becoming a feminist fan 'was a slow process and I am still learning'. These narratives bear resemblance to those articulated by Jackson's (2018) research participants. In her research on girls' digital feminisms in New Zealand, Jackson notes young people's commitment to identity work and self-development in their feminist frameworks, observing that 'the construction of feminism within a pedagogical framework was striking ... girls commonly located themselves within a developmental trajectory as "growing" in their feminism through using social media sites as a learning tool' (41). Similarly, Kanai's (2020b, 11) feminist research participants emphasized that 'self-education was a highly important facet of life that was almost taken for granted as an everyday, responsible feminist activity'. This understanding of feminism as an ongoing learning process is something many feminists articulate (see Ahmed 2017).

Thus, throughout these self-narratives, we witness a move away from the paratextual grounding of the first two discursive themes and can instead identify an emphasis on the processual nature of fannish feminist becoming.

These narratives position fandom as a site where fans collectively struggle over meanings of feminism and locate feminist becoming as an ongoing form of group and individual identity work that corresponds to broader discursive shifts in feminism, particularly concerning concepts such as 'intersectionality' and 'white feminism'. Additionally, these narratives of feminist becoming are punctuated by discourses about regulating and improving the feminist (and, thus, fannish) self. In most cases, these are bound up with anxiety about the articulation of privilege and normative identities, although several respondents also explore youth and marginalized identity positions through this discursive framework. More broadly, these self-narratives can be unified through their emphasis on the importance of self-awareness, ongoing processes of education and learning, and a broader commitment to the group identity work taking place within feminist fandom.

Conclusion

Throughout this chapter, I have explored my participants' self-narratives of becoming a feminist fan to reveal how digital media fandom might offer a pathway that is conducive to feminist becoming. In doing so, I move away from popular narratives within feminist cultural studies which position formal education contexts and participation in largely ephemeral and episodic acts of digital feminism as dominant pathways towards feminist becoming and instead examine the processes of feminist becoming which are unique to the cultural and social specificities of media fandom. Through examining my participants' self-narratives, I also reveal how the relatively dichotomous understanding of identity development within both feminist cultural studies and fan studies does not account for the nuances and complexities of my participants' self-narratives, which in many cases utilize discursive themes of both continuity and change.

While media fandom does not, of course, *determine* or guarantee feminist becoming, my participants' self-narratives offer insight into how, under certain circumstances, it does provide a space conducive to it. Additionally, these narratives should be interpreted within their broader social, cultural, and political context. As my participants' narratives of emergent feminisms indicate, the kinds of feminism articulated by fans correspond to discursive shirts in feminism taking place within both the academy and the popular domain. These self-narratives also correspond to the social locations and positionalities of individuals. My participants' self-narratives point to the importance of identity markers such as race, gender identity, and sexuality, in narratives of becoming a feminist fan. These differences, in turn, subsequently shape fannish activities and practices, as well as fandom more broadly. Thus, to identify as a feminist fan is to inhabit a fluid and emergent identity position that is contingent upon other salient identity markers and social, cultural, and political contexts.

Belonging as a feminist fan on Tumblr

Over the past two decades, the concept of belonging has become a subject of lively sociological inquiry. Building upon critically oriented conceptual and theoretical understandings of identities as fluid and processual, as I discussed in the previous chapter, scholars such as Elspeth Probyn (1996) argue that conceptualizations of belonging can augment our understandings of identity. The concept of belonging, Probyn argues, allows us to account for the relational aspects of identity. It accounts for 'what identity really is for' (9). The concept, she argues, thus,

> [c]aptures more accurately the desire for some sort of attachment, be it to people, places, or modes of being, and the ways in which individuals and groups are caught within wanting to belong, wanting to become, a process that is fuelled by yearning rather than the positing of identity as a stable state.
>
> (Probyn 1996, 19)

In these discussions, too, belonging is tied to becoming and is similarly approached as multiplicitous, dynamic, and processual. In their overview of the use of the concept of belonging in contemporary research, Lähdesmäki et al. (2016, 242) argue that belonging comprises of 'situational relationships with other people and social and cultural practices stemming from these relationships, which are fundamentally political and include emotional and/ or affective orientations'. More broadly, the concept of belonging is taken up as a framework for examining the entanglement of the multiple and intersecting spatial, temporal, cultural, and socio-political dimensions of identity.

Unlike the self-narratives of becoming that I explored in the previous chapter, which were often self-contained within responses to specific questions within my narrative survey, my participants' accounts of belonging within feminist fandom were dispersed across their responses. Examining these accounts grants us insight into the ways in which feminist fan communities on Tumblr bring together fannish and feminist discourses, practices, and positionalities.

Due to the taken-for-grantedness of belonging (May 2011), as an everyday mode of being that is largely habitual, unmomentous, and unconscious (Felski 2002), my analysis of my participants' experiences of belonging had to account for the *implicit* ways in which notions of belonging were embedded into my participants' discursive understandings of concepts such as community, inclusion, participation, recognition, and reciprocity within the context of feminist fandom.

Feminist identity work and/as belonging work

In Chapter 1, I positioned *becoming feminist* (be that within, or without, fandom) as an ongoing and open-ended process, as a form of group identity work corresponding with broader discursive shifts in feminism within both academic and popular domains. Before I delve further into my ethnographic data to examine feminist fans' implicit sense of *belongingness* within feminist fandom, I would first like to turn to Kuurne and Vieno's (2022) theorization of 'belonging work' to allow us to better understand feminist fans' individual and group feminist identity work detailed in Chapter 1 (and, later, in Chapter 4) as a form of belonging work. The concept of belonging work, Kuurne and Vieno argue, locates the active and processual nature of belonging as a form of *work* that is relationally negotiated. While Kuurne and Vieno recognize that belonging work is 'always complex, ambiguous, and messy' (293), and thus evades rigid empirical definition, the concept invites a greater attentiveness to the complex relational landscape in which belonging is achieved. Belonging work, they write,

> [t]ackles the agentic aspect of belonging, asking how actors can shape their own or others' inclusion and exclusion, or closeness and distance, in relation to social groups and categories ... Belonging work is thus relational work that actors embedded in social structures engage in to shape and modify their social relations and positions ... The work of belonging is made up of a tremendous amount of constant activity, which may be habitual and/or intentional and often involves conscious and subconscious dimensions.
>
> (Kuurne and Vieno 2022, 292)

Here, they attend to the ongoing work, be that intentionally, routinely, or subconsciously, involved in *doing* or accomplishing belonging (also see May 2011). Within feminist fandom, we can see belonging work play out across feminist fans' accounts of their feminism as *in process*, as well as in their efforts to position themselves as open to new concepts, discourses, and practices, as willing to undertake the identity work required of a 'good' feminist subject.

This reflexive feminist identity work, then, encapsulates the relationally negotiated work that feminist fans continuously undertake to negotiate and accomplish belonging within feminist fandom. To belong within feminist fandom, one must be willing (or, at least, perform a willingness) to actively and continually undertake feminist identity work. To engage in an ongoing process of *becoming*, one necessarily undertakes *belonging work*: wanting to 'become' and wanting to 'belong' are interrelated (Probyn 1996). This is something I will also return to in Chapter 4, where I explore feminist fans' conscious commitment to an ongoing process of reflection and un/learning as a form of relational feminist identity work *and* belonging work within feminist fandom. It is for this reason that the feminist identity work undertaken within, and through, feminist fandom is best understood *and/as* a form of belonging work: as an ongoing, complex, messy process of feminist becoming that mediates one's access to (non/)belonging (see Chapter 3) within feminist fandom.

Throughout the remainder of this chapter, I examine my ethnographic data to explore the interrelated affective, spatial, and relational dimensions of belonging within feminist fandom on Tumblr. Firstly, I explore how feminist fandom is discursively (re)produced as an imagined community of 'like-minded' feminist fans by my participants, as well as the importance of shared *feeling*, of shared affective states, to a sense of belonging within this imagined community. I subsequently position feminist fandom on Tumblr as an 'intimate public' (Berlant 2011) rooted in the expectation that feminist fans always already share a worldview and emotional, or affective, knowledge tied to one's fannish feminisms. I then explore how my participants' pursuit of connection with like-minded fans works to produce spatial understandings of belonging to feminist fandom closely tied to the perception of Tumblr as a 'safe space'. Within these accounts of spatial belonging, the platform is positioned as a 'safe space' because of its reputation as a space conducive to 'counterpublic' address (Fraser 1990), as well as the sense of privacy produced by the technological affordances and 'silosocial' (Tiidenberg, Hendry, and Abidin 2021) vernacular of the platform. Building upon these claims, I argue that my participants' positioning of Tumblr as a 'safe space' to engage with feminist fandom without fear of judgement counters recent claims within fan studies about the mainstreaming and increasing acceptance of fandom and fan cultures within the twenty-first century (Jenkins 2007; Coppa 2014; Jenner 2017).

Imagined community and affective belonging

One of the most prominent themes that emerged across my participants' accounts of feminist fandom involved the centrality of 'community' to their sense of belonging. As Sarah (#64), for example, explained, '[t]hat sense of community is, to me, one of the most integral aspects of fandom. I can't really consider myself part of a fandom unless I'm engaging on a pretty deep level with other people in it'. Morgan (#322) similarly positioned community membership as the 'primary experience of being involved in fandom'. The term 'community' and synonyms and derivatives such as 'communal' and 'collective' were mentioned over three hundred times across my data set, and many responses established strong demarcations between the first subjective appearance of individual fannish identities and first 'real' encounters with fandom through access to a community of fans. Belonging to an 'imagined community' (Anderson 1983) of feminist fans, based not in geographic proximity but in mutual recognition of shared practices, identifications, and norms, is thus highly important and meaningful to my participants. Community, in this sense, 'exists in the *minds* of its members' (Cohen 1985, 98; my emphasis).

The concept of community has been taken up in many iterations within fan studies, and Morimoto and Chin (2017) observe that the understanding of media fandoms as imagined communities forms a 'central truism' (174) of English-language fan studies. They add that the concept of imagined community within contemporary fan studies foregrounds 'the transborder, transnational reach of the Internet in creating a sense of a simultaneous, shared popular culture experience' (174). My research includes participants from thirty-nine countries in total, although the vast majority were from Anglophone countries in the Global North. Nevertheless, the understanding of fandom as an imagined transnational and transborder community rooted in shared popular cultural experience was articulated by a number of my respondents. Florangel (#9), for example, explained that she loved fandom because of 'how united and connected I felt with people from many different backgrounds and places in the world'. Likewise, HelloMissSunshine (#8) told me that she enjoys 'the open and friendly community from all over the world', and TheGirlNoOneKnows5 (#61) wrote that she loves fandom because it provides a way to 'communicate' and 'share interests' with 'people from all over the world that you may never have met otherwise'.

For Laura (#40), the benefits of belonging to a seemingly transnational community of feminist fans were twofold: 'I like it because it includes people from all around the world and it gives you that bit of anonymity that makes you feel safe even if you are talking/interacting with people you don't know personally.' Laura not only values the understanding of fandom as a transcultural space, she also values the relative anonymity that it affords. For Laura, the sense of anonymity within an imagined community of fans helped her to feel a sense of safety. The importance of 'feeling safe' within Laura's response highlights the interplay between both the relational and affective content of belonging (see May 2011; Murphy 2011).[1] While the invocation of a 'sense of belonging' is itself affective (see Ferreday 2011), belonging is often described in affective terms as feeling 'safe' (Ignatieff 2001) or feeling a 'sense of ease' (Lugones 1990; Miller 2003; May 2011, 2013), and many of my participants articulated their understandings of the imagined community of feminist fans using similar affect-laden descriptions that evoke safety, comfort, and ease. Twenty-three-year-old Alicia (#128), for example, explained that it 'felt cosy and nice', Alejandra (#16) described the community as 'supportive', and tiny-steve (#232) described it as 'welcoming'. Similarly, Sabrina (#205) used the phrase 'family-like feeling' to refer to her experiences, while Renee (#42) described the community as marked by a 'feeling of union'. These affect-laden descriptions produce a sense of closeness, trust, and connection that are important to the constitution and maintenance of feminist fandom as an imagined community.

Like-mindedness as shared affective practice

Many of my participants emphasized the importance of feminist fandom as a space to connect with 'like-minded' people and forge new friendships based on mutual recognition. As Gauntlett (2000, 13) notes, coming into close proximity with 'like-minded people' online is crucial to the formation of online communities (also see Korobkova 2014; Mendes, Keller, and Ringrose 2019; Tiidenberg, Hendry, and Abidin 2021). Elly (#108), for example, explained how her engagement with fanfiction led her to engage with a community of like-minded fans who shared her tastes, practices, interests, and world view. For Elly, connecting with like-minded fans produced powerful feelings of inclusion and recognition:

> I found the fanfiction community and started reading everything – good, bad, great, awful. And then I started talking to the people behind the stories. They are awesome. I feel like I'm amongst equals of the mind and it doesn't matter who we are on the other side of the screen.
>
> (Elly, #108)

Beyond shared interests, one important criteria for determining like-mindedness across these responses was through a sense of shared 'affective practice' (Wetherell 2012) between oneself and other members of the imagined community of feminist fans. Many participants emphasized the significance of not only interacting with 'like-minded' people but more specifically interacting with 'people who *felt the same way*' (theclexachronicles, #80; my emphasis). Here, the sense of *shared feeling*, of shared affects, within feminist fandom is crucial to theclexachronicles's sense of belonging, weaving together both the affective and the relational. Indeed, both feminism and fandom have been described as deeply affective. As numerous fan studies scholars have highlighted, affect plays a key role in the formation of both individual and collective fannish identities (Busse 2013; Stein 2015, 2019; Lamerichs 2018), and intense affective experience is fundamental to the formation and operation of media fandom (Stein 2018, 2015). Similarly, feminist theorist Hemmings (2012, 150) asserts that affect 'gives feminism its life', and Stanley and Wise (1993, 66) highlight that 'feminism appeals because it means something – it touches deeply felt needs, feelings and emotions.' It is 'suffused with feelings, passions, and emotions' (Gorton 2007, 345). Fandom and feminism can thus be understood as intensely affective, and for many of my participants the shared experience of these 'affective intensities' (Papacharissi 2014) formed an important aspect of belonging to an imagined community constituted by its both *fannish* and *feminist* valences. As McCracken (2017, 152–3; my emphasis) notes, Tumblr users blur the 'boundaries between affect and social critique'; they are 'bonded primarily by common, passionate affective *and* progressive interests'. Similarly, Tiidenberg, Hendry, and Abidin (2021, 48) highlight that Tumblr users engagements with cultural texts are 'fuelled primarily by affective investments and political stakes'.

Across my data collection, feminist fans used a wide range of terms, both positive and negative, to describe their affectively charged engagements with the fantext and with feminist fandom. These include, for example, terms such as 'happy', 'overwhelmed', 'thrilled', 'excited', 'awe', 'love', 'enjoy', 'hate', 'touched', 'passion', 'fascinating', 'annoyed', 'obsessed', 'adore', 'squee', 'frustrated', and 'upset'. Zellieh (#87), for instance, reported feeling 'overjoyed' upon discovering fandom, while Lane (#63; original emphasis) explained that she was 'THRILLED' to discover other fans like her. Similarly, theclexachronicles (#80) reported feeling 'awe and general happiness when realising that there were fellow people out there feeling the same way as me'. Here, the affective intensities produced by these feelings of recognition fulfil the desire for attachment that Probyn (1996) argues is central to belonging. Not only do these accounts support May's (2013, 93) assertion that 'a sense of belonging can lead to experiences of joy, contentment, happiness, or fulfilment', they also demonstrate how the act of articulating emotional states can create imagined communities of feeling (Ferreday 2003, 2011).

Passion and anger

Two of the most prominent shared affective states that emerged across the responses were both *passion* and *anger*. Passion most often emerged in reference to participants' shared interest in the fantext, wherein a sense of belonging was expressed in relation to the recognition of shared passion towards the practice of consuming and producing the fantext. Seventeen-year-old Max (#112), for example, explained:

> Fandom is something that is very present in my everyday life, ... it's something my friends are also involved in. I feel like fandom can be a wonderful thing that brings people closer and has them bond over stories, and characters they both love and/or identify with.
>
> (Max, #112)

Here, Max argues that shared passion for the fantext can 'bring people closer', wherein shared passion for the fantext becomes a source of connection and bonding between fans. The feelings of contentment produced by this are clear through Max's description of this as a 'wonderful thing' that is very present in their everyday life. Similarly, Morgan (#322) also articulated a sense of belonging not only through shared interest but through a shared *passion* for the fantext. Morgan emphasized that the expansion of his 'sense of connectedness to others through the things I had passions for' was central to his involvement in media fandom, going so far as to describe it as his 'primary experience' of fandom. The recognition of shared passion and the feelings of connectedness it produces is thus important to a sense of belonging within feminist fandom.

On the other hand, many feminist fans also emphasized how central shared anger and frustration are to their sense of belonging within the feminist fan community. Feminist fans share a common understanding of cultural texts as the 'object' of their feminist anger (Ahmed 2004b). Sarah (#308), for example, explained the feeling of catharsis produced by discovering other fans who shared her sense of frustration with the object of fandom. A fan of the American fantasy-drama television series *Supernatural* (2005–2020),[2] she wrote:

I got sucked into the [Supernatural] fandom because I was no longer satisfied with the content and tried to reach out and see if other people felt the same way. I honestly thought I was the only one in the world to be depressed because of a TV show, so it was a nice surprise to find other people who took it as personally as I did.

(Sarah, #308)

Above, she describes the importance of connecting with like-minded fans who shared her feelings of frustration and dissatisfaction towards the object of fandom. Discovering other fans who also felt so intensely about the programme was a 'nice surprise' and helped to reduce her sense of isolation. The recognition of these intensely affective states in others, who 'took it as personally as I did', thus provided an important sense of belonging for Sarah. As Ferreday (2011) notes, such moments of recognition often come to be articulated as a sense of belonging. Affective belonging to an imagined community of fans therefore rests on the recognition of shared intense affects that are not only positive (joy, celebration, passion), but also negative (anger, frustration, upset) or even 'ugly' (Ngai 2005).

As I previously argued, fandom can operate as an interpretative tool to *make sense of* feminism, as well as *make feminist sense* of fandom and all that it encompasses. In turn, many of my participants made sense of, organized, and articulated their shared affective investments in the fantext through feminist discourses and frameworks. When I asked Sarah (#308), for example, to elaborate on the feelings of frustration that she shared with other fans, she explained that many of her frustrations coalesced around a central 'feminist debate' within the community of *Supernatural* fans to which she belongs: 'where are the women and why do they keep dying?' Here, Sarah frames fans' shared feelings of frustration with the fantext through feminist discourses about cultural representations and media critique.

Across my research participants' survey responses, this process of articulating shared affects through feminist frameworks applied to feelings of anger and frustration as much as it did passion, and in many cases my participants reported feeling an ambivalent mix of both passion and anger, often simultaneously, towards the fantext. As fan studies scholar Louisa Stein (2019, 83) highlights, 'fan love is almost always in constant interplay with a spectrum of negative emotions, from ambivalence to frustration to fear to dissatisfaction to hate'. Additionally, this is typical of the kinds of impassioned fourth-wave feminist critique that I discussed in the introduction. Media fandom is marked by expressions of both 'frustration and fascination' (Jenkins 2006a, 247), as my participants' experiences confirm, just as feminist popular culture critique can be characterized by its displays of 'outrage and delight' (Piepmeier 2009, 174). Molly (#342), for example, explained how belonging to a community of feminist fans provides her with a space to work through shared feelings of both passion and anger towards the fantext with like-minded fans who also *make feminist sense* of the fantext. Her fannish affective investments in popular cultural texts are subsequently framed and articulated through feminist discourses about cultural representations:

> Fandom is a great way to keep track of what media is known for good female characters and which media continues to be really horrible to its female characters. It's a way to vent to like-minded people about franchises you love, and how much you wish they would do better on representation of women and minorities.

> (Molly, #342)

Evaluating the fantext

For my participants, the affective intensities of their fannish investments in texts are organized and reproduced by their investments in a feminist politics of recognition and vice versa. Furthermore, for participants such as Zellieh (#87), the affective intensities produced by their fannish investment in media texts and those produced by their identities as feminists are indistinct. As Zellieh reflected, 'there was never a fannish experience for me that was separate from criticism and analysis of the source media, and that naturally included feminism, equal rights, representation, and racism and homophobia, etc.' Autumn (#31) similarly emphasized the reciprocity between her fandom and her feminism, highlighting the pleasure she derives from engaging in feminist commentary and critique with an imagined community of like-minded fans:

> Many of the fandoms I'm involved in have something to do with feminism, whether it's just the fans themselves or also the content we love. In the fandom, I love discussing the importance of representation, and listening and learning from people about their thoughts and experiences.

> (Autumn, #31)

Shared feminist interpretative frameworks thus operate as a way for participants like Sarah, Molly, Zellieh, and Autumn to organize their affective investments in texts and connect with like-minded fans. Here, we can turn to Grossberg (1992b) assertion that affect organizes and structures *why things matter* to understand the work that affect performs to produce valuations of the fantext within feminist fandom. Within the imagined community of feminist fandom, then, connection with 'like-minded' fans rests not only on shared interests and the recognition of shared affective investments in the objects of fandom but also on the affective force produced by shared feminist identities, and how these feminist identities influence one's relationship to and interpretation of the fantext – be that through feelings of fascination or frustration. To turn to Tumblr, briefly, it is in this sense that Tiidenberg, Hendry, and Abidin (2021, 48) highlight that participation in a given community on Tumblr necessitates a 'combinatory literacy' (Kanai 2019):

> It spans pop culture literacies (i.e., knowledge of TV shows, pop music, memes), transmedia literacies (i.e., GIF making), ideological literacies (i.e., sensitivity to social justice and intersectionality), representational literacies (i.e., an antiracist and antisexist stance in assessing pop-cultural representations), and affective literacies (i.e., a shared imaginary that allows a joke to work, or disapproval to be expressed), in addition to whatever interest-driven literacy is needed to partake in a particular conversation.

We can see this complex and combinatory literacy at work across my research participants accounts of affective belonging within feminist fandom on Tumblr, where one routinely moves indeterminately across, within, between, and beyond these literacies. Feminist fandom is thus imagined by my participants as a fruitful space to engage and establish connections with other 'like-minded' fans who share their affective investments in feminist causes (especially a politics of recognition) as much as they do fannish ones. Building upon the work of Hemmings (2012), Keller, Mendes, and Ringrose (2016) refer to such feminist connections rooted in shared emotional responses as a form of 'affective solidarity' which, they argue, can provide comfort and connection. This was certainly true for my participants, who positioned shared feelings and emotional responses as central to the production and maintenance of an imagined community of feminist fans.

Imagined community, imagined intimacy

Lauren Berlant's theorization of intimate publics offers a useful framework for understanding the complexities of affective belonging within feminist fandom. Berlant (2008, viii) argues that the intimacy of an 'intimate public' lies in 'the expectation that consumers of its particular stuff *already* share a worldview and emotional knowledge that they have derived from a broadly common historical experience' (original emphasis). Thus, Renee's (#42) description of a 'feeling of union', or Morgan's (#322) description of feeling a 'sense of connectedness to others through the things I had passions for', adheres to this understanding of shared emotional and cultural knowledge derived from common experience central to Berlant's notion of an intimate public. Moreover, the expectation of a shared world view also mirrors my participants' expectation of like-mindedness central to their understanding of feminist fandom as an imagined community. Berlant (2008) later adds:

> An intimate public is an achievement. Whether linked to women or other non-dominant people, it flourishes as a porous, affective scene of identification among strangers that promises a certain experience of belonging and provides a complex of consolation, confirmation, discipline, and discussion about how to live as an *x*.
>
> (Berlant 2008, viii)

Berlant's characterization of intimate publics easily fits my participants' experiences of affective belonging within feminist fandom, in that it accounts for their understanding of feminist fandom as a place where like-minded strangers with shared affects, affinities, knowledge, and experiences come together and experience, or *work* towards developing (Kuurne and Vieno 2022), a sense of belonging. Moreover, the concept of the intimate public encapsulates a 'common sense or a vernacular sense of belonging to a community' (Berlant 2008, 10) in a manner that also speaks to my participants' common sense of belonging to an *imagined community* built upon *imagined intimacy* on Tumblr (also see Hendry 2020a, b; Brett and Maslen 2021). Affective belonging, and the forms of imagined community it produces, therefore rests upon an imagined intimacy that becomes spatially anchored to Tumblr.

Spatial belonging on Tumblr

In Chapter 1, I examined the self-narratives produced by my research participants which locate Tumblr as an important space for the development of young people's feminist identities. My research participants situated the platform as their first sustained point of contact with feminist frameworks, concepts, and discourses. It is therefore not surprising that they subsequently reported seeking out an imagined community of like-minded feminist fans on the platform, particularly given that the need to connect with like-minded people (Enli and Thumim 2012) and feel a sense of belonging has been cited as a significant motivator for use of social networking sites (Nadkarni and Hofmann 2012; Agosto, Abbas, and Naughton 2012). This is something that, as Tiidenberg, Hendry, and Abidin (2021, 41–61) highlight, makes Tumblr particularly appealing given its unique affordances, vernacular, and sensibility rooted in shared interests and affinities. My participants' pursuit of connection with an imagined community of like-minded feminist fans on Tumblr *in particular* therefore produces understandings of belonging to feminist fandom that are not only *affective* but *spatial*.

Many scholars have noted that affective dimensions of belonging are often articulated through spatial frameworks. The experience of belonging within particular spaces is, for example, marked by what Thrift (2004) describes as 'intensities of feeling' or what Anderson (2009) calls the 'affective atmospheres' of place. Affective belongings can subsequently 'stick' (Ahmed 2004b) to specific spaces, and the affective component of belonging is often spatially situated. Sociologists of youth suggest that virtual spaces are particularly important for young people to negotiate their identities and develop a sense of belonging (boyd 2014; Bennett and Robards 2014), and online communities have in turn been described as fostering place-connected identities and belongings (Baym 2015; Habib and Ward 2019). This has been explored in relation to both feminist and fannish online communities, where young people's sense of belonging within these spaces is frequently theorized using spatial metaphors and frameworks. Within fan studies, for example, online fandom has been characterized as a feminist room of one's own (Bury 2005; Warner 2015), while feminist scholars have positioned social networking and microblogging websites, including Tumblr, as 'safe spaces' for feminist consciousness-raising (Keller 2016b).

A safe space

One of the most significant ways that my participants constructed a sense of spatial belonging on Tumblr was by positioning the platform as a *safe space*. While I briefly explored the importance of feeling 'safe' to affective belonging earlier, it is worth considering in more detail with regard to spatial belonging. Initially emerging out of feminist, queer, and anti-racist social movements in the late twentieth century, the concept of the safe space, as Kenney (2001, 24) explains, refers to 'a certain license to speak and act freely, form collective strength, and generate strategies for resistance'. More recently, the concept has been adopted as a framework to explore feminist understandings of 'safe spaces' within a digital context. The repeated, almost ritualistic, invocation of Tumblr as a 'safe space' across my survey responses suggests that, for many feminist fans, Tumblr provides them with the sense that they are able to openly discuss experiences, share interests and information, and connect with like-minded people 'without shame' (Tabitha, #185) and 'without fear of being judged' (happyb33ps, #284). For example, Alicia (#128) noted the sense of solidarity she felt with other fans who 'were all like me and wanted to just talk about something they liked without being judged'. Happyb33ps (#284) similarly positioned Tumblr as a 'way to connect with likeminded people and to enthuse about passions without fear of being judged'.

Across many of these responses, feminist fans express fear about being negatively judged by peers due to their participation in fandom as well as their feminist identities. As many scholars have noted, the forms of transformative fandom associated primarily with girls and young women are often subject to public ridicule based on negative fan stereotypes that are inherently gendered (Scott 2019; Hannell 2020a). As many feminist scholars have noted, there is often a gendered element to the pathologization of the fan, where girls' and young women's fandom is cast in 'disparaged terms' (Pomerantz 2008, 50). Behaviour perceived as fundamentally irrational, excessively emotional, and passive has made the fan normatively feminine and youthful – leading to what Dare-Edwards (2015), building upon Jensen's (1992) notion of 'fandom as pathology', describes as *fangirl* as pathology'. Anti-fandom is often configured along gendered lines, through which the affective intensities of fandom are 'criticised for being *too girly* or *too juvenile*' (Busse 2013, 76; my emphasis). For feminist fan studies scholar Suzanne Scott (2019), this gendered logic has been intensified in recent years at the intersection of the growth of anti-feminist 'toxic technocultures' (Massanari 2017) that espouse what Banet-Weiser (2018) calls 'popular misogyny' and the increasing 'industrial privileging' of an extremely narrow 'white, straight, cisgendered male conception of the fan' (Scott 2019, 77) within the media and entertainment industries.

Furthermore, within the context of *feminist* fandom and the hybridization of fannish and feminist identities, *fangirl as pathology* is compounded by the often-ridiculed figure of the 'SJW' or 'social justice warrior', a figure discursively associated with Tumblr and maligned, especially within anti-feminist, right-wing, and reactionary contexts, for their excessive over-investment 'in identity politics and political correctness' (Massanari and Chess 2018, 141).[3] Within feminist fandom, where the affective intensities, or *excesses*, of one's fannish investments in cultural texts are structured by their investments in a feminist politics of recognition, *fangirl as pathology* transmutes into *SJW fangirl as pathology*.[4] The evasion of these negative stereotypes subsequently necessitates the pursuit of shared interests and affinities with other feminist fans within a 'safe space'.

This stands in contrast to broader debates in fan studies about the mainstreaming and acceptability of fandom and fannish practices in the twenty-first century. For example, Booth and Kelly (2013, 69) argue that the visibility of online fandoms in the twenty-first century has had a 'mainstreaming' effect, making fan cultures a '*more visible* and thus *more acceptable* a cultural identity' (original emphasis). Elsewhere, fandom has been described as the dominant mode of consumption in late modernity, leading to the 'fanification' (Nikunen 2007) of media audiences. Fans are increasingly hailed as a lucrative target market and the sharing economy of fandom is often used as a key method for marketing texts (Affuso 2018). Jenner (2017) draws upon the phenomenon of 'binge-watching' as an example of the mainstreaming of fandom. She argues that the contemporary media environment strongly encourages fan-like behaviours such as binge-watching and live-tweeting in ways that blur the lines between fans and non-fans (see Gray 2003). For Jenner (2017, 314), binge-watching typifies the process wherein fan discourses and practices, as well as a 'close audience-text relationship', are adopted as mainstream media practice. Through the normalization of such behaviours, fannish practices, such as binge-watching and engaging in extremely close readings and analyses of a text, that enable audience-text closeness are increasingly positioned as a form of 'socially legitimised excess' (317).

Many fan studies scholars have built upon these debates about the mainstreaming of fandom to dispute Henry Jenkins's (1992, 23) early claim that 'to speak as a fan is to accept what has been labelled a subordinated position within the cultural hierarchy, to accept an identity constantly belittled or criticised'. However, feminist fans' fear of being negatively judged and pathologized for their participation in *feminized* (and *feminist*) forms of fandom highlights the limits of debates about the mainstreaming of fandom and fan culture, particularly for young people and those with marginalized identities who engage in transformative fandom and its associated affectively intense and close yet critical modes of engagement with popular cultural texts. This aligns with Suzanne Scott's (2019, 107) argument that the conditional embrace of *some* segments of fan culture while others are marginalized has produced an 'isolationist' (108) response in marginalized and minoritarian fans who withdraw to spaces less hostile to the 'fangirl' and all she represents. We see this isolationist impulse at work across these accounts from feminist fans pursuing a 'safe space' on Tumblr.

Feminist fans' positioning of Tumblr as a safe space where they can enjoy common understanding and acceptance with like-minded fans without fear of judgement, of alignment with negative gendered fan stereotypes or reactionary disparagements of the social justice warrior, thus adheres to Kenney's (2001) understanding of safe spaces as spaces containing a certain license to speak and act freely. Moreover, it also affirms Scott's (2019, 13) assertion that fan culture's shift from the 'margins to the mainstream' has been unevenly distributed, having (re)produced a 'structured secondariness' (5) for fangirls, fans of colour, and queer fans and their preferred modes of engagement with popular culture.

Tumblr as a home

Many of my participants' survey responses which emphasized this sense of comfort and ease frequently employed spatial metaphors to position Tumblr as a 'home'. Tiny-steve (#232), for example, noted that, while she has been less active in fandom in recent years since graduating from university, Tumblr nevertheless 'was home for a very long time, the people on my dashboard providing familiarity and comfort'. Bobbisnose (#251) also positioned Tumblr using similar discursive themes, noting that while she has 'been on and off it since high school', she ultimately 'never really found anywhere else I can comfortably fit in'. Rebecca (#129) similarly remarked that 'Tumblr remains my home base', while Lily (#53) explained that Tumblr 'still has my community on there. It's my place'. Here, participants characterize their experiences of belonging within feminist fandom through descriptions of Tumblr as a *built space,* as not only a 'safe space' but a 'place' and a 'home'. Belonging within feminist fandom is thus both spatially and temporally situated.

Notably, similar understandings of Tumblr have been articulated within fan studies. Stein (2018, 87), for instance, makes use of spatial metaphors to describe the relationship between fan communities and Tumblr, remarking that the platform 'remained (and remains) a home to fan communities'. As many sociologists have noted, belonging is often discursively associated with the trope of home through the entrenched understanding of belonging as 'feeling at home' (Yuval-Davis 2006; hooks 2009; May 2013). In my participants' accounts of spatial belonging, their framing of Tumblr as a 'home' produces an understanding of Tumblr as a symbolic space of familiarity, comfort, safety, security, ease, and nostalgic emotional attachment. In doing so, the affective experience of feelings of comfort and safety within feminist fandom becomes anchored to Tumblr in particular. Spatial belonging on the site subsequently has a deeply affective character.

Feminist fans' descriptions of Tumblr as their 'home' – be that past or present – also echo Tiidenberg, Hendry, and Abidin's (2021, 117–28) theorization of 'Tumblr meta-fandom', as a self-referential fandom of the platform itself, 'focused almost entirely on Tumblr as a culture and community'. Tumblr meta-fandom, they write, centres Tumblr users' performance of fannishness towards the platform's 'various histories, contexts, features, functions, affordances, and even glitches' (128). In doing so, they write, Tumblr users demonstrate their fannish 'love, loyalty, and longing' (128) for the platform. This 'love, loyalty, and longing' is most certainly mobilized in my participants' affect-laden descriptions of Tumblr as their 'home'. As Kuntsman (2012, 6) notes, internet sites can in this sense operate as 'objects and anchors of feeling'.

Tumblr's affordances and platform vernacular

Tumblr's distinct affordances and 'platform vernacular' (Gibbs et al. 2015), as a multimodal, multivocal, and multiplicitous site whose users are committed to a politics of social justice, are central to these accounts of spatial belonging on the platform. Gibbs et al. (2015) emphasize that platform vernaculars emerge as the result of the interaction between, on the one hand, the technological affordances of particular digital platforms and, on the other, the mediated practices and communicative habits of the users of the platform. They emerge from *within* platforms through the interaction between technological affordances and use (Renninger 2015; Warfield 2016). This vernacular, according to Tiidenberg, Hendry, and Abidin (2021), produces a distinct 'sensibility' on Tumblr characterized by

> [a] broader recognisable normative, ethical, and political sensibility, which can be described as *an orientation toward social justice* … and a related commitment to maintaining one's experience of tumblr as a *safe space*.
>
> (Tiidenberg, Hendry, and Abidin 2021, 50)

This sensibility, they write, emerges from Tumblr's distinct affordances beyond those typical of most social networking sites (boyd 2011). According to Tiidenberg, Hendry, and Abidin (2021, 43–5), Tumblr's platform-specific affordances include its combination of *high pseudonymity* (the ease of remaining pseudonymous on the platform given its lack of formal identity cues as noted in the introduction); *high scalability* (potentiality for content to scale up its reach to more varied audiences); *low searchability* (given its non-standardized folksonomic tagging systems); *high multimodality* (with users posting across text, images, videos, audio, hyperlinks, tags, and more); *high interactivity* (nuanced range of interactive and communicative features); *low reactivity* (lack of reactive sentiment-measuring metrics); and *high nonlinear temporality* (given the archival function of blogs and the uneven recirculation of content on a user's dashboard). Combined, these affordances, and their role in shaping the platform's vernacular, produce distinct cultures of use and forms of sociality on the site. Tiidenberg, Hendry, and Abidin (2021) use the term 'silosociality' to refer to the forms of connection, or community, that emerge on the platform (also see Sharp and Shannon 2020) rooted in shared sensibilities, interests, and affinities. While Tumblr silos are not hermetically sealed and rigidly bounded (hence the coming together of fandom and social justice on the platform), they are

> *felt* and *imagined* and experienced as somewhat sequestered from each other. That is why they feel so nice. That is why they are referred to as safe spaces. That is why they offer a sense of escape … People within silos have put in the effort to find others with whom they share something they consider important – an identity, a lifestyle, an attitude, love for a fictional pairing. They have learned the vernacular and they accept the shared sensibility.
>
> (Tiidenberg, Hendry, and Abidin 2021, 52–4)

Within silos, they write, both *affect* and *affinity* are intensified. We see this at work in feminist fans' accounts of affective belonging to an imagined, intimate community detailed above. Indeed, for many of feminist fans involved in my research, Tumblr's platform vernacular positions it as a safe space for feminist fans to indulge in Tumblr's silosociality and openly discuss experiences, share interests and information, and connect with like-minded people who share their affective investments in both fandom and feminism. Sanne (#155), for instance, explained that Tumblr is her favourite digital platform because the interface enables her to easily combine her interests and 'passions' within a singular space. She explained, 'Tumblr has been my favourite platform so far because there's a mix of different things that I enjoy: fan-related content, feminist/social justice content and also very importantly, lots and lots of deadly funny content.' Sanne's sense of spatial belonging on Tumblr, then, relies not only on the wide range of content produced and circulated by its users but on the ways in which Tumblr's technological affordances, its *high scalability*, enable this content to circulate and 'spread' (Jenkins, Ford, and Green 2013). Similarly, jokesandgays (#163) explained:

> I like that Tumblr is anonymous ... and it's just kind of a space where I can dump all of that stuff without needing to sift through it or worry about how to present it. My blog is also a hot mess, it's my personal blog and a political blog and a fandom blog all at once, so that also makes it easier in that I don't have to worry about fitting a theme or anything else.
>
> (jokesandgays, #163)

While I will examine the importance of anonymity, pseudonymity, and privacy to spatial belonging in more detail shortly, here jokesandgays more broadly highlights how the interaction between affordances and use produced particular modes of expression central to her sense of belonging on the platform. Like Sanne, jokesandgays draws attention to the value in being able to draw upon their 'combinatory literacies' (Kanai 2019) to mix up a range of personal and political material on her blog, and the sense of freedom this affords in terms of self-expression. She explains, 'It's my personal blog and a political blog and a fandom blog all at once.' Sanne and jokesandgays thus position their Tumblr blogs as multiplicitous and multimodal repositories, or archives, of their interests, emphasizing the ease with which they mix up personal and political interests and modes of expression in a manner that echoes Harris's (2008b) description of online DIY cultures discussed in the introduction.

One of the most important communicative aspects of Tumblr's platform vernacular and sensibility is the prevalence of discourses about feminism and social justice on the platform. As noted throughout *Feminist Fandom*, the networked and 'silosocial' (Tiidenberg, Hendry, and Abidin 2021) nature of Tumblr brings discourses of media fandom, feminist activism, and media consumption into contact with each other (Hillman, Procyk, and Neustaedter 2014a; Naylor 2016; McCracken 2017), and, for my participants, the prevalence of feminist discourses within Tumblr's platform vernacular and sensibility is central to their sense of safety and spatial belonging. Sahvana (#321), for example, described Tumblr as her 'primary fandom platform' and explained how the 'attitude towards social issues that Tumblr [users] generally [have]' makes her 'feel safe':

When I first forayed into fandom, I used Facebook group pages for a brief amount of time. I quickly transitioned exclusively to Tumblr, which is my primary fandom platform. It feels like an actual community, I like the aesthetic, I like the dashboard setup, and most importantly I prefer the attitude towards social issues that Tumblr generally has. Tumblr's general commitment towards reacting against bigotry has kept my fandom experience 'clean' so to speak and has made it infinitely more enjoyable. Without Tumblr, I don't think I'd be able to stay as involved in fandom … I feel safe with the commitment Tumblr has towards speaking out against injustice and bigotry.

(Sahvana, #321)

Sahvana constructs an opposition between the 'attitude towards social issues' on Tumblr and other social media platforms, such as Facebook, explaining that she much prefers engaging with fandom on Tumblr because of the platform's 'general commitment towards reacting against bigotry'. Sahvana's response positions the integration of a feminist social justice politic into media fandom as a central to Tumblr's platform vernacular and as an important aspect of her sense of spatial belonging. Additionally, Sahvana's emphasis on the sense of safety and comfort produced by Tumblr users' active commitment to 'speaking out against injustice and bigotry' adheres to The Roestone Collective's (2014, 1348) understanding of a 'safe space' as a form of 'relational work'. Their relational understanding of safe spaces accounts for the situatedness and multiplicity of the concept and allows an understanding of safe spaces as the fluid and reflexive result of interpersonal social processes and belonging work, much like those described by Sahvana. Across their responses to my survey, many of my participants perform a willingness to undertake the relational work, the feminist identity work and belonging work, required to create and maintain their understanding of feminist fandom on Tumblr as a safe space. This is particularly explicit with regard to reflexively *listening* and *learning* as part of their processual and ongoing feminist becoming. Recall, for example, Josie's (#227) willingness to 'check myself and learn/unlearn new ways of thinking'. This is something that I will explore in more depth in Chapter 4.

Moreover, such an understanding of Tumblr's platform vernacular, as a space committed to open and progressive dialogue about pertinent social issues, adheres to Nancy Fraser's (1990) conceptualization of 'subaltern counterpublics', as 'parallel discursive arenas' (67) that elaborate alternative styles of political behaviour and 'norms of public speech' (61). Indeed, as I noted in the introduction, the analysis of online feminist communities often draws upon

Fraser's concept of subaltern counterpublics, and Tumblr has been described as particularly conducive to 'counterpublic address' (Renninger 2015, 1513) through its communicative 'affinity with social justice dialogues' (Sills et al. 2016). As I argued in Chapter 2, fan-created paratexts circulated on Tumblr can prompt powerful processes of transformation in fans' development of a feminist identity, providing fans with a framework through which they come to both *make sense of* feminism and *make feminist sense* of texts. This process adheres to Fraser's conceptualization of counterpublics as spaces that permit members of subordinated social groups to 'invent and circulate counter-discourses, which in turn permit them to formulate oppositional interpretations of their identities, interests, and needs' (Fraser 1990, 67). While, due to the nature of my research, many of my participants discussed the process of formulating oppositional interpretations of their identities with regard to their feminism, many also referred to other salient aspects of their identities. Alex (#278), a bisexual and transgender man, for example, explained how fandom called his attention to a myriad of social issues and subsequently led him to reinterpret his own identities, interests, and needs. While he cautions against the tendency to ascribe utopian forms of resistance to fandom (which I shall discuss in more detail in Chapter 3), Alex nevertheless describes fandom as his prototypical safe space:

> Fandom is where I met people against bi-erasure, not my first LGBT groups IRL/in meatspace. Fandom is where I met my first trans mentors, genderqueer folks, other spoonies, and we could hear each other out without reservations or doubts. It is not a perfect space and there are many problems, … and overall we fans are less "woke" than we pat ourselves on the back for – but it was a safe space for me before I knew about the idea of safe spaces. It helped me question.
>
> (Alex, #278)

Many of my participants emphasized the importance of privacy to spatial belonging on the platform. This is in part due to the technological affordances of the site, arising from Tumblr's *high pseudonymity* and *low searchability*, as well as the broader privacy norms of fandom. My participants' sense of privacy on Tumblr thus emerges from the interaction between technological affordances and use and can be considered as another important aspect of the site's platform vernacular. Unlike social networking sites such as Facebook, where explicit 'identity cues' (Baym 2015), including one's real name, age, location, occupation, relationship status, etc., are required for meaningful participation, the only identity information Tumblr requires a user to provide is their age, email address, and a username. Tumblr therefore affords users a high level of control over their self-presentation that many other social networking sites do not (see boyd 2012; Renninger 2015; Tiidenberg, Hendry, and Abidin 2021). The Tumblr platform interface does not seek to engineer self-presentation by providing predetermined sets of identity categories through which users are expected to build digital identities. Instead, it operates as a relatively 'sparse-cue' (Baym 2015, 130) platform which affords users a high level of control over the identity information they disclose. It thus affords *high pseudonymity* (Tiidenberg, Hendry, and Abidin 2021). This is something my participants valued highly. As joslynnyc (#157) noted, 'I appreciate that there is less expectation on Tumblr to reveal details of yourself [in real life], there is more [of] a culture of anonymity'.

What is invoked in many of these accounts of spatial belonging is the construction of spaces both real and virtual which are imagined, or in some cases lived, as either *less safe* or *unsafe* (see The Roestone Collective 2014) compared to Tumblr. Unlike platforms such as Facebook, where a user's profile is associated with one's real name and tightly wedded to unmediated social communities based on familial, educational, and occupational networks (see van Dijck 2013), the technological affordances of Tumblr enable young people to create 'firewalls of visibility' (Jenkins, Ito, and boyd 2016, 57) and evade surveillance from unsympathetic peers and family members (boyd 2014; Marwick and boyd 2014; Shorey 2015; Livingstone and Sefton-Green 2016; McCracken 2017). Recent studies have indeed noted the discomfort many young people experience using Facebook due to the risk of being monitored by adults in their lives (Madden et al. 2013). For many of my participants, the perceived risk of surveillance by peers and adults on platforms such as Facebook is compounded by the fear of negative judgement and alignment with negative *SJW fangirl as pathology* stereotypes that I discussed earlier. For example, ripley-stark (#289) told me, 'I'm afraid … that people I know in real life will find me and use my beliefs against me. The vast majority of people I interact with are privileged enough to really not care about representation at all.' Similarly, Dinah (#98) explained:

> I never use Facebook for fandom purposes … because Facebook is my most public profile, in my opinion. I'm friends with family friends, my mom's co-workers, distant family members, etc. I don't want the parts of me I hold dear-especially more controversial parts-on that profile.
>
> (Dinah, #98)

Moreover, while Tumblr is not a closed-access or password-protected site, and users can even browse through personal blogs and tracked tags without an account, many online fan spaces are commonly perceived as semi-public, if not private, and therefore as safe from censorship and incursion from those unfamiliar with fannish norms and practices (Busse and Hellekson 2012; Zubernis and Larsen 2012). Many scholars have explored how fannish identities and practices can restructure notions of public/private (Harrington and Bielby 1995; Zubernis and Larsen 2012; Duffett 2013), and, within fandom on Tumblr, participants are expected to adhere to an 'implicit code of conduct' (boyd 2014, 35) that privileges an expectation of privacy (Shorey 2015; McCracken 2017) based upon Tumblr's silosociality and low searchability. To expose a fellow fan through the loss of privacy without their consent is considered a gross 'norm violation' (McLaughlin and Vitak 2011) on Tumblr. Exposure can seriously undermine one's sense of comfort, safety, and belongingness within feminist fandom and can cause 'context collapse' (Marwick and boyd 2010). For example, 25-year-old Sarah, following the discovery of her Tumblr blog by acquaintances she knew in real life, subsequently withdrew from publicly engaging in fandom for three years:

> When I was 14, I withdrew from public fandom activity due to my Tumblr being discovered by acquaintances I knew in real life, though I still wrote (or attempted to write; a vast majority of the stories I attempted were never finished) fic in private. I spent a few years lurking extensively through so many fandoms … I didn't start publicly posting my work again until I was 17.
>
> (Sarah, #64)

The sense of privacy produced by Tumblr's affordances and vernacular, and the feelings of spatial belonging it produces, is important to my participants precisely because it reduces the risk of exposure to the negative *SJW fangirl as pathology* stereotypes I discussed earlier by those unfamiliar with the norms, values, and practices of feminist fandom. My participants' descriptions of adverse reactions to their fandom from peers and acquaintances, or their fear of exposure to their friends, family, and colleagues, once again highlight the limits of debates about the mainstreaming of fandom. As joslynnyc (#157) explained, the sense of privacy afforded by Tumblr's high pseudonymity 'allow[s] a pure expression of fannish love that I think is less possible on [other platforms] unless you have a protected or entirely anonymous account'. Indeed, previous research on the relationship between anonymity and self-disclosure online indicates that users who feel a stronger sense of anonymity often feel that they can self-disclose more freely, more often, and more intensely than they would in person (Suler 2004). This is reflected in joslynnyc's comments, and she later added, 'Tumblr was the first place I truly saw fans be their unbound, unapologetic fangirl selves, so I will always be grateful for it for that alone.'

While, as Sarah's (#64) experience indicates, the privacy norms and technological affordances of Tumblr cannot definitively protect users from exposure or harm, more broadly my participants affectively experience Tumblr as feeling *more private* and thus *more safe* than other online spaces. The sense of privacy afforded by the technological architecture and vernacular of Tumblr, as well as its reputation as a platform conducive to counterpublic address, thus demarcates the platform as a safe space and as an important site of spatial belonging for my participants. The discursive construction of Tumblr as a safe space by my participants can subsequently be understood in contrast to their broader understanding of other online spaces as *less safe*, if not entirely *unsafe*.

Queer normativity

For my queer participants who explore their gender and sexuality through fandom, the lack of anonymity on more public platforms such as Facebook, which are more or less 'tied to the maintenance of a true identity' associated with one's 'real name' (Renninger 2015, 1519), puts them at risk of significant harm and thus positions these alternative online spaces as *unsafe* in ways that work to reinforce a sense of spatial belonging on Tumblr. For these feminist fans, the consequences of exposure to unsympathetic family members or peers are potentially severe. For Nicole (#101), a 21-year-old who describes herself as queer and pansexual, visibly engaging with her queerness through feminist fandom on platforms such as Facebook, could expose her to harm because of her identity as a queer and closeted young woman. For Nicole, the risk of surveillance of her online activity by family members could thus have 'catastrophic consequences'. The sense of privacy afforded by Tumblr is thus crucial to her sense of safety and well-being. She explained:

> I would never ever ever use Facebook for any fandom activity because I need
> to keep my private interests separate from my Facebook, especially now that
> I have family members as friends who can see my profile. My family isn't the

most supportive of anything LGBTQ* centred and they don't know about my own orientation so I avoid posting on platforms where they can easily find me to avoid any suspicion/possible catastrophic consequences.

(Nicole, #101)

Many scholars have positioned fandom as a site for queer identity work (Lothian, Busse, and Reid 2007; Hellekson and Busse 2014; Russo and Ng 2017; Anselmo 2018), especially with regard to queer community building and queer spectatorship. For young people like Nicole, the use of fandom as a conduit for such queer identity work necessitates that the spaces in which she engages in fandom are not visible to her family members and acquaintances. On Tumblr, then, as a platform popular among queer and trans youth (Cho 2015; Dame 2016; Cavalcante 2019; Sharp and Shannon 2020), this fannish queer identity work is at once both enabled and intensified by the platform's affordances, vernacular, and resultant 'queer silosociality' (Tiidenberg, Hendry, and Abidin 2021).

Moreover, according to Tiidenberg, Hendry, and Abidin (2021), this gives rise to a tacit assumption that Tumblr is *the* definitively queer platform (see Cavalcante 2019), thus inverting the *imagined* and *lived* heteronormativity of other online spaces (see Cover 2019). This produces, they argue, the platform's queer normativity:

> Tumblr fosters *queer normativity*. In general, Tumblr is a platform that is welcoming to LGBT users and cultures, having been cited by generations of queer people as a safe space, where they learned a lot, found a voice, experimented with facets of their identity, and figured themselves out … this validation is often experienced as a super intense affective utopian bubble.
>
> (Tiidenberg, Hendry, and Abidin 2021, 72)

For Nicole, Tumblr's queer silosociality and queer normativity provides a space 'to freely engage in queer content and be myself on a platform that I feel I can't really do elsewhere'. We see Tumblr's intensely affective 'queer utopic' (Cavalcante 2019) potential at work elsewhere across my ethnographic data, where Mai (#327), for example, similarly explained:

> [Tumblr] is a huge source of support for me. Without Tumblr, I wouldn't have found my queer identity or recognised my own mental health issues. Both of those things are unknown to the people around me, making Tumblr an important safe space for self-expression, comfort and validation.
>
> (Mai, #327)

Mai's remarks reveal, once again, how the platform vernacular and (queer) silosociality of Tumblr designate it as a 'safe space' in ways that are central to my participants' sense of spatial belonging. For Mai, the interaction between the sense of privacy produced by Tumblr's technological affordances, combined with the platform's popularity among queer and trans youth, made it an important space for 'self-expression, comfort and validation'. As Baym (2015) notes, the anonymity afforded by sparse cue online spaces, such as Tumblr, enable people to engage in riskier acts of self-disclosure which, when affirmed, can create positive changes in people's self-concepts. For Mai, then, the anonymity afforded by Tumblr's culture of queer silosociality and queer normativity enabled her to engage in acts of self-disclosure about her queer identity which were then affirmed by other queer users on the platform.

The relationship between Tumblr's queer normativity and spatial belonging was particularly important for my young, queer, and *rural* participants. These participants, by virtue of their age, sexuality, and geographic location, cannot access the urban metropolis as a normatively queer, or 'metronormative' (Halberstam 2005; Herring 2010; Podmore and Bain 2021), place and space. For example, 15-year-old Tizzy (#50), like many of my participants, positioned feminist fandom on Tumblr as one of the few spaces in which she could speak freely about her sexuality. However, she also emphasized that, as a young person living in a rural area without access to 'support structures or even an LGBT+ group', her ability to 'openly' engage in acts of self-disclosure about her sexuality on Tumblr was a crucial, life-affirming source of support. She explained:

> When I was about to turn thirteen, I started properly using [Tumblr], and I have done so since. I use the platform very often, as it is to this day my only social media profile on the major sites, and to be honest, despite many of the problems with it and the things I have seen on here, I keep using it because it is one of the only places I can talk about my sexuality really openly without making people feel uncomfortable. … I don't live in a big town with support structures or even an LGBT+ group, so the internet, or Tumblr specifically, is pretty much the only place I can talk about things like my sexuality.
>
> (Tizzy, #50)

According to youth sociologist Mary Gray (2009), rural life for queer young people increasingly involves the types of 'entanglements' with online spaces that Tizzy describes, wherein rural queer youth use new media technologies to 'enhance their sense of inclusion to broader, imagined queer communities beyond their home towns' (Gray 2009, 15). These experiences of spatial belonging on Tumblr thus highlight not only the tightly wedded relationship between platform vernacular and notions of safety but also how one's sense of spatial belonging is configured in accordance with one's identities and the kinds of belonging they wish to access.

Platform un/safety

As Bondi and Rose (2003) note, perceptions of safety are socially, spatially, and temporally contingent, varying greatly according to one's positionality, yet the idea of safety generally relies on the perception of an underlying threat of physical and/or symbolic violence. For many of my participants, the perception of such an underlying threat goes beyond both the fear of judgement and alignment with negative fan stereotypes, as well as the fear of surveillance from unsympathetic peers and adults. While *Feminist Fandom* more broadly concerns the relationship between fourth-wave feminism and media fandom, feminist scholars have emphasized that we need to 'think together' (Gill 2016a, 617) the rise of popular feminism and new forms of feminist practice and activism alongside, and in tandem with, 'new mediations of gender and sexual violence' (Phipps et al. 2017, 2).

Feminist research suggests that popular misogyny (Banet-Weiser 2015a, 2018) and anti-feminism (Anderson 2015) are steadily increasing, as new forms of 'networked misogyny' emerge (Banet-Weiser and Miltner 2015, 171). Just as social networking websites can become key spaces for feminist education and activism, they can also become 'aggregators of online misogyny' (Rentschler 2014), giving rise to new forms of 'networked harassment' (Filipovic 2007; Megarry 2014; Marwick and Caplan 2018). This online misogyny is compounded when it intersects with racism, homophobia, transphobia, and ableism (Daniels 2009; Gray 2012; Noble and Tynes 2016). The broader demarcation of Tumblr as a *safe*, or as a *safer*,[5] space by many of my participants is thus significant given this context.

Drawing upon this broader social, political, and cultural context, a number of my research participants' accounts of *unsafe* spaces framed their sense of spatial belonging on Tumblr through the anticipation of symbolic violence and online harassment elsewhere, particularly through reference to platforms such as Reddit and 4chan, which are discursively associated with the 'toxic technocultures' (Massanari 2017) of popular misogyny (also see Ging and

Siapera 2019). As Nagle (2017, 69) notes, Tumblr is often positioned as 'very much the reverse mirror image' of sites such as Reddit and 4chan, and my participants' responses reinforce this. Similarly, Tiidenberg, Hendry, and Abidin (2021, 10) observe:

> The general consensus ... seems to be that compared to most alternatives, Tumblr has offered an inhabitable space for people and communities, especially those with minoritarian identities, identifications, lifestyles, and values.

We see this consensus at work across my ethnographic data, which offers insight into the way Tumblr circulates within the popular fannish and feminist imaginary in opposition to other established social networking and social media platforms. Damdamfino (#147), for example, explained, 'I refuse to use Reddit. From what little experience I've had with it and from other's accounts, it seems pretty toxic. Many people I know have experienced extreme sexual and emotional harassment [there].' Likewise, Shea (#246) emphasized, 'I have avoided Reddit because I have an expectation of an anti-feminist atmosphere on that platform', and Sara (#288) explained that, while she 'lurks' on Reddit, 'it's generally too white and/or male-dominated for me to want to engage'. While these alternative digital platforms are, of course, not inherently misogynistic or anti-feminist, the hypervisibility of Reddit as a 'nexus for various toxic technocultures' (Massanari 2017, 333) nevertheless designates the space as largely *unsafe* for my participants and works to reinforce their sense of spatial belonging on Tumblr. As Portwood-Stacer (2012) notes, personal politics, as well as resistance to wider cultural phenomena, may factor into decisions to resist participation on certain social networking websites.

Conclusion

Throughout this chapter I have detailed the various interrelated narratives of affective, spatial, and relational belonging to feminist fandom produced my participants across my ethnographic data. Firstly, I characterized the kinds of feminist identity work detailed in Chapter 1 as a form of *belonging work* in order to better theorize the relational work feminist fans undertake in order to negotiate their access to belonging. I then explored my participants' positioning of feminist fandom on Tumblr as an imagined community, highlighting how their desire to seek out like-minded fans who *felt* the same way revealed the affective character of belonging to feminist fandom. Secondly, I examined their accounts of spatial belonging in order to highlight how Tumblr's affordances, vernacular, and queer normativity produced a sense of safety for my participants. In the following chapter, I will explore the experiences of feminist fans which raised questions about their *differential access* to, as well as their *desire to access*, feelings of belonging within feminist fandom on Tumblr. These accounts trouble the celebratory, utopian imaginaries at work across many of the accounts of belonging I have detailed throughout this chapter.

3

Non-belonging and exclusion

In Chapter 2, I explored my participants' experiences of belonging to feminist fandom, focusing on their spatial, affective, and imagined notions of belonging, as well as the *work* undertaken to accomplish and maintain these. However, despite my participants' shared identities as feminist fans, they did not *universally* align themselves with an overarching sense of belonging to feminist fandom, both on and beyond Tumblr. While it is possible to identify oneself with a particular group, Lähdesmäki et al. (2016, 240; original emphasis) highlight that 'in order to belong, the question is whether the person *can* belong or not'. The counter-narratives of non-belonging I detail throughout this chapter thus complicate the dominant narratives of belonging detailed in Chapter 2 in several ways, resisting the oversimplification at work in the more utopian imaginaries, both popular and academic, that 'stick' (Ahmed 2004a) both to feminist fandom and to Tumblr.

Firstly, the experiences captured within this chapter highlight how the dominant narratives of belonging produced by the majority of my research participants' risk obscuring the social and structural barriers which can prevent access to belonging within feminist fandom. They also reveal the fluidity and contingent nature of belonging to the imagined, deeply affective, intimate public on Tumblr detailed in Chapter 2. Belonging, of course, *presupposes* access (Anthias 2002; Christensen 2017), and, as May (2013, 126) highlights, a focus on belonging must, in turn, be attentive to the 'barriers that may obstruct a person's ability to feel they belong'. Secondly, these experiences of non-belonging interrogate the normative positioning of belonging as an ideal state and instead offer an insight into the negotiation of more tentative, contingent, and precarious modes of 'differential belonging' (Carrillo 2005) within feminist fandom (also see Yodovich 2021, 2022). Thirdly, they reveal the fluidity between categories of belonging and non-belonging (Savage, Bagnall, and Longhurst 2005; Christensen 2017), emphasizing that belonging is always a dynamic, fluid, and contingent process, rather than a 'reified fixity' (Yuval-Davis 2006, 199).[1] It is in this sense that these accounts of non-belonging highlight how the perception of a sense of community is fluid, unstable, and ephemeral (Beck 1992). Finally, they make the politics of belonging visible and disrupt normative assumptions about fandom, both within fan studies and within fandom itself, as an inherently progressive, resistant, or emancipatory space (Coppa 2014).

Methodological dilemmas

As I noted in the introduction, feminist methodologies are central to the work I have undertaken in developing, researching, and writing *Feminist Fandom*. Feminist methodologists recommend an approach to data collection and data analysis that privileges 'listening, recording, and a non-judgmental stance' (Kelly, Burton, and Regan 1994, 39). Lewis and Marine (2015), for example, call for a compassionate approach to feminist research comprised of 'empathy, kindness, and recognition of commonalities' (128). However, they emphasize that a compassionate approach to the research process does not forsake due criticality. Feminist compassion, they argue, 'does not foreclose critique of the work under review, but encourages constructive engagement rather than simply judging it, and finding it wanting' (Lewis and Marine 2015, 130). In mapping experiences of non-belonging within feminist fandom throughout this chapter, I found myself navigating this complex territory between, and across, feminist compassion and feminist critique. In doing so, I found solace in Rosalind Gill's (2007a) theorization of 'critical respect'. Describing the concept of 'critical respect' with regard to the act of 'respectful listening' within the research process, Gill argues:

> [Respectful listening] is the beginning, not the end, of the process and our job is surely to contextualise these stories, to situate them, to look at their patterns and variability, to examine their silences and exclusions, and, above all, to locate them in a wider context.
>
> (Gill 2007a, 77)

Respectful listening thus produces an approach to data analysis which involves 'attentive, respectful listening, to be sure, but it does not abdicate the right to question or interrogate' (Gill 2007a, 78). Similarly, as fan studies scholar Hills (2002) notes, as researchers we should be mindful to avoid interpreting fan talk at face value as direct 'evidence' of the fannish experience:

> Fan-talk cannot be accepted merely as evidence of fan knowledge. It must also be interpreted and analysed in order to focus upon its gaps and dislocations, its moments of failure within narratives of self-consciousness and self-reflexivity, and its repetitions or privileged narrative constructions ... Asking the audience cannot act as a guarantee of knowledge.
>
> (Hills 2002, 38)

Hills later adds that analyses should in turn account for the 'potential gaps' and 'absences' in fans' reflections on their identities and cultures (42). Following these assertions, I approached my participants' narratives compassionately and respectfully yet remained mindful of the need to critically situate their stories and accounts of feminist fandom on Tumblr within their wider contexts and to, as Gill and Hills note, examine their silences and exclusions. As García-Rapp (2018, 620) notes, it is the work of researchers to both 'clarify and complicate' our understandings of the social world. In doing so, I foreground how the narratives about feminist fandom produced by the feminist fans involved in my research are rich and varied and yet, at times, contradict one another in ways that reveal the powerful processes of inclusion and exclusion, of 'expansion and foreclosure' (Pande 2020b, 7), at work within feminist fandom, as well as digital feminist spaces more broadly.

In what follows, then, I enact a necessary feminist project of 'critical respect' (Gill 2007a) in my efforts to expose and examine the ambivalences, the gaps and silences, of the accounts of belonging to feminist fandom detailed in Chapter 1. As Pande (2020b, 9) notes, within fan studies it is increasingly important that we interrogate 'the stories that fans tell on multiple axes, as those occupying marginalised positions can and do replicate structures of white supremacy while laying claim to a broader progressive politics'. My analysis of non-belonging subsequently contributes to an emergent body of literature which examines and interrogates the structuring force of whiteness within both fannish (Morimoto 2018; Pande 2018a, 2020a; Warner 2018; Woo 2018; Yodovich 2022) and feminist online spaces (Loza 2014; Daniels 2016).

Multiple non-belongings

Multiple non-belongings were articulated across the responses to my narrative survey which correspond with various degrees of access to, and identification with, positions of relative power and privilege. Several respondents articulated a lower sense of belonging, for example, due to their reduced or intermittent levels of activity within feminist fandom, subsequently describing themselves as more 'passive' fans or as 'lurkers' (see Preece, Nonnecke, and Andrews 2004). In turn, they used anxiety-laden discourses to express concern about the extent to which they felt they could claim an identity within fandom without being continuously textually productive (Fiske 1992). Here, we may return to some of the discourses about regulating and improving the feminist and fannish self that I discussed in Chapter 1. MB (#228), for example, wrote, 'I wouldn't really consider myself part of a fandom other than being a viewer/reader, a passive fan,' and Ludmila (#125) explained, 'I love fandom, but I'm kind of a passive participant, I never wrote any fanfics or produced any gifs or fanart.' These fans notably replicate narratives common within fan studies which operationalize a binary between participatory and non-participatory fans (Hellekson and Busse 2006). However, these narratives have in turn been criticized for devaluing and deemphasizing the myriad practices engaged in by 'non-participatory' fans (see Sandvoss 2005; Gray, Sandvoss, and Harrington 2007; Bury 2018). This is something I will return to in Chapter 4 in more depth.

Fluctuations in fannish productivity and participation, in the level of contribution one makes to the production of the fantext, therefore reduced some participants' access to a 'sense of *continuous* belonging' (Kanai 2017, 300; my emphasis), highlighting how belonging to feminist fandom is often both fluid and temporally contingent. Note here that these feminist fans position their *fannishness*, rather than their feminist identities, as contingent and temporally bounded. This is in keeping with their emphasis, detailed in Chapter 1, on their feminist identities as open-ended and ever emergent. These narratives subsequently imply that feminist narratives of the self will continue to be at work after, and beyond, their fannish ones. This is something I will reflect on further as I conclude *Feminist Fandom*.

Conflict and call-outs

To characterize feminist fandom on Tumblr as an inherently utopic space would undercut the many accounts, and evidence, of conflict, disagreement, and in-fighting within feminist fandom that I encountered while writing this book. While media fandoms are often characterized by intra- and inter-fandom conflict (Guerrero-Pico, Establés, and Ventura 2018; Reinhard 2018), within my research, many feminist fans' accounts of non-belonging centred their complex and uneasy relationship with strategies of 'accountability' within feminist fandom on Tumblr, citing them as sources of 'severe anxiety' (junkshop-disco, #13) and 'fear of targeted harassment' (LD, #81), resulting in a 'toxic environment' (Frida, #117).

Their accounts of conflict within feminist fandom, often described through encounters with – in fannish parlance – 'antis' or 'discourse', are marked by distinct 'patterns of social surveillance and discipline' (Kanai 2020a, 30). This is reflective of a wider trend within popular feminist digital cultures, which are characterized by 'digital accountability praxis' (Clark 2020) and anxieties surrounding what it means to be a 'good' feminist (Kanai 2020a). This is typified in the practice of 'calling out'. While 'call-out' culture is often portrayed disparagingly within the popular press (see Clark 2020), Tiidenberg, Hendry, and Abidin (2021, 114) note that, among many Tumblr users, given their assumed commitment to social justice, 'calling out unjustness is a central ... task'. Tumblr call-out culture, they write, is produced by Tumblr's platform vernacular, which asserts that 'the most socially aware and informed users should be attuned to structural inequalities and social faux pas' (65). Within the context of feminist and anti-racist digital spaces, Nakamura (2015) characterizes the act of 'calling out' as a labour-intensive form of 'community management' intended to protect more marginalized and vulnerable members of a given community. The call-out, then, functions as a moral evaluation (and condemnation) of particular beliefs, practices, or behaviours, with the intention of prescribing a remedy or corrective through the collective reasoning of members of a given (social justice-oriented) community (Meraz and Papacharissi 2013). Calling out is often (but not exclusively) intended to operate as a *learning moment* rather than an act of expulsion (see Chapter 4). Within the context of fandom, these strategies are often mobilized and directed outwards to media texts and producers 'as a potential force in the push for ... media change' (Johnson 2018, 396). However, on Tumblr, given the forms of affective and spatial belonging detailed in Chapter 2, this accountability praxis between feminist fans is intensified, where shared, intense, affects and affinities incentivize efforts to maintain and preserve a 'community' or 'silo' on the platform:

> This, in turn, introduces call-outs, virtue-signalling, and normative performances of the 'right way' of being in order to protect or maintain that experience.
>
> (Tiidenberg, Hendry, and Abidin 2021, 56)

Likewise, Robards et al. (2020, 288) highlight that, on Tumblr, the intense drive to 'define vocabulary, circulate perspectives on power, and generally tackle … challenging ideas … can be experienced and levied as a negative style of policing'. Thus, while many Tumblr users view the moral imperative to 'call out' as a necessary one, the practice is also met with ambivalence and uneasiness. Given the risks of 'context collapse' (Marwick and boyd 2010) that Tumblr's *high scalability* and *nonlinear temporality* produce, it puts one at risk of dogpiling, trolling, and abuse, which produces the fears and anxieties I detailed earlier. The same affordances and vernacular so central to spatial belonging on Tumblr can also be its undoing: 'the anonymity that can help people communicate their story also leaves room for people to attack you indiscriminately and that can be deeply upsetting' (Rita, #51). Consequently, as Tiidenberg, Hendry, and Abidin (2021, 141) highlight, many Tumblr users are 'highly reflexive about the limits and problems surrounding SJWs and social justice Tumblr'. This is where we see a more contradictory and complex engagement with the 'social justice warrior' (SJW) stereotype than I detailed in Chapter 2: an engagement that moves away from the illiberal uses of the term within right-wing, reactionary context towards its varied and contradictory usage *within* feminist fandom.

Across my ethnographic data, I subsequently identify what I refer to as *SJW fatigue* on two distinct counts. Firstly, *SJW fatigue* emerges because the feminist fan-as-SJW is herself *tired*. Feminist fandom, by virtue of its feminist politics and its emergent nature, is necessarily fraught and is deeply affective. It is also a site of contestation, as I have noted throughout this book, over the meanings of feminism/s. An engagement in this project can be emotionally intense and tiring given the affective and relational labour, alongside the belonging work, required to sustain it and protect its most vulnerable members (see Kanai and McGrane 2020). Leah (#296) encapsulates this mode of *SJW fatigue*, when she tells me that 'being socially conscious in fandom … sometimes feels like just endless screaming into the void. It can be very tiring'.

This use of the metaphor of the 'void' to describe Tumblr, with its connotations of unbounded chaos and darkness, reoccurred across my data, with evakuality (#70), Em (#136), Lily (#53), and Emily (#248) using the term in similar ways. Their description of Tumblr as a potential 'void' echoes the claims made by Andre Cavalcante's research participants in his research on queer utopias on Tumblr (also see Keller 2019; Burton 2020). Drawing upon Whannel's (2010) theorization of vortextuality, Cavalcante uses the metaphor of the 'vortex' to explore the pitfalls and risks of the affectively intense forms of silosociality that have emerged on Tumblr given its users' affinity with social justice discourses:

In the context of media audiences, vortextuality is a process of intense user engagement with media ... It is the experience of being sucked in, of falling into a mediated black hole. Although media users do not entirely drown out other sources of information, the attention paid to alternative voices in the media landscape is reduced ... Vortextuality ... is facilitated by the character of digital social media such as Tumblr: their portability, networked structure, customisability, and capacity to allow users to be perpetually connected to technology and to each other across time and space.

(Cavalcante 2019, 1727)

Tiidenberg, Hendry, and Abidin (2021, 135) also emphasize that a sense of spatial belonging on Tumblr is not inherently static, where a given user 'may embrace learning about issues and building skills to participate in personal and social change, but later find the same silo that made it possible to feel overwhelming or even "toxic"'. We can see this play out through Leah's (#296) description of her exhaustion, which implies that affective intensities of feminist fandom on Tumblr, and the resultant efforts to maintain and regulate particular ways of being within that space, may be harder to sustain for longer periods of time.

In the second mode of *SJW fatigue*, the feminist fan is *tired of* the 'SJW' and their unwelcome incursion into feminist fannish spaces. Here, the SJW, and the call-out culture they symbolize, is positioned as an antagonistic, inauthentic, and disciplinary figure who poses a threat to the sanctity of a given fannish space. The 'SJW' is positioned as a 'moralising Other' (Phelan 2019) from *within* feminist fandom, who engages in practices of monitoring, scrutinizing, and policing other fans, becoming the site of anxiety, conflict, and distress. This is emblematic of wider fannish debates surrounding 'toxic' fandom, intra-fandom conflict, and (anti-)fan practices (Guerrero-Pico, Establés, and Ventura 2018; Johnson 2017, 2018). Moreover, this demonstrates how the cynicism underpinning a critique and 'discursive repositioning' (Robards et al. 2020, 288) of the SJW, as Sobande, Kanai, and Zeng (2022) and Phelan (2019) note, is not exclusive to a right-wing political position.

Crucially, within this discourse, the SJW is positioned by feminist fans as posing a threat to feminist fandom's capacity for 'escapism' for its members. What is implicit here is a normative assumption within media fandom that fannish 'affect towards an object' ought to 'supersede personal, cultural, and societal identification' (Hornsby 2020, 19). Feminist fandom's call-out culture on Tumblr, as embodied in the SJW, subsequently threatens their enjoyment of the fannish object and the fantext:

> Fandom for me has always been about escaping reality … The more fandom insists that all things problematic needs to be discussed *ad nauseam* the less enchanted I am.
>
> (Yiva, #39)

In the quote above, we see a fundamental tension between the figure of the SJW and the feminist fan's ability to maintain the escapism and enchantment of feminist fandom on Tumblr. Yet this begs the question: for whom, exactly, is feminist fandom a form of escape and enchantment?

Language and culture

In addition to their anxieties about participation and textual productivity, as well as their concerns about conflict and call-out culture, participants expressed concerns about language and cultural barriers preventing them from accessing feelings of belonging. For example, the dominance of monolingual English speakers within feminist fandom on Tumblr, particularly from Anglophone nations in the Global North, proved daunting for a number of my participants who speak English as a second, or even third, language (also see Bussoletti 2022). Carolina (#120), a 23-year-old from Brazil, for example, explained, 'English is not my first language, so I have a little bit of struggle to express myself.' She later noted, '[T]hat doesn't happen when I write in Portuguese.' Similarly, Ukrainian 19-year-old Marichka (#86) described the feelings of alienation that result from the perceived lack of linguistic diversity on the platform, writing that 'I still find total domination of English language is what makes it feel distant and detouched for many people'.

Language barriers proved particularly troublesome for my research participants within the context of engaging in discussions about feminism within fandom. They once again employed anxiety-laden discourses to express concern about how their communicative competence in English might hinder their ability to fully participate in feminist discussions and debates within feminist fandom. Participants such as Giorgia (#301), an Italian who speaks English as a second language, explained that 'most of the time there may be a language barrier. Talking about feminism isn't easy when you're talking in a language that isn't your first language'. Similarly, a German participant named mybabysteps (#82) told me that 'it's not easy for me to explain complex social issues in a language that isn't mine'. For mybabysteps, this apprehension towards engaging in feminist debate in her second language, and the resulting risk of being misunderstood or misinterpreted, reduced her level of activity within feminist fandom, producing fannish practices and behaviours more in line with the 'lurking' that I discussed earlier. Language barriers, she explained, are the reason 'why I limit my interaction to reblogs'. Within these narratives of non-belonging, then, language barriers reduce access to feelings of belonging within feminist fandom. As Latina and Docherty (2014, 1104) ask, who might be excluded from participating in feminist discourse 'by way of not knowing the languages that are being spoken?'

Cultural barriers also prevented access to feelings of belonging within feminist fandom. While many of my participants emphasized the pleasures of shared intense affective investments in predominantly Anglo-American objects of fandom, several expressed concern about the overwhelming focus on discussing feminist issues within a US-centric context. Belgian Dreamywritingdragon (#22), for example, noted that 'lots of what we talk about is US-centric', and Norwegian Ylva (#31) lamented that 'the discourse is so USA-centric in many cases it's not even funny'. However, for my participants from the Global South, such as Rebecca (#129), a 23-year-old from Iran, the privileging and hypervisibility of white, Western, and Anglo-American feminisms within feminist fandom, produced more pronounced feelings of alienation. She explained:

> I still think my take on feminism is entirely different from a person living in the USA or Europe or Japan. Based on my culture and my country's history, I have some very specific factors that I as, an Iranian feminist, care about that might seem like second nature to someone elsewhere or absurd and unacceptable to another.
>
> (Rebecca, #129)

Here, Rebecca's account raises questions about the transnational and transcultural reach of the feminist discourses that circulate within media fandom. As many feminist scholars have noted, mainstream digital feminism has often excluded the voices of non-white and non-Western women (Loza 2014; Daniels 2016) and has rather myopically focused on the North American and European context (Altınay 2014; Losh 2014; Kim 2017), thus extending the forces of neocolonialization and neo-imperialism within a digital context (Taylor and Zine 2014; Maxfield 2016). So, too, scholars such as Rukmini Pande (2018a, b, 2020a) note, has Anglophonic media fandom excluded and marginalized fans of colour and non-Western fans. Rebecca's account thus raises questions about the extent to which feminist media fandom reinscribes these unequal digital feminist hierarchies, and the impact this may have on different feminist fans' access to belonging, subsequently mediating their *desire to belong*.

White and cisgendered fantexts

Like Rebecca, many of my participants who articulated a sense of non-belonging often did so at the level of social location, demonstrating the myriad ways in which intersecting relationships between gender, class, race, ethnicity, nationality, and other social divisions are central to identities and belonging (Yuval-Davis 2006; Christensen 2017). As Carrillo (2005) notes, the presumption of belonging and belongingness often implicitly reproduces dominant identity formations, such as whiteness (see Anthias 2015). Within the context of belonging, these dominant identity positions tend to be 'naturalised' (Yuval-Davis 2006) and are only articulated or interrogated when exposed by those who do not inhabit them. This is much the case across my ethnographic data. Many feminist fans' accounts of non-belonging referred to the ways in which fannish spaces are often structured around the valourization of white characters, for example, and particularly heterosexual and cisgender white men (Pande 2018a). For eiqhties (#111), for example, the dominant focus on white and cisgender men within fan communities risks excluding fans with trans, non-binary, or genderqueer identities, as well as fans of colour (who may, of course, themselves be gender diverse):

> I think that a lot of the time fandom can perpetuate stereotypes and problematic opinions without even meaning it. There are still primarily ships which only involve two males, often two cisgender, white males – which means that a lot of the approach is very inherent on the white, cisgender LGB experience, which can leave out a lot of people that don't conform to these categories.
>
> (eiqhties, #111)

Indeed, trans participant Jason (#224) explained his difficulty reconciling his fannish interests in 'male/male content' with his emergent identity as a transman, explaining:

> I have only recently discovered I am trans and I am still coming to terms with it. I am learning how my views on feminism and the female experience still affect my life, and how I view my own body ... Tying that to fandom and the ships that I am interested in has also added a twist to this process.
>
> (Jason, #224)

Similarly, feminist fans of colour described how feminist media fandom's broader 'elevation of white characters' (Pande 2018a, 94) within the fantext shapes and reinforces their sense of non-belonging. My participants of colour discussed their uneasy relationship with the lack of representation of people of colour within the fantext. For example, Ashling (#305), an Asian American 23-year-old, discussed her concerns about the predominant focus on (cisgender) white men within the fantext and broader fan community, particularly within the context of fanfiction. She wrote:

> I am worried that fandom … is subconsciously training people to write, think, and care about white men more at the expense of everybody else. In most fandoms, a m/m fic about white boys will get the most views, kudos, likes, reblogs, whatever. I am deeply worried about the cultural implications of this. Fanfiction can serve as a mechanism by which internalised misogyny and racism is reinforced, and that's just not what I want from it at all.
>
> (Ashling, #305)

While Ashling's critique centres fanfiction, her comments reflect broader claims about the reification of privileged racial, gender, and cultural representations within fan communities (Warner 2015, 2018; Pande 2018a, 2020a). Additionally, the experiences of feminist fandom captured within Ashling's responses subsequently problematize the extent to which my participants' emphasis on the importance of centring women in their production of the fantext, as I discussed in Chapter 1, extends to women of colour. To what extent is whiteness centred as the invisible norm in feminist fandom? As many scholars of critical whiteness studies have noted, whiteness tends to be invisible or unmarked to those who inhabit it (Frankenberg 1993; Dyer 1997). Yet, as Ahmed (2004c) notes, for those who do not inhabit whiteness, it has always been visible as a racialized identity. Participants of colour like Ashling thus express frustration with, firstly, fandom's elevation of white (cisgender) characters and, secondly, its subsequent failure to address whiteness itself 'as a racialised identity' (Pande 2018a, 82). This exposes the limits of the feminist fandom's queer normativity on Tumblr, highlighting how not all subjects are granted equal access to the utopic and intensely affective modes of belonging detailed in Chapter 2.

Fandom racism and non-belonging

For instance, Alex (#28), a Latinx 25-year-old from the United States, discussed the hostility and backlash she encounters when trying to engage in critical discussions about problematic aspects of feminist fandom when it comes to race and whiteness:

I have dear friends who are still not all there when my feminist rant involves race. It's been very difficult to even bring up facts that whole *x* female character is treated badly, *x* female character of colour is treated worse. So that's the major issue. Tumblr has grown into this place where a conversation can't happen without insults, people don't like to feel uncomfortable and want to learn, but part of that is learning to deal with their own guilt instead of lashing out.

(Alex, #28)

Alex's reference to the reluctance of (assumedly white) feminist fans to engage in dialogue about race, lest they 'feel uncomfortable', adheres to Robin DiAngelo's (2011, 2018, 2021) theorization of white fragility, which has been used to explain the tendency of white people to flee from racial discomfort and subsequently distance 'whiteness from examination and critique' (Yancy 2012, 153). White fragility, DiAngelo argues, is the 'state in which even a minimum amount of racial stress becomes intolerable, triggering a range of defensive moves' (2011, 54). These defensive moves, or 'distancing strategies' (Applebaum 2010, 42), include the outward display of emotions such as anger, fear, and guilt, or behaviours including argumentation, silence, or even flight from the racial stress-inducing situation. This becomes particularly problematic in supposedly 'progressive' spaces, such as feminist fandom, where self-avowed progressive white people's moral objection to racism increases their resistance to acknowledging their complicity within it (Applebaum 2010; DiAngelo 2018, 2021). We can see these defensive moves at work in Alex's description of her white friends' feelings of guilt and subsequent 'lashing out' in response to Alex's attempts to integrate an intersectional feminist framework into her participation in feminist fandom. Alex's description of her friends' reluctance, if not refusal, to engage in dialogue about these issues is significant, and it has important implications for the feelings of belonging Alex can, or rather *cannot*, access within this context. If, as Ferreday (2011) observes, belonging within online communities arises from one's willingness to engage in 'acts of self-erasure' (101), to become *unmarked* by difference, it follows that non-white feminist fans' non-belongings rest precisely on their refusal to perform the role of the unmarked, and thus implicitly *white* (see Puwar 2004; Yancy 2017), subject when engaging in critique of the fantext. Alex's experience highlights how this refusal to go unmarked within feminist fandom can be disruptive and can produce in others the defensive moves symptomatic of white fragility. Within feminist fandom, then, the operation of white fragility works to stifle discussions which address or challenge racism, subsequently producing feelings of non-belonging and in/visibility for feminist fans who occupy more marginal, and especially racialized, identity positions.

The anti-racist killjoy fan

I argue that we should subsequently *think together* two things: firstly, on the one hand, the forms of *SJW fatigue* I examined earlier, where feminist fans themselves frame the SJW, or 'anti', as an antagonistic figure within feminist fandom; and, secondly, on the other hand, the racist hostility experienced by feminist fans of colour and anti-racist fans detailed above. This understanding of the SJW as an antagonistic, negative figure within feminist fandom aligns them with that of the 'killjoy'. In *The Promise of Happiness*, feminist theorist Sara Ahmed (2010) discusses the relationship between feminist critique and unhappiness and in doing so introduces the figure of the 'feminist killjoy'. The feminist killjoy is a figure whose expressions of their 'consciousness of injustice' are attributed by others 'as the cause of unhappiness' (61), rather than the injustice itself. The feminist killjoy's failure to be happy and joyful in the light of injustice is thus read as sabotaging the joy and happiness of others. Ahmed describes the racial logics underpinning the feminist killjoy, examining the killjoy's relationship to unhappiness within feminism itself:

> Within feminism, some bodies more than others can be attributed as the cause of unhappiness. We can place the figure of the feminist killjoy alongside the figure of the angry black woman … The angry black woman can be described as a killjoy; she may even kill feminist joy, for example, by pointing out forms of racism within feminist politics.
>
> (Ahmed 2010, 67)

The feminist killjoy can therefore kill joy, or cause unhappiness and tension, within feminist spaces precisely because they discuss and expose forms of racism at work within them. Gloria Wekker (2016, 167) offers the 'anti-racist killjoy' as a term to explicitly foreground this intersectional, anti-racist engagement with the feminist killjoy politic. Combined, this understanding of the *anti-racist (feminist) killjoy* has real currency within the context of producing anti-racist critique within feminist fandom. Within feminist fandom, the anti-racist (feminist) fan kills joy, as a shared affect directed towards the fantext, through their refusal to feel joy towards the fantext. This refusal is also a refusal to perform the role of the unmarked, and thus implicitly *white*, subject when engaging in a feminist (anti-racist) critique of the fantext and of representational politics within popular culture at large. Black feminist scholar bell hooks (2003, 35) alludes to a similar process in noting that

> [w]hen people of colour attempt to critically intervene and oppose white supremacy, particularly around the issue of representation, we are often dismissed as pushing narrow political correctness, or simply characterised as being no fun.

The anti-racist killjoy fan's refusal to engage in fannish (joyful and celebratory) affect is thus read as 'sabotaging the happiness' (Ahmed 2010, 66), the positive affects and affinities, of other feminist fans. They kill joy because, in exposing, challenging, and resisting racism, they are 'no fun' (hooks 2003, 35). It is here that the anti-racist killjoy fan is implicated in the *SJW fatigue* detailed above. We can see further evidence of white fans' resistance to this anti-racist killing of (fannish) joy in Rukmini Pande's description of the 'fandom killjoy'. Pande (2018a, 99) identifies 'patterns of erasure and discrimination' in supposedly liberal fannish spaces, like feminist media fandom, where 'questions of racial identity and discrimination' are characterized by some fans as '*too fraught* to be engaged with in arenas that are meant to be for *fun and enjoyment*' (my emphasis). Here, an engagement with anti-racist critique is represented as causing unhappiness, tension, and 'toxicity' and is thus discouraged. This is underpinned by an assumption that fannish affect should supersede one's social location (assuming, of course, that one is white) and thus prevent the risk of killing fannish joy.

Several participants expressed an awareness of this racialized logic within feminist fandom, connecting the *anti-racist killjoy fan* and *SJW fatigue*. For example, Leah (#296), a 21-year-old Jewish woman from the United States, explained: 'Being socially conscious in fandom is often seen as ruining people's fun or being an "anti" (apparently now the fandom term for "SJW").' As digital media scholar Lisa Nakamura (2015, 106) notes, it is often 'women of colour, queer and trans people, and racial minorities' who undertake the work required of a killjoy, who 'call out, educate, protest, and … intervene in racist and sexist discourse online'. However, given that these users are often racially othered, like many of the anti-racist killjoy fans whose experiences I detail, Nakamura adds that this work is often 'rewarded differently and under different conditions' (107), often resulting in 'being harassed, trolled, and threatened on these fora' (108). We see this in the accounts of non-white fans like Alex (#28), who are viewed as causing unhappiness and are at heightened risk of abuse on Tumblr.

To be clear, I am not arguing that *all* forms of *SJW fatigue* arise from these racialized logics and tensions within feminist fandom. Other forms of conflict, hostility, boundary-policing, and disagreement within undoubtedly occur (see Johnson 2017). However, I do believe that it is worth asking ourselves: to what extent are these dominant discourses of unhappiness, frustration, and fatigue within feminist fandom on Tumblr used as an attempt to silence anti-racist critique and prevent the anti-racist killjoy fan from killing the 'fun and enjoyment' (Pande 2018a, 99) of other (implicitly white) fans? To what extent do they locate unhappiness and tension within feminist fandom in the bodies of feminist fans of colour? The experiences of the anti-racist killjoy fan subsequently reveal the 'fault lines' (McCracken 2017, 160–1) between the convergence of the affective investments of fandom with progressive and feminist politics, distinguishing between 'users who can shift out of progressive politicised media reception from those who cannot' (McCracken 2017, 160–1) on the grounds of their more marginal social locations as *marked* (and implicitly racialized) subjects.

Moreover, this is where the *SJW fangirl as pathology* stereotype I detailed in Chapter 2 becomes implicitly racialized, rather than gendered, when mobilized from *within* feminist fandom, where the *SJW fangirl* is *pathologized* on account of their *anti-racist killjoy* politic and their refusal to engage in 'acts of self-erasure' (Ferreday 2011, 101) in order to be 'happy' (Ahmed 2010) and belong within feminist fandom. This contrasts with the exogenous pathologization of the SJW fangirl on account of their gender (or, at least, their proximity to femininity and feminized forms of cultural consumption) and age (see Scott 2019). Within feminist fandom, governed by a common-sense assumption that members are already marginalized in terms of their gender and/or sexuality, SJW fangirls are pathologized because they kill (white) fannish and feminist joy. They are pathologized because their presence risks rupturing the kinds of affective belonging to feminist fandom detailed in Chapter 2. The shared feminist anger so central to affective belonging within feminist fandom, then, does not necessarily extend beyond communal critique of gender and sexuality within the fantext. Producing fannish and feminist critique that explicitly foregrounds race (as well as, or instead of, gender and sexuality) risks being characterized as *excessive* in its anger, much like the trope of the angry Black woman (Lorde 1984; Yancy 2012; hooks 2014), which can lead to expulsion and exclusion from a given community in an act of intra-fandom boundary-policing. Ahmed (2010, 67) subsequently describes the affective alienation that this produces in the killjoy:

You can be affectively alien because you affect others in the wrong way: your proximity gets in the way of other people's enjoyment of the right things, functioning as an unwanted reminder of histories that are disturbing, that disturb an atmosphere ... The body of colour is attributed as the cause of becoming tense, which is also the loss of a shared atmosphere ... As a feminist of colour you do not even have to say anything to cause tension.

Within feminist fandom, the tension caused by the presence of the anti-racist killjoy produces the defensive moves of white fragility in an effort to protect or maintain the experience of normative (white) belonging to feminist fandom. To be a feminist of colour and(/or) an anti-racist killjoy *and* engage in feminist fandom subsequently necessitates a more precarious and contingent mode of belonging in order to navigate the forms of alienation detailed by Ahmed (2010). As Pande (2018a, 99; my emphasis) highlights:

The enjoyment of fannish spaces is clearly far more contingent and precarious for some fans rather than for others. ... Escape relies on switching off but also finding like-minded fans – not just in terms of fannish texts but also in terms of *not* being able to discuss problematic aspects of fandom's safe spaces.

Negotiating differential belonging

According to my participants, such moments of racial tension between white fans and fans of colour often result in fans of colour adopting a range of strategies and techniques to connect with like-minded anti-racist killjoy fans and attempt to evade these forms of racism within feminist fandom, thus producing alternative, more precarious modes of belonging. For example, some utilize Tumblr's affordances to further reduce the (already low) *searchability* of their posts by deliberately omitting tags from their posts. Others make efforts to decrease the potential for *interactivity* with and *reactivity* to their posts by altering the required conditions that enable Tumblr users to 'reply' to their post, by altering their 'Ask' settings to disallow anonymous questions and comments from other Tumblr users, by using the 'Block' user function, and/or by restricting their 'Messages' to only receive incoming messages from users they already follow. These strategies require a sophisticated level of familiarity with Tumblr's affordances and vernacular, while also requiring a notable amount of work, both *with* and *against* the platform's architecture, to reduce, yet not *eliminate*, their exposure to these forms of racist fannish hostility.

Alternatively, participants also described occasions where they had instead decided to take their anti-racist critiques of the fantext off Tumblr entirely, instead preferring private communications on other platforms with sympathetic feminist fans, in their effort to *eliminate* their encounters with this racist hostility as an ethic of care to the (racialized) self. For example, Yasmin (#1), a mixed-raced 26-year-old, explained that, despite her desire to integrate an intersectional feminism into her fandom experience on Tumblr, she noted, '[O]ften I just don't have the energy to get into prolonged debates with people, so I won't discuss these issues publicly and will usually reserve them for group messages with close friends.'[2] African American 19-year-old bobbisnose (#251) similarly described her feelings of exhaustion produced by the overwhelming whiteness of feminist fandom. She lamented, '[F]andom is large, and many times White Feminism seems to reign, which can be exhausting. So a lot of times it's block and move on.' It is in this sense that the platform vernacular of Tumblr does not produce feelings of safety to speak and act freely, openly discuss experiences, share interests and information, and connect with like-minded people for *all* of my participants. While the queer normativity of feminist fandom on Tumblr might operate as a safe space for, say, queer (white) women to openly discuss their sexuality, this feeling of safety does not necessarily extend to fans with other intersecting marginalized identity positions, who have to develop complex strategies to negotiate their position within feminist fandom.

For Ashling (#305), the choice to continue actively engaging with feminist fandom on Tumblr in a public capacity inevitably involves employing a range of strategies, both technologically and discursively, to alleviate the white fragility of other members of feminist fandom while still attempting to enact her anti-racist killjoy politic. Discussing her experiences running a blog exclusively for engaging with the fandom surrounding the television series *Peaky Blinders* (2013–22), a British crime drama set during the early twentieth century, she described the feelings of ambivalence that this complex negotiation produces:

> I have one freewheeling personal blog and one blog that's strictly *Peaky Blinders*, and the way that I approach intersectional feminism on them is radically different. In the former, I mostly do what I want. In the latter, it's a predominantly white, European crowd of women, and sometimes I feel I have to be more diplomatic because there's more internalised misogyny in that crowd, a lot more irrational hating of women or double standards. Navigating that (which is a more recent project of mine) has been uncomfortable at times, and I sometimes think that if I abandon that fandom it may make life easier. Nonetheless, I've made some friends and I'm fond of the canon, so … It's just weird. I'm not sure.
>
> (Ashling, #305)

Above, Ashling explains that engaging in a predominantly white, European, and female fandom on her secondary fandom-specific blog necessarily produces engagements with 'intersectional feminism' that are 'radically different' to those she performs on her 'personal blog'. Ashling tells me that she feels she has to be 'more diplomatic' when engaging with feminist fandom in a predominantly white and European setting in order to lessen the chances of being subject to the racial hostility produced by white fragility, of being marked as the cause of tension and unhappiness. She describes this process of negotiating her engagement with (white) feminist fandom as 'uncomfortable' and even notes that she has considered abandoning fandom entirely. Ashling's experience thus highlights how this process of negotiation can produce feelings of unease and discomfort in feminist fans of colour, generating ambivalence towards and alienation from feminist fandom, which ultimately results in feelings of non-belonging. However, her admission that she has nevertheless made some meaningful friendships within feminist fandom points to the possibility of being able to negotiate more marginal, precarious, contingent, and at times contradictory forms of belonging to feminist fandom.

Carrillo's (2005) conceptualization of 'differential belonging' provides a useful framework to consider how these feminist fans negotiate a more precarious sense of belonging within feminist media fandom. Carrillo offers the concept of 'differential belonging' as a way for subjects to reverse processes of interpellation and to resist the 'discourses of hegemonic belonging' (28) which centre whiteness and heterosexuality. Differential belongings allow for contextual movement between various modes of belonging according to one's needs. This process, she writes, involves negotiating the navigation 'across such boundaries of different to build intimate knowledge of that which lies between self and other' (38). Due to broader lack of resources, fans of colour 'have long had to "make do" and consequently will recalibrate the limits of fandom experience to suit their own need for participation and community amongst themselves' (Warner 2018, 256). As Pande (2018a, 100) and Yodovich (2022) have noted, marginal fans often have to employ contradictory strategies to keep enjoying fannish spaces. Ashling's description of modifying her behaviour to be 'more diplomatic', despite her anti-racist killjoy understanding of feminist fandom as a mechanism through which racism is 'reinforced', serves as a good example of such contradictory strategies. Under Carrillo's (2005) schema, Ashling's negotiation of this process allows for movement between various modes of belonging according to her desire to continue to meaningfully engage with the fan communities surrounding the objects of fandom in which she is invested.

Sara (#288) similarly described her process of negotiating a more differential, contingent, and precarious form of belonging to feminist fandom. While she explained that fans of colour 'still have to deal with a lot of racism and sexism from fandom as a whole', feminist fandom was nevertheless important to her because it provided a space where she could establish meaningful connections and solidarities with other women of colour who also come up against the pathologization of the anti-racist killjoy fan:

> It is the only place where I can choose to primarily engage with other WOC, which makes participating in fandom a lot more bearable. We still have to deal with a lot of racism and sexism from fandom as a whole (as well as canon content itself), but it's easier to deal with when people call it out along with you rather than call you oversensitive for critiquing it.
>
> (Sara, #288)

Such accounts highlight how the fans who cannot access the feelings of belonging captured by the dominant narratives of belonging to feminist fandom may, under some circumstances, negotiate a more precarious, ambivalent, and marginal form of belonging to feminist fandom.

Additionally, these accounts of non-belonging and, to some extent, differential belonging trouble how fan communities are often imagined, both within fandom itself and within fan studies (see Pande 2018a, 2020a). Within fan studies, for instance, media fandom is normatively framed as subversive, liberatory, and resistant due to its willingness to explore gender and queer sexualities (Lothian, Busse, and Reid 2007; Coppa 2014, 2006), which falls in line with my discussion of queer normativity in Chapter 2. These assertions are likewise mirrored within popular journalistic commentary, particularly concerning the fan communities that convene on Tumblr (Madden 2019; Watercutter 2019). However, Pande (2018a) also notes that these ideals are circulated within media fandom itself (also see Stein 2015, 2018). Indeed, my participants' dominant constructions of belonging to feminist fandom detailed in Chapter 2 demonstrate how this progressive vision of media fandom is explicitly declared and circulated within the fannish imaginary on Tumblr. This normative framing of feminist fandom, within both fandom and the study of it, elides the structural forces which differentially distribute access to belonging, as well as the *desire* to belong, within feminist fandom. This is something that Ashling notably alluded to. She explained:

Fandom is often looked at as a vehicle for progressive, intersectional, and feminist values. But in action, it often reinforces the patriarchy instead by training young writers to value white men characters and relationships involving white men characters. … People can yawp all they want about the transformative powers of fanfiction, but if we're all just replicating the racist and patriarchal focus on white men that's already present in the Western canon, then what even is the fucking point? You know? Tumblr is a part of this.

(Ashling, #305)

Without an intersectional and critical lens, it's relatively easy to be seduced by the utopian promise of these celebratory framings of feminist media fandom as a 'vehicle for progressive, intersectional, and feminist values'. However, when considered within the context of the experiences detailed by participants like Ashling, the dominant celebratory narratives about media fandom are rendered increasingly complex and contradictory and are instead infused with ambivalence.

The narratives of non- and differential belonging produced by my participants complicate dominant constructions of belonging to feminist fandom in several ways. Firstly, they reveal how understandings of feminist fandom as a utopian imagined community flatten difference (see Morimoto and Chin 2017) and risk obscuring the embodied raced, gendered, and classed hierarchies that extend into the virtual world (Kolko 2000; Nakamura 2002; Hobson 2008). Consider Elly's (#108) remark that I discussed earlier, for instance: 'I feel like I'm amongst equals of the mind and it doesn't matter who we are on the other side of the screen.' To what extent do such remarks flatten difference and assume whiteness? To what extent is whiteness a 'condition of belonging' (Carrillo 2005, 29) to feminist fandom? These counter-narratives of non- or differential belonging raise questions about the extent to which feminist fandom is imagined as a homogenous and assumedly *white*, Anglophone community, wherein feeling a sense of belonging with 'like-minded' individuals naturalizes dominant hegemonic identity positions and subsequently risks reproducing 'white ignorance' (Applebaum 2010).

Secondly, these counter-narratives of non-belonging complicate the positioning of feminist fandom as a 'safe space' for all. As these counter-narratives highlight, not *all* of my participants affectively experienced participating in feminist fandom on Tumblr as *safe*. As Clark-Parsons (2018) notes, the relational work required to establish and maintain safe spaces inevitably creates boundaries, and the process of cultivating a safe space often raises questions of difference (The Roestone Collective 2014). While the technological affordances and platform vernacular of Tumblr produce certain types of belonging for feminist fans, they do not necessarily extend access to belonging to participants like Alex (#28), Sara (#288), and Ashling (#305) with more marginal intersecting identities and social locations.

The politics of intersectionality

This suggests that, despite feminist fans' broader willingness to performatively and discursively position themselves as 'intersectional' feminists, as I discussed previously, this does not necessarily produce a willingness to thoroughly attend to the lived particularities of *all* intersecting identities and experiences (see Rivers 2017; Kanai 2020a). As Flood (2019, 424) notes, 'it is all too easy to claim an intersectional identity but not actually live out an intersectional politic'.

Additionally, the narratives detailed throughout this chapter raise additional questions about whether my participants' anxieties surrounding (white) privilege, normative identities, whiteness, and white feminism do the anti-racist and intersectional work that it purports to. As Sara Ahmed (2004c) notes, even when white people learn about racism and learn to recognize whiteness as a structure of racism and white supremacy, this does not necessarily challenge racism. For white people, recognizing and declaring whiteness is often understood as in itself an anti-racist act, whereby the declaration of whiteness is assumed to put in place the conditions in which racism can be 'transcended'. Ahmed subsequently describes these disavowals of whiteness 'non-performative' in that they do not perform the work they purport to (also see Ahmed 2012). As I noted in Chapter 1, many of my participants performatively position themselves as intersectional feminists, demonstrating awareness of white feminism and openly critiquing, if not disavowing, it. Yet the experiences of non-white fans, and of the anti-racist killjoy, detailed throughout this chapter suggest that this does not necessarily extend to the *doing* of an intersectional feminism within feminist fandom. This affirms my suggestion in Chapter 1 that the disavowal of whiteness, and white feminism, often involves a gesture towards white moral purity and moral integrity that obfuscates the dominance of whiteness in this supposedly progressive, or 'intersectional', setting. As Applebaum (2010, 9; original emphasis) highlights:

> White people can reproduce and maintain racist practices even when, and *especially when,* they believe themselves to be morally good.

Within feminist fandom, then, there is a risk that intersectionality functions as an 'empty performative', as a 'gesture that produces nothing' (Skeggs 2019, 29). Moreover, as Black feminist scholars including Jennifer Nash (2019) have noted, what does this (non-)performative disavowal of 'white feminism' and avowal of 'intersectional feminism' mean for the explanatory potency of intersectionality? To what extent does it sever it from its origins in Black feminist epistemologies?

Here we arrive at the politics of intersectionality, where feminist fans of colour's narratives of non-belonging, and resulting critique of the celebratory framing of feminist fandom, subsequently mirror broader debates taking place within intersectional feminist theory about the dominance of white cisgender women as the 'architects and defenders of a particular framework of feminism in the digital era' (Daniels 2016, 42). Their accounts reveal how mainstream digital feminism's extension of 'a cultural map of assumed whiteness' (Kolko 2000, 225) subsequently pervades feminist fandom. As many feminist fans have emphasized, digital feminist spaces, including those occupied by media fandom on Tumblr, undoubtedly facilitate consciousness-raising and community building. Yet they, as Fischer (2016) argues, do not miraculously provide transformative political participation and engagement precisely because intersecting oppressions, and particularly the 'centrality of whiteness' (756), continue to permeate and structure these spaces in ways that resonate throughout feminist fandom. This once again reminds us that fannish engagements with feminist identities, discourses, and practices do not take place in a vacuum but remain embedded within social, political, cultural, and economic processes and structures that reproduce uneven power differentials.

Conclusion

The narratives of belonging captured within the previous chapter produce a decidedly utopian vision of feminist fandom as an inherently progressive space, in many ways affirming dominant conceptions of fandom circulating within fan studies as well as within fandom itself (both media fandom *and* Tumblr metafandom (Tiidenberg, Hendry, and Abidin 2021)). However, such utopian narratives flatten difference and universalize the experiences of fans with less marginal identity positions, particularly in terms of race. This demonstrates the crucial need to make room for competing visions of feminist fandom and take seriously the multiplicity and multivalency of feminist fans' experiences, practices, and identities.

Across the accounts of belonging and non-belonging detailed throughout Chapters 2–3, feminist fandom emerges as an increasingly complex and contradictory space that can be about both upending power hierarchies and reinscribing them. Throughout the process of writing this chapter, I tried to avoid hierarchical distinctions between 'good' and 'bad' feminist fans, as I feel this is not productive and is incongruent with my ethos of 'critical respect' (Gill 2007a). Feminist fandom is meaningful to *all* of my participants, as evidenced most saliently by the depth and breadth of their responses to my research survey, their willingness to participate in follow-up interviews, and their eagerness to grant me permission to examine their blogs for research purposes. In many cases, feminist fandom produces powerful feelings of safety, comfort, recognition, and belongingness. However, it is also important to critically attend to the ways in which power differentials structure these spaces and unevenly distribute access to these feelings of safety and belonging. As Cervenak et al. (2002, 346) note, 'the condition of subordination does not prevent us from reproducing similar dynamics of power'. Feminist fandom can be fraught and messy in ways that are not conducive to easy formulations of subversion and resistance found within various scholarly accounts of fandom (Coppa 2014, 2006; Lothian, Busse, and Reid 2007).

While fannish spaces and communities can facilitate feminist becoming as detailed in Chapter 1, they can also operate as spaces of contention and conflict over the meanings of feminism, and over which identities, practices, and positionalities are most recognized within the feminist project. Nevertheless, for many participants whose responses emphasized non-belongingness, their narratives of non-belonging were often configured through feminist intersectional frameworks, and many articulated some form of oppositional or differential belonging within smaller enclaves of feminist fandom. This works as a particularly notable example of how feminist fandom operates as a site of struggle over the meanings of contemporary fourth-wave feminism. Through the discrepancies between the accounts of belonging and non-belonging I have explored across Chapters 2 and 3, we can see how competing understandings of feminism operate within feminist fandom in complex and contradictory ways.

The processual nature of feminist fan identities might offer a more generative, hopeful, and promising outcome for feminist fandom through its emphasis on the value of reflexivity, learning, and self-education. Feminist fans' emphasis

on the developmental, ever-changing nature of feminist fan identities that
I discussed in Chapter 1 offers a potentially productive avenue towards more
inclusive digital feminist and fannish spaces. Their insistence on locating
themselves within a developmental trajectory of reflexive feminist growth
and self-learning, emphasizing their willingness to commit to the ongoing
identity work required of feminism, as well as the ongoing relational work
and belonging work involved in crafting and sustaining feminist spaces, might
offer a more generative outcome for feminist fandom. This is something I will
explore in more depth in the following chapter.

Fandom and/as feminist pedagogy

Both fannish and feminist digital spaces have long been lauded for their pedagogical potential for young people. A significant number of feminist researchers have emphasized the pedagogical value of platforms like Tumblr for social justice and feminist-oriented praxis. For instance, they have highlighted how feminists cultivate new modes of feminist cultural critique online (Keller 2019), creating feminist memes (Rentschler and Thrift 2015) and critiquing the portrayals of girls and women in popular media culture (Eckert and Steiner 2016). Beyond this, self-education and the sharing of knowledge have been described as highly important to digital feminisms (Keller 2016a; Jackson 2018; Mendes, Keller, and Ringrose 2019). Furthermore, media fandom has been described as a type of informal learning culture where fans can collectively develop critical cultural and media literacies through their attachments to the fantext (Jenkins, Ito, and boyd 2016). Bringing together these perspectives, fan studies scholars have more recently emphasized the connections between media fandom and feminist pedagogy (Popova 2020). For McCracken (2017, 151), the connections between media fandom and feminist pedagogy are exemplified by Tumblr's 'convergence of popular culture, socially critical discourse, and peer education'. This discourse also resonates throughout popular journalistic coverage of the platform. For instance, in a 2019 *Pitchfork* article, journalist Emma Madden (2019) positions Tumblr as a 'home' for marginalized communities, 'where they became educated and politicised'. She later aligns Tumblr's pedagogical impetus with the popularization of queer and feminist discourses in the 2010s, adding that 'the new language used to articulate gender and sexual identity has been popularized in lockstep with the platform'.

The importance of fandom and/as feminist pedagogy dominates my ethnographic data, and the pedagogical significance of feminist fandom has punctuated the preceding chapters. As I discussed in Chapters 1 and 2, the pedagogical function of feminist fandom emerged as important to my participants' feminist becoming, as well as their articulations of a sense of belonging to feminist fandom. For example, in Chapter 1, I examined the role of media fandom in educating young people about different meanings of feminism. I subsequently positioned fandom as a site at which meanings of feminism are paratextually constructed, negotiated, and contested in an ongoing process. In Chapter 2, I examined feminist fans' perception of Tumblr as a safe space for young people to learn about gender and sexuality, as well as other salient aspects of their identities, sharing information and resources, and mixing up personal and political material on their blogs. However, the accounts of fandom racism detailed in Chapter 3 raise questions about the extent to which (white) feminist fans are willing to unlearn the trappings of white feminism they expressed so much anxiety about in Chapter 1.

Throughout this chapter, I attend to the complex and multifaceted relationship between fandom and feminist pedagogy in more depth. In the first section, I explore the role of feminist fandom as an informal learning culture that fosters the development of critical feminist media literacy. My analysis locates feminist fandom as a site at which feminist media critique is routinely produced and circulated in an informal and everyday setting. Discussion of cultural texts within feminist fandom thus offers an informal and accessible entry point for fans to move outwards from the text to address broader social issues from a feminist and social justice-oriented perspective, serving a consciousness-raising function within the feminist fan community. In the second section, I demonstrate how the critical feminist media literacies my participants developed both *within* and *through* feminist fandom are carried forwards into their communal production of the fantext. I frame the circulation of fan-created paratexts informed by these critical media literacies as a valuable mode of feminist knowledge sharing that aligns with fannish gift economies. Finally, I return to my earlier understanding of feminist identities as active, ongoing and processual to explore my participants' accounts of engaging in an open-ended and lifelong process of *learning* and *unlearning* within feminist fandom to which a politics of listening is central. Drawing upon feminist perspectives on the relationship between feminist pedagogy and un/learning *through* listening, I position listening as central to the relational belonging work required of creating and maintaining feminist fans' understanding of feminist fandom as a safe space.

Media literacy and informal learning within feminist fandom

In Chapter 1 I discussed the role of fannish paratexts, through the lens of the *fantext*, and their role in the development of feminist identity. Across feminist fans' responses to my narrative survey, they emphasized the importance of the fantext to the continuous, informal process of learning about feminism *through* fandom. I subsequently argued that the paratextual framing and reframing of texts within feminist fandom is important to the process of *making meaning of feminism*, and hence to feminist becoming, as well as to the process of *making feminist meaning* of popular cultural texts. While I briefly discussed the process of *making meaning of feminism* in Chapter 1, here I would like to attend to the process of *making feminist meaning* in more detail as it grants us considerable insight into the pedagogical value of feminist fandom. Across my ethnographic data, feminist fans positioned feminist fandom as a pedagogical space wherein, through routine and everyday fannish practices, fans learn about a wide range of issues concerning media representation and diversity, social justice and inequality, digital technologies, and the media industry. As one Tumblr post from October 2014 noted, 'Tumblr taught me so much about representation tho[ugh] …. today I literally can't watch a film without thinking "why is everyone so white" [or] "why is everyone straight"' (Figure 3). The popular post, which at the time of the writing has accrued almost 225,000 notes, has been reblogged countless times with the addition of hundreds of affirmative comments. In many ways, this Tumblr post captures the sentiments expressed by many feminist fans about the role of feminist fandom in developing critical media literacy. The term 'representation', for example, appears more than sixty times across my data, while the term 'learned' occurs almost ninety times.

Zellieh (#87), for instance, reflected, '[T]here was never a fannish experience for me that was separate from criticism and analysis of the source media, and that naturally included feminism, equal rights, representation, racism and homophobia, etc.' For Zellieh, engaging in critical media discussion from a feminist perspective is intimately and innately intertwined with her fannish experience and with the pleasures of engaging in the practices of fandom.

We can also see a similar process at work in Isolde-thelady's (#315) account of learning how to critically engage with texts through fandom. She explained how the process of developing her critical skills 'started small' involving 'reading

bombshellssz

tumblr taught me so much about representation tho.... today i literally can't watch a film without thinking

"why is everyone so white"

"why is everyone straight"

 mchalemac

#why aren't there any women in the credits

Figure 3 Author screenshot of October 2014 blog post by *bombshellssz*.

[Tumblr] posts and articles about how the world works and microaggressions and studies about stereotypes', before 'snowballing' into a more complex and comprehensive understanding of 'patriarchy and systematic racism and ableism and every other ism'. Here, she highlights the importance of engaging with media critique on Tumblr, in the form of the 'posts and articles' she mentions, to the process of developing her feminist media literacy, as well as her broader understanding of a more intersectional feminism, as captured by her knowing reference to 'and every other ism'. Thus, the same fan-created paratexts that can interrupt and redirect interpretations of a text can, in turn, function as feminist teaching moments that enable fans to develop critical media literacy. De Kosnik (2016, 179) highlights that these paratexts have an educative function through the 'internal changes that such [fanworks] might effect in fans themselves'. Indeed, feminist fans like Elizabeth (#303) noted how engaging with feminist fandom on Tumblr opened her 'eyes to different ways of thinking' and ultimately transformed her entire 'belief system'. Fannish identities and practices can therefore catalyse critical political-intellectual shifts.

Feminist fandom's capacity to catalyse such shifts aligns it with the forms of learning associated with 'passionate affinity spaces'. In *Language and Learning in the Digital Age*, Gee and Hayes (2011) define passionate affinity spaces as out-of-school learning systems rooted in learning *as* and *through* popular culture (also see Gee and Hayes 2010). Passionate affinity-based learning is an interest-driven form of learning that occurs

[w]hen people organise themselves in the real world and/or via the Internet ... to learn something connected to a shared endeavour, interest, or

passion. The people have an affinity (attraction) to the shared endeavour, interest, or passion first and foremost and then to others because of their shared affinity.

(Gee and Hayes 2011, 69)

Passionate affinity spaces encourage their members to engage in forms of learning that are complex, deep, and knowledge-producing. These forms of learning are rooted in their members' shared interests that are often related to popular culture. As fandom itself is built on shared interests, affects, and affinities, the concept of the passionate affinity space has been widely employed to examine informal learning within fandom (Jenkins, Ito, and boyd 2016; Min, Jin, and Han 2018), as well as on Tumblr in particular (McCracken et al. 2020; Tiidenberg, Hendry, and Abidin 2021). We see passionate affinity-based learning at work throughout my ethnographic data on feminist fandom, where feminist fans' deep passion, as a *shared affect* as detailed in Chapter 2, 'for the common endeavour' (Gee and Hayes 2011, 71) fuels learning, locating *all* members of the feminist fan community as the potential producers of shared knowledge about society, culture, and media.

Critical media literacies

Across my ethnographic data, feminist fandom on Tumblr emerged as an affinity-driven space that enables young people to develop critical feminist and social justice-oriented media literacies based on their shared affinities and interests as feminists and fans. According to Kellner and Share (2007, 4), the concept of *critical media literacy*

[e]xpands the notion of literacy to include different forms of mass communication and popular culture as well as deepens the potential of education to critically analyse relationships between media and audiences, information and power. It involves cultivating skills in analysing media codes and conventions, abilities to criticise stereotypes, dominant values, and ideologies, and competencies to interpret the multiple meanings and messages generated by media texts.

Furthermore, Kellner and Share emphasize that feminist pedagogical approaches to critical media literacy emphasize the importance of 'addressing principles of equity and social justice related to representation' (10) and subsequently attend to issues of gender, race, sexuality, and power. These interest-driven processes of developing skills in analysing media codes and conventions, criticizing representational stereotypes, and questioning dominant values and ideology within media texts, all while attending to principles of social justice from a feminist perspective, are evidenced across my data and are subsequently central to the operation of feminist fandom.

Within feminist fandom, as a passionate affinity space, the cultivation of this feminist media literacy is primarily interest-driven and is, in many cases, fuelled by the fans' desire to foster a greater level of understanding of the fantext, as fans' 'common interest' (Gee and Hayes 2011), in line with their identities as both feminists and as fans. Moreover, as Jessica (#280) highlights in a response that is worth citing at length, discussions of media texts offer an informal and accessible entry point for fans to address broader social issues, thus functioning as a democratizing pedagogical tool. She explained:

> In real life, I talk about discrimination in fandom a lot, often through dialogue with similarly minded friends, but also through challenging people in my life ('why do you think Kylo Ren is a more sympathetic character than Finn? I don't know much about *Star Wars*, but I know one is pretty unambiguously the villain and one is black, so … '). The media we consume is sometimes an easier way to talk about tendencies of racism, sexism, homophobia, etc. … I engage with issues of oppression and inequality in just about everything I do, to the extent that sometimes my family roll their eyes at me, and fandom is no different. We can't talk about how much we love Tolkien if we don't unpack what it means that *The Hobbit* has no female characters, that the dwarves are pretty heavily Jewish-coded, and so on. We can't talk about the historically progressive nature of the *Star Trek* fandom without discussing some of the fairly heavy racism underlying Spock/Kirk fic, especially since the release of the recent movies.
>
> (Jessica, #280)

Here, Jessica's (#280) response reveals how the shared affinity and interest-driven nature of feminist fandom on Tumblr enable feminist fans to learn about feminism in an 'intense, autonomous, and interest-driven way' (Ito et al. 2009, 28), where one's feminist and fannish interest in the fantext provides a shared framework for cultivating critical feminist media literacies. Once again, we see the passionate affinity space's capacity to facilitate knowledge production and knowledge sharing at work here. Furthermore, note that Jessica's commentary moves far beyond the representational politics of just gender. Here, she refers to the representational politics of (a)sexuality, race and ethnicity, religion, and other salient identity markers, demonstrating her knowledge of the 'intersectional turn' (Carbin and Edenheim 2013) within digital feminist spaces. Like Jessica, joslynnyc (#157) also noted the interest-driven nature of learning within feminist fandom. She reflected, 'We use the things we love as a jumping off point to examine feminist issues and share things we've learned.' As a result, she later noted, 'I've learned a ton about queer and intersectional feminism through Tumblr and fandom and I use the platforms to listen and engage with other women/[non-binary] people.'

For projecitdespatio (#165), the interest-driven process of learning on Tumblr is central to her continued use of the platform and is underpinned by a civic impulse. She explained, 'I continue to use Tumblr because it has such a diverse community coming together to celebrate and appreciate different things, but at the same time enables you to learn about diversity and experiences faced by other people.' Similarly, Jessica (#280) highlighted that 'Tumblr is my biggest location for fandom activity because it allows me to do my favourite thing: lurk, learn, and shape my own views and opinions'. Here, Jessica (#280) derives pleasure from the process of learning itself in relation to fandom. From this, we can see how the interest-driven processes of learning on Tumblr are central to the pleasures many feminist fans derive from participating in feminist fandom.

Like projecitdespatio and Jessica, many of my participants reported using these passionate affinity spaces within feminist fandom to learn about, and make appeals for, what Beltran (2010) describes as 'equitable representation' and 'meaningful diversity' beyond the mere inclusion of actors and characters who occupy more marginal social locations. Peyton (#59), for example, noted that 'I think that joining fandom has really increased my understanding of how important and great it is to actually have diverse characters and casts in our media,' and C (#187) explained that her identity as a feminist and fan 'pushes me to seek more female "heavy" and diverse content and be more interested in those characters and points of view'. Moreover, participants such as Sarah (#308) emphasized the importance of more *meaningful* forms of diversity, highlighting that 'being diverse just for the sake of it often leads to stories that just don't work'. This suggests that a more reflexive, critical engagement with a feminist politics of recognition can be at work within feminist fandom. Kohnen (2018) made similar observations in her research on Tumblr pedagogies, highlighting that 'fandom on Tumblr often includes discussions of diversity in media representation and the intersections of fandom and social justice' (465). McCracken (2017, 157) takes this one step further, noting that 'media representation is a chief concern' to Tumblr users, forming 'the subject of much of their sophisticated criticism, creative production, and pleasure'. Tumblr has subsequently secured a reputation within the feminist and fannish imaginary for its users' in-depth analyses of representational politics and social issues.

Transformative learning

Many participants emphasized the transformative power of affinity-based learning within feminist fandom beyond critical media literacy. In addition to the narratives of feminist becoming detailed in Chapter 1, feminist fans highlighted that their time within feminist fandom had fostered a greater level of self-awareness and self-assuredness, enabling them to develop their empathy and understanding towards others who do not share their experiences and subject positions. Josie (#227), for instance, noted the transformative educational function of fan-created paratexts, not only for developing critical media literacy but also for learning interpersonal social skills through fostering a greater understanding of other members of the feminist fan community:

> People spend so much time thinking and writing and engaging in discussions about reasons behind/implications of so many things (and not just in source material, but also within the fandom). … *Reading about what other people have to say deepens my understanding not only of the source material, but also of other people.*

> (my emphasis)

These acts of informal learning within feminist fandom emerged as particularly important to my queer and gender nonconforming participants, who used feminist fandom to 'explore and learn about … different sexualities and genders' (Lunylovegoodlover, #96). Bisexual and genderqueer 24-year-old Gull (#32), for example, explained how they learned about bisexuality and genderqueer identities through their engagement with feminist fandom, and particularly through consuming the fanworks produced by other feminist fans. Reflecting on their experience reading 'slash' (same sex) fanfiction, they explained:

> [I was] learning a lot about myself thanks to being involved in fandom. I read a lot of slash fic and became a lot more comfortable thinking about/talking about sex, and I would definitely attribute my finally coming out to myself as bisexual (and, later, genderqueer) as greatly influenced by the widespread acceptance I saw in fandom. (That, and Tumblr genuinely had a lot of good information about what it meant to be bisexual, which I hadn't encountered anywhere else in my life and hadn't really realised it was even much of an option).

> (Gull, #32)

Additionally, Gull emphasizes that the information they encountered on Tumblr about gender and sexuality was not available to them elsewhere. As they noted, they hadn't had access to 'good information about what it means to be bisexual ... anywhere else in my life'. Xyresic (#97) similarly noted that 'fandom tries to open the conversation to more than what you would hear in everyday life. I discovered who I was and my sexuality by reading through some things and going "hot damn, that sounds exactly like me". I learned that it's okay to like what you like and to be open about it to people'. This affirms Gee and Hayes's (2011, 74) assertion that passionate affinity spaces foster learning that is distinctly 'not on offer in schools' (also see Tuck and Yang 2013).

As I discussed previously, feminist fandom on Tumblr can be positioned as a counterpublic in that it functions as a space that permits members of subordinate social groups 'to formulate oppositional interpretations of their identities, interests, and needs' (Fraser 1990, 67). Given Tumblr's queer silosociality and queer normativity, this performs a particularly important educative function for my queer, trans, and gender-diverse research participants. For instance, in Chapter 2, I discussed the example of Alex (#278), a bisexual transgender man, who explained that feminist fandom was the first place he had encountered 'people against bi-erasure', which he contrasted to his experiences in LGBT groups 'in real life', as well as the place where he met his 'first trans mentors, genderqueer folks, other spoonies'. He explained, '[W]e could hear each other out without reservations or doubts'. While I previously explored Alex's experiences in relation to his sense of safety and spatial belonging on Tumblr, experiences like his are also worth considering with regard to their pedagogical value. Like Gull (#32), Alex (#278) notes that engaging in feminist fandom on Tumblr granted him access to other people who shared experiences and identities he could learn from and be affirmed by. This echoes queer young people's claims in research conducted by Cavalcante (2019), Byron et al. (2019), and Robards et al. (2020), who note:

> When queer and gender diverse people are hidden or erased in education and accessible cultural forms, stumbling across 'people like me' on Tumblr can be revelatory and also a moment of learning and discovery: new words, new languages for self-expression, and new opportunities to connect one's own experiences with others through learned language.
>
> (Robards et al. 2020, 286)

Moreover, these forms of learning are a typical feature of feminist pedagogy. As Shrewsbury (1993, 13) argues, 'the personal can be recognised as political in a classroom with some sense of mutual community', where 'students may find connections with themselves, their individual and collective pasts, with others, and with the future'. Feminist fandom's function as a counterpublic sphere, where members of subordinated social groups can formulate oppositional interpretations of their identities, therefore enables participants like Alex (#278) to engage in the feminist pedagogical practice of coming to recognize the personal as political. According to Naples (2013, 661), this process is a core feature of intersectional feminist pedagogical practice, where safe spaces provide the deliberative 'context in which individuals can critically reflect on their experiences' and generate situated knowledge 'in dialogue with others'. Moreover, Cervenak et al. (2002, 345) argue that feminist pedagogies work to produce the modes of 'oppositional thinking' captured within Alex's response.

Alex also emphasized that such shared experiences were absent elsewhere in his life, thus serving as a crucial resource for connecting to and learning from queer and gender-diverse peers based on shared interests, affects, and affinities. As hooks (1994b) argues, for subordinated people, formal education can be a place of punishment, confinement, and control, rather than of learning and enrichment. My research subsequently affirms the research findings of Byron et al. (2019), whose participants described learning about gender fluidity, non-binary genders, experiences of asexuality, and distinctions between bisexuality and pansexuality through Tumblr.[1] Many of my participants thus associate Tumblr with learning about their own identities, as well as the textual representations of these identities within popular culture, in ways they otherwise would be unable to access. Although, as J's (#90) experience highlights, this education is not limited to one's own identities and social location but rather extends to a much broader knowledge of social issues surrounding gender and sexuality:

Tumblr allowed me to read posts by other queer people and connect with them. That exposure helped me feel less alone in my discovery of my queerness, and I think that was an important step along the way to engaging with queer issues, not just in terms of my identity, but in terms of activism. Tumblr is one of the only places that I've read personal accounts of nonbinary and trans people, for example, which helped me understand a side of feminist/queer activism that I'm not sure I would have learned about in the same way otherwise.

(J, #90)

For many feminist fans, the processes of informal learning they accessed within fandom enabled them to redress some of the constraints produced by the social, cultural, and educational norms of their local contexts, where the passionate affinity space of feminist fandom provides them with access to information and knowledge they would seldom access otherwise. Eighteen-year-old Sahvana (#321), for instance, wrote in length about the significance of fandom as an informal learning opportunity that she otherwise wouldn't experience in her predominantly white, rural, and conservative community in Idaho, USA. She explained:

> I grew up in a tiny North Idaho town that was only 20 minutes away from the founding place of the Aryan Nations. It was very homogenous, very white, very straight, very Christian, very Conservative, and very misogynistic. ... Once I left that town and was exposed by fandom to new concepts, less 'socially acceptable' (in my hometown) concepts, I learned to actively work against my own racism. This opened the doors to learning to stop being bigoted in other senses: ableism, transphobia, and misogyny as well. The biggest part in my journey to becoming a feminist wasn't actually letting go of misogyny, it was letting go of the passive racism that had prevented my enlightenment in other social aspects. There was no actual moment that made me say 'I'm a feminist'. It was just a long process of detoxing my bigotry that ended with me as a better person in general.
>
> (Sahvana, #321)

While she frames this experience with reference to the process of becoming feminist, she touches on a range of hugely transformative learning experiences she accessed through feminist fandom. As Jenkins, Ito, and boyd (2016) highlight, the interest-driven and participatory forms of learning detailed by feminist fans were previously only available to privileged young people with access to specialized enrichment activities, as well as access to further education. Yet the advancement of new media technologies has lowered the barriers to accessing these spheres of community-oriented and interest-driven informal learning typical of the passionate affinity space. For many of my participants, the opportunity to share resources, information, experiences, and knowledge with like-minded feminist fans who shared their interests is subsequently of immense value. Like Sahvana, a South African respondent named Isa (#104), for example, positioned feminist fandom as 'incredibly freeing' and as a safe space to learn about concepts and world views 'frowned upon in my conservative community'. Similarly, 16-year-old HelloMissSunshine (#6) from

Germany commended the educational value of the imagined transnational nature of feminist fandom, explaining that 'fandom taught me a lot by showing new perspectives and differences around the world'. Meanwhile, 26-year-old Martina (#33) from Slovakia emphasized the role of feminist fandom in accounting for the shortcomings of the formal education she had accessed in Slovakia. She explained how she relied on her access to Tumblr to teach her about social issues from a feminist perspective, 'Tumblr taught me about [feminism], because sadly in my country no one will ever teach you about it or other social problems. Which sucks.' For these respondents, then, the pedagogical value of feminist fandom on Tumblr lies primarily in its ability to redress the learning constraints of one's local context and facilitate processes of 'transcultural and transnational awareness and education' (McCracken 2017, 154). It is in this sense, as Gee and Hayes (2011) highlight, that passionate affinity spaces create distinctly out-of-school learning spaces.

Thus, my participants' understanding of feminist fandom on Tumblr as an imagined transnational community rooted in shared popular cultural experience worked to reinforce their understandings of feminist fandom as a pedagogical space. Moreover, responses from participants like Martina (#33) and Sahvana (#321), which emphasize the role of feminist fandom in addressing some of the shortcomings of their formal education, problematize perspectives from fan studies scholars, such as Booth (2015), which position fandom as a *supplementary* educational space. Booth describes fandom as 'the classroom of the future', highlighting that it 'may be one of the few places where people are encouraged to think critically, to write, and to make thoughtful and critical judgments about hegemonic culture *once formal schooling is complete*' (my emphasis). As many of my participants emphasize, for many young people, feminist fandom is one of the *only* spaces they can access the kinds of informal learning opportunities detailed above. As McCracken (2017, 153) notes:

> In an era in which traditional educational institutions have faced the narrowing of their curriculum in the areas of critical thinking, the arts, sex education, and progressive politics, it is in social media's spaces of community and contestation that many young people develop their critical skills, engage in creative work, and construct a sense of themselves as desiring individuals and social actors.

Fandom and feminist knowledge sharing on Tumblr

Feminist fans emphasized that they were not only *learning* about feminism through fandom; they were also actively engaged in the ongoing project of educating, or rather *teaching*, their peers in turn. Many feminist fans, for example, discussed how the critical feminist media literacies they had developed within feminist fandom are carried forwards into their communal production of the fantext, of the paratextual assemblages surrounding popular cultural texts. As Kellner and Share (2007, 4) note, these modes of cultural production can encourage young people to 'challenge media texts and narratives that appear natural and transparent' and thus perform an important pedagogical function. For example, Acme146 (#54) explained, '[I]f my fandoms have disappointed me in terms of representation, I do my best to address that in my fanfiction.' While these forms of cultural production operate as a way for young people to put their feminist knowledge into practice, they also have the potential to function as teaching moments for other fans. The circulation of fan-created paratexts within fandom, then, functions as a valuable means of feminist knowledge sharing.

Knowledge sharing thus forms a core part of the group identity work required of being a feminist fan. According to Gee (2005), passionate affinity spaces, like fandom, encourage members to gain and spread both extensive, in-depth knowledge and distributed and dispersed knowledge that is shared across its membership. We see this at work in feminist fans' framing of feminist knowledge sharing as an obligation and as a central component of participation within feminist fandom. Dinah (#98), for example, who noted that she was 'introduced to important threads I missed, issues I was blind to, through Tumblr and Twitter', emphasizes that she, in turn, puts a great deal of effort into seeking out in-depth information and helping to share it with other Tumblr users to distribute and disperse knowledge throughout feminist fandom. Max (#112) similarly positions themself as the agent of feminist knowledge sharing, explaining that 'I try to do my part teaching the people around me about intersectional feminism by amplifying the voices of the marginalised people who speak up about it'. Not only does Max frame feminist knowledge sharing, or 'teaching', as an obligation, as doing 'my part', within feminist fandom, they also highlight the pedagogical importance of sharing the feminist knowledge produced by more 'marginalised people', thus marking an attempt to engage with more intersectional approaches to feminist knowledge sharing and commit to learning across difference. Max later emphasized their awareness of the *work* that goes into producing and sharing feminist knowledge on Tumblr: 'I'm very grateful to all those who take the time to provide us with information, explanations and testimonies, which is time-consuming and mentally/physically exhausting.'

Even for feminist fans unable to produce pedagogical materials first-hand, sharing and distributing feminist knowledge they encountered on Tumblr remained highly important and meaningful. Emmie (#164), for example, explained:

> I engage with feminist issues in fandom mostly through reblogging posts that I come across that bring light to or engage with important issues – poor treatment of women in fandom, or fanworks, or in the film/TV industry, or in the source material, or lack of representation or intersectionality in any of these spheres. I don't really dedicate time to producing this sort of content myself, but I think it's important to amplify these discussions and voices when I see them.
>
> (Emmie, #164)

Across my participants' responses, the practice of reblogging feminist knowledge on Tumblr operates as a form of *sharing feminist knowledge*. Reblogging feminist knowledge, and thus recirculating information to one's own network of followers, on Tumblr thus 'extends that critique beyond the individual, where it can continue to live and resonate with others' (McCracken 2017, 161) through Tumblr's *high nonlinear temporality*. Again, this highlights feminist fandom's operation as a passionate affinity space, as feminist fans strategically utilize 'tools and technologies that store and facilitate knowledge' (Gee and Hayes 2011, 70). Many feminist fans do so with the hopes that doing so might facilitate the educative process of feminist consciousness-raising among their peers.

In turn, they placed great emphasis on the personal impact of these processes of feminist knowledge sharing. For example, Ingrid (#313), writing about her process of feminist becoming, explained how following a particular Tumblr blog, that routinely shared information about feminism, particularly concerning disability, taught her a great deal about feminism and initiated a long-term process of self-education. She explained at length:

> I didn't really start understanding feminism until one of the authors from AO3[2] I was following reblogged a post about a Tumblr that helped writers find people they could talk to if they needed to understand a particular culture or disability or circumstance to write about it sensibly. That Tumblr had a database of people

offering their services, which I browsed through, and found a particular profile that interested me, possibly only because the person sounded nice. I followed the link to their Tumblr. That was how it all really started. ... I felt like they kept explaining things that I had always felt to be true but had never really considered, or would've had the words to explain ... I became obsessed with that Tumblr [blog] for what must've been months. Most of my early feminist learnings came from it, although only about a few weeks in I must've started following other feminist Tumblrs. I identified as a feminist the moment I learned what the word really meant. I never really studied it formally, but since then I've been educating myself constantly.

(Ingrid, #313)

Here, Tumblr's affordances of *high scalability*, where a post reblogged (and thus shared) by another user, brought a list of feminist educational resources on disability to Ingrid's attention, and *high nonlinear temporality*, which enabled Ingrid to subsequently examine a user's archive of blog posts in her own time, granted Ingrid access to invaluable knowledge about feminism and disability.

Feminist fandom's gift economy

By engaging in this reciprocal and ongoing process of knowledge sharing, my participants strategically utilize the gift economy of fandom, combined with the technological affordances of Tumblr, to engage in acts of feminist knowledge sharing. Fandom, as Hellekson (2009) argues, involves three elements of exchange that, together, comprise fandom's gift economy: *giving, receiving,* and *reciprocity.* The 'gifts' that fans exchange take many forms and might include, for example, fanworks such as fanfiction, fanvids, or fanart, meta analysis, or other aggregates of information. These gifts, Hellekson (2009, 115–16) argues, 'are designed to create and cement a social structure ... with the goal of creating and maintaining social solidarity'. The gifts exchanged between fans contribute to the overall composition of the fantext, as well as the constitution of a given fan community. When applying this understanding of fandom's gift economy to feminist fans' experiences, the sharing of feminist knowledge thus becomes a 'gift' that one anticipates other fans to 'receive' and 'reciprocate' in turn. For example, one fan's blog post detailing the kinds of critique described by Emmie (#164) that 'bring[s] to light or engage[s] with important issues' from a feminist perspective operates as a *gift* that, through the act of reblogging, Emmie can *receive* and then *reciprocate* the act of *gifting* by *regifting* the blog post to her own followers, in turn. From this, we can see the co-constitutive relationship between fandom's gift economy and feminist knowledge sharing on Tumblr.

Moreover, as Turk (2014) notes, fandom's gift economy is not merely 'an accumulation of contiguous reciprocal relationships between individuals but a complex system in which the reciprocation of gifts … is distributed across the community rather than concentrated in a single transaction'. As noted above, this *distribution* and *dispersal* of knowledge is typical of a passionate affinity space, where working towards collaboratively building a replenishing repository of public goods and information is central to the operation of a given online community. Within the context of feminist fandom on Tumblr, this act of establishing a repository of public goods is facilitated by the platform's *high nonlinear temporality*, which allows networks of Tumblr blogs to function as archives of information. These public goods and information, Baym (2015) argues, are intended for use by imagined and unknown recipients one might never encounter again and one might not expect the recipient to reciprocate immediately. From this, feminist fandom's gift economy results in the establishment of a broader repository of public goods and information intended for use by other feminist fans who share one's affinities, interests, and affects.[3] Thus, under this schema, the reciprocal sharing of feminist knowledge functions as a form of 'open-ended gifting' (Turk 2014) within feminist fandom that has a powerful educative function. The process of producing affinity-based feminist knowledge within feminist fandom is thus deeply, inherently collaborative in nature.

Multi-generationality

To extend this metaphor of feminist fandom's gift economy further, feminist scholars have notably conceived of feminism as an inter-generational 'gift'. Concurrently, feminist fans emphasized that one of the benefits of feminist knowledge sharing on Tumblr is its multi-generational character. While Tumblr is culturally and discursively associated with youth, and the modal age of the 342 feminist fans who participated in my research was 21 years old, many feminist fans nevertheless emphasized the multi-generationality of feminist knowledge sharing within feminist fandom. For example, recall in Chapter 1, where I explored Emily's experiences of feminist becoming which emphasized the significance of multi- and inter-generational feminist knowledge sharing. Emily (#71) explained:

I don't think I really identified as a feminist until I … interacted with other [fans] who were older and gave me a lot of words and pedagogy and theory for things I had felt and experienced but didn't have the verbiage to explain.

Here, Emily explicitly aligns the multi-generationality of feminist on fandom Tumblr with its pedagogical value. For Emily, interacting with older fans was central to her process of feminist consciousness-raising, enabling her to learn about, and name, the things she 'had felt and experienced but didn't have the verbiage to explain'. While generational logics are often employed within scholarly and popular commentary on feminism to understand *conflict* (Quinn 1997), here a generational logic is utilized to describe practices of reciprocity and learning. As McCracken (2017, 154) notes, the kinds of intra- and inter-generational mentoring Emily alludes to here are 'an important aspect of the cultural functioning of the [Tumblr] platform'. Likewise, many of my other participants also discussed similar processes of inter-generational mentoring and consciousness-raising. For instance, Carla (#211), when reflecting on her process of feminist becoming within fandom, noted that 'there were always older women I could talk to and ask questions about my feeling towards things and that influenced me a lot'. This is something that Tumblr users themselves often encourage (Figure 4).

Sabrina (#25) also discussed the value of multi-generationality:

Older people in the fandom usually helped me realise how to be a better person/ feminist regarding women in fandom. … It was very useful to me that older fans provided examples on how to grow and be as people. In retrospect, I also appreciate that these older fans very much kept their distance from younger fans, but didn't shy away from providing advice to them, again, whether in life or writing or whatever.

(Sabrina, #25)

 firewxtch

to my younger followers: if u ever have questions u want answering but arent sure who to talk to you can ask me. i am ur honorary big sister now ok

Figure 4 Author screenshot of an April 2015 blog post by *firewxtch*.

Sabrina later explained how she carried forwards this ethos into her approach to feminist fandom as she herself grew older. She wrote, '[A]s well, I think especially I got older, I tried to create safe, open platforms. I didn't engage in fandom "drama", but would try and write work that represented women and LGBTQIA+ people well.' Here, we can see the gift economy of fandom at work in Sabrina's desire to re-gift the knowledge she was gifted by older fans through the process of crafting safe and open platforms for younger fans to engage with.

Older feminist fans often demonstrated awareness of their roles in this capacity. For example, 40-year-old Willow (#75), when responding to a question about how she primarily engages with feminism through fandom, responded that she felt engaging 'in conversation with other women, especially younger women' was a fundamental part of the group identity work required of being a feminist fan. Once again, here we may return to the idea of feminist knowledge sharing as an *obligation* one takes on if they are to meaningfully participate in the passionate affinity space of feminist fandom on Tumblr. Playfully and ironically referring to herself as a 'Tumblr old', Willow expressed her sense of 'responsibility for this'. She later added that these conversations can be a productive place to share knowledge about and 'explore intersectional feminism' through the lens of fandom:

> I think that the issues of relevance to feminism in canon/source material can be a safer platform for discussion than making people expose themselves and their lives. In particular, it's a slightly removed place to explore intersectional feminism. When we discuss [the] lack of female agency in [the] source material, and then talk about how black women are portrayed differently, and then how sex work is always viewed as either desperate or amoral, and also a black women's space – we can start to understand how images harm everyone.
>
> (Willow, #75)

Thirty-three-year-old laughingpinecone (#259) similarly discussed taking on a role that younger people within the community would benefit from, explaining that 'I think a good deal of the content I create is stuff that would've helped a younger me feel like she belonged'. Older members of feminist fandom are thus positioned as particularly knowledgeable and thus more able to engage in acts of feminist knowledge sharing that can facilitate the process of feminist consciousness-raising.[4] This is something that participants such as 43-year-old Zellieh (#87) articulated, explaining:

I mostly feel like fandom and media criticism … it's more about what used to be called 'consciousness-raising' – the first part of the process of making change, which is important because we need to keep doing that for every new generation of teens and young adults who are coming to these ideas for the first time.

These narratives subsequently adhere to Stein's (2015, 175) understanding of contemporary media fandom as a 'safe but multi-generational environment', where multi-generational dialogue can offer 'an empowering route to knowledge within a supportive community'. With regard to feminist fandom, this functions as a route to *feminist* knowledge within a largely supportive and multi-generational community. More significantly, however, the experiences of multi-generational feminist knowledge sharing and mentoring detailed by my participants trouble Yodovich's (2022, 104) assertion that older women fans are often rendered 'invisible' within feminist-fannish spaces.

Archival practices

Thus far, I have discussed the relationship between fandom's gift economy and feminist knowledge sharing, as well as the multigenerational character of feminist knowledge sharing on Tumblr. Now, I will move on to discuss the practices of one of my research participants, named centrumlumina (#298), in more detail to examine how an individual fan might approach the work of feminist knowledge sharing within feminist fandom. This grants us more detailed insight into how feminist fans facilitate the process of feminist knowledge sharing on an individual level. Firstly, I will attend to her involvement in the *femslashrevolution* Tumblr blog before discussing her AO3 Fandom Statistics project.

Centrumlumina's (#298) role as the co-creator of an archival Tumblr blog named *femslashrevolution* ('Femslash Revolution') offers a useful example of how an individual feminist fan might approach the work of feminist knowledge sharing within feminist fandom on Tumblr. Notably, while discussing centrumlumina's experiences in Chapter 1, I explored how her positionality as a queer woman and a feminist inflected her entry into, and production of, the fantext. Here, I will attend to the ways in which her approach to the (re)production of the fantext, particularly through her involvement with *femslashrevolution* as well as her AO3 Statistics project, has a critical-pedagogical impetus. *femslashrevolution*, which centrumlumina describes as a 'pan-fandom F/F blog', was created in late 2013 and operates as a collection of fanworks, meta analyses, advice, and fannish commentary all centred around female/female, also known as 'femslash', 'wlw' (women loving women), or 'f/f', relationships (see Figure 5).

The blog compiles and archives a wide range of Tumblr posts from other users featuring fanworks that centre female/female relationships within popular culture texts, thus functioning as a public repository or archive of fanworks that centre female/female relationships. Such fanworks might include, for example, fanart, fanfiction, fanvids, and meta analysis. In doing so, *femslashrevolution* adheres to McCracken's (2017, 156) characterization of a particular type of Tumblr fan blog 'run by groups of moderators devoted to specific intersections of popular culture and politics (and/or social marginalization) about which they offer advice and counsel'. Beyond utilizing Tumblr's *high nonlinear temporality* to offer a space for queer women to congregate, celebrate, and *archive* their shared identities and fannish interests, *femslashrevolution* more broadly calls attention

Figure 5 Author screenshot of *femslashrevolution* Tumblr blog.

to the invisibility of queer women within contemporary Anglo-American media culture and in doing so performs a kind of 'curatorial activism' (Reilly 2018).

As a queer feminist fan, centrumlumina adheres to Abigail De Kosnik's (2016) model of the queer fan archivist. Drawing upon the work of Cvetkovich (2003) and Halberstam (2005), De Kosnik characterizes fan archives, like those maintained by centrumlumina, as queer archives engaged in queer cultural memory-making:

> Queer archives are frequently, at least partially, fan archives. Both queer and fan groups grasp the power of appropriating and transforming received cultural texts, and therefore, any archive that hopes to adequately represent either queer or fan sensibilities must archive queer and fannish ... productions ... They safeguard fans' histories of explorations of, and experiments with, possibilities (including possibilities of sexual identifications, desires, and fantasies) that are not recorded or documented anywhere else.
>
> (De Kosnik 2016, 153)

The forms of queer, feminist, and fannish cultural memory-making facilitated by *femslashrevolution* also operate as a form of 'critical paratextuality' (Gray 2010) that educates its readers about the representation, of absence, of female/female relationships within both popular culture and fandom itself. Writing about the blog, centrumlumina explains:

> My femslash blog tries to support queer women in fandom to relate their experiences to the characters onscreen, whether or not the character is canonically queer. We also run events to boost the representation of minorities within F/F, such as Femslash Diversity Bingo, a tongue-in-cheek way for writers to create 5 fics featuring diverse women and NB [(non-binary)] people along axes such as race, gender identity, sexual orientation, disability, body type and class.
>
> (centrumlumina, #298)

Moreover, through the running of events to encourage other fans to produce and share fanworks – often under a unifying folksonomic Tumblr tag – that centre femslash pairings through an intersectional lens, *femslashrevolution* encourages other fans to take seriously two things. Firstly, a feminist politics of recognition and, secondly and more specifically, the politics of the intersection of sexuality and gender with other identity markers. In doing so, they raise individual fans' awareness of the systemic biases of media representation and encourage them to think critically about the invisibility of queer women and non-binary people both within popular culture texts and within fandom itself. This subsequently functions in a consciousness-raising capacity and strives for meaningful inclusivity and diversity within the fantext, while also strengthening the archival and cultural memory-making impetus at the heart of initiatives like *femslashrevolution*. These events, unified under a searchable Tumblr tag and collated on the *femslashrevolution* blog, encourage feminist fans to embed archival practices into their cultural production, which, within the context of feminist fandom's gift economy and Tumblr's technological affordances, then operate as a 'gift' passed onto other queer feminist fans. As De Kosnik (2016, 137–8) notes:

> Archives allow users to access the documents that constitute the cultural tradition of a community. Archives allow users to develop an understanding of what cultural texts the archive's community has produced over time.

This enables and encourages other fans to learn about feminist issues *through* their practices of cultural production, embedding the process of feminist learning into the pleasures of fannish cultural production. Moreover, through the process of sharing their fanworks with other fans, feminist fans are in turn able to teach others through raising awareness of the lack of representation and diversity within the portrayal of female/female relationships. Thus, a continual process of learning and (archival) knowledge sharing is central to the process of cultural production within feminist fandom.

Another fan project associated with centrumlumina is her 'AO3 Statistics' project, a project she has been running since 2013. Archive of Our Own, more commonly referred to within fannish spaces as the abbreviated 'AO3', is a non-profit and open-source repository of fanworks, although predominantly fanfiction, created and operated by the fan-led Organisation for Transformative Works. Organized and indexed through a folksonomic tagging system (see Price 2019), AO3's tagging system can be easily mined to generate quantitative data about the features and content of fanworks being produced and shared by fans on the platform.[5] Centrumlumina's AO3 Statistics project subsequently involves her conducting an annual content analysis of the most popular relationships, or 'ships', within AO3 fanworks on her Tumblr blog. From a post collating her work on the AO3 Statistics project (see Figure 6), you can see that this involves posting an annual 'Top 100' list of statistics, alongside annual lists dedicated exclusively to femslash ships.

In addition to this, centrumlumina also directs her readers towards a range of supplementary meta analyses she has authored over the years, written from

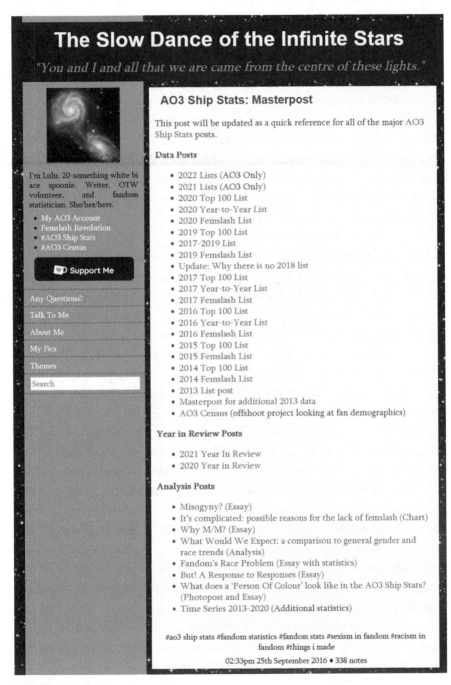

The Slow Dance of the Infinite Stars

"You and I and all that we are came from the centre of these lights."

I'm Lulu. 20-something white bi ace spoonie. Writer, OTW volunteer, and fandom statistician. She/her/hers.

- My AO3 Account
- Femslash Revolution
- #AO3 Ship Stats
- #AO3 Census

☕ Support Me

Any Questions?

Talk To Me

About Me

My Fics

Themes

Search

AO3 Ship Stats: Masterpost

This post will be updated as a quick reference for all of the major AO3 Ship Stats posts.

Data Posts

- 2022 Lists (AO3 Only)
- 2021 Lists (AO3 Only)
- 2020 Top 100 List
- 2020 Year-to-Year List
- 2020 Femslash List
- 2019 Top 100 List
- 2017-2019 List
- 2019 Femslash List
- Update: Why there is no 2018 list
- 2017 Top 100 List
- 2017 Year-to-Year List
- 2017 Femslash List
- 2016 Top 100 List
- 2016 Year-to-Year List
- 2016 Femslash List
- 2015 Top 100 List
- 2015 Femslash List
- 2014 Top 100 List
- 2014 Femslash List
- 2013 List post
- Masterpost for additional 2013 data
- AO3 Census (offshoot project looking at fan demographics)

Year in Review Posts

- 2021 Year In Review
- 2020 Year in Review

Analysis Posts

- Misogyny? (Essay)
- It's complicated: possible reasons for the lack of femslash (Chart)
- Why M/M? (Essay)
- What Would We Expect: a comparison to general gender and race trends (Analysis)
- Fandom's Race Problem (Essay with statistics)
- But! A Response to Responses (Essay)
- What does a 'Person Of Colour' look like in the AO3 Ship Stats? (Photopost and Essay)
- Time Series 2013-2020 (Additional statistics)

#ao3 ship stats #fandom statistics #fandom stats #sexism in fandom #racism in fandom #things i made

02:33pm 25th September 2016 ♦ 338 notes

Figure 6 Author screenshot of *centrumlumina*'s AO3 Statistics masterpost.

a queer, feminist, and anti-racist perspective, which reflexively examine her findings with regard to the intersection of race, gender, and sexuality. Meta analyses such as these have an important pedagogical function within feminist fandom on Tumblr. For example, in an August 2016 post titled 'Fandom's Race Problem and the AO3 Ship Stats', she draws upon her research to explore the structural racism of fannish spaces and examine how the fantext largely reproduces the pervasive whiteness of contemporary Anglo-American media cultures, as I discussed previously in Chapter 3. In this blog post, she calls attention to the structural racism implicated in the statistics she gathered, which revealed that just 12.5 per cent of the characters featured within the fanworks based on Western media fandoms on AO3 are people of colour, over half of whom are mixed-raced and/or light-skinned.

Using quali-quantitative methods of data collection and analysis that would not be amiss within a university classroom, including the citation of a large-scale content analysis conducted by Smith et al. (2015) examining gender, race, and sexuality within the US film industry alongside US census data, centrumlumina draws upon her research to explore colourism and 'anti-Blackness in fandom' (centrumlumina 2016b). The methods used by centrumlumina to critically examine and reflect upon fandom are commonplace within feminist cultural studies and feminist media studies, where such techniques are used to 'reveal scales of presence and absence in identified texts, groups, and sites, as well as patterns of inclusion and exclusion' (Harvey 2020, 43).

Indeed, feminist media critique is by no means the exclusive domain of academic researchers, just as academic language and expertise itself, as fan studies scholar Matt Hills (2002, 21) argues, 'cannot be kept safely "in" the academy'. This fannish democratization of knowledge production and knowledge sharing resonates distinctly across Tumblr, where fannish pedagogies on the platform frequently reproduce academic methods of media analysis, often accruing notable visibility through the platform's *high scalability* and *nonlinear temporality*. As Gee and Hayes (2011, 67) note in their research on online learning and passionate affinity spaces, 'a considerable amount of important knowledge today is produced outside of academic institutions … it is produced … across the internet, and, most distinctively, in popular culture activities using digital media'. Feminist fandom's bringing together of feminist frameworks and discourses with an intense investment in popular culture, then, harbours unique potential for (feminist) knowledge production and knowledge sharing *through* media consumption, production, and critique. This is something

De Kosnik examines in her analysis of activist-fannish archival practices like those undertaken by centrumlumina:

> In foregrounding non-white and non-Western characters … drawing attention to nonnormative sexual practices … [they] try to disrupt the individual fan reader's private belief systems, which are likely heavily shaped by the racial/sexual/national/regional hierarchies of mass media presentation.
>
> (De Kosnik 2016, 180)

The circulation of these forms of feminist and fannish media critique, especially when turned inwards towards fandom itself, thus operates as a powerful and accessible form of feminist knowledge sharing. Beyond this, they play an important role in encouraging fans to more critically attend to fandom's failure to address whiteness itself 'as a racialised identity' (Pande 2018a, 82).

Moreover, centrumlumina's analysis anticipates some of the 'defensive moves' (DiAngelo 2011, 54) of white fragility that I discussed in Chapter 3 and offers anticipatory counterarguments to these defensive moves in turn. Here, given that centrumlumina is white, we can see a move away from the types of anti-racist critiques produced almost *exclusively* by my non-white feminist fans detailed in Chapter 3. This is particularly evident in a follow-up blog post authored by centrumlumina titled 'But! A Response to Responses', which she describes as 'a rebuttal to some of the criticisms of myself and other's work on sexism and racism in fandom that I've seen in the past' (centrumlumina 2016a). She ends her 'Fandom's Race Problem' post urging other fans to learn from her observations and work towards producing 'even greater moves towards diversity':

> [F]or fandom to make good on its promises of diversity, we must all contemplate the part we play in supporting or erasing characters of colour in our fics and other fanworks. It is my hope that future AO3 Ship Stats lists will reflect even greater moves towards diversity, but this can only be achieved by a conscious, concentrated effort on the parts of fans.
>
> (centrumlumina 2016a)

Here, centrumlumina encourages fans to reflexively point their social and cultural critiques inwards towards fandom itself, encouraging them to challenge their biases and blind spots, particularly in terms of race and whiteness. By urging her peers to 'contemplate the part *we* play in supporting or erasing characters of colour in our fics and other fanworks' (my emphasis), she encourages her peers to engage in acts of feminist consciousness-raising and self-education in line with the intersectional feminist frameworks many feminist fans, at least at a discursive level, endeavour to align themselves with. Her call to fans to consider their complacency in reproducing the valourization of white characters, and particularly canonically heterosexual and cisgender white men, as detailed in Chapter 3, within the fantext exposes whiteness as a racialized identity and thus functions as an act of anti-racist feminist knowledge sharing (Applebaum 2010). Notably, here we can once again see how the kinds of feminisms articulated by fans correspond to broader discursive shifts taking place within both the academy and the popular domain with regard to the intersectional turn.

The circulation of her 'Fandom's Race Problem' blog post on Tumblr is punctuated by comments and contributions from other users adding additional commentary and analysis to the post. While some responses are symptomatic of the kinds of white fragility detailed earlier, a significant number of users add additional insight and commentary to centrumlumina's original meta analysis, thus utilizing Tumblr's technological affordances to engage in a communal process of feminist knowledge production and feminist knowledge sharing on Tumblr (also see Popova 2020).[6] Moreover, through the visibility of these discussions on Tumblr, given its *high scalability*, people far beyond those immediately involved can 'listen in' (Thelandersson 2014, 529) and learn from the knowledge being shared between users.

Centrumlumina's experiences demonstrate the high value feminist fans place on the importance of both educating oneself and educating other members of the feminist fan community. For many of my participants, the act of taking their feminist critical media literacy forwards into their production of the fantext – be that through the production of fanworks, through engaging in critical discussion, or through producing meta analysis and archival practices as centrumlumina does – operates as a way of *sharing* their feminist knowledge with other members of the fan community. As I highlighted in Chapter 1, these meta analyses function as a form of 'critical paratextuality' (Gray 2010) and have the capacity to radically interrupt and redirect interpretations of a text, teaching other fans about feminism and *making feminist meaning* in turn.

The pedagogical impact of centrumlumina's analyses was mentioned by another one of my participants. Ashling (#305) alluded to centrumlumina's production of feminist knowledge in her responses to my survey, as well as during our follow-up interview. When describing her concern over the elevation of white characters within fandom, she suggested that I 'look at centrumlumina and the many other Tumblr's that conduct fandom statistics analysis for this'. Two things are worth noting here. Firstly, Ashling highlights that the kinds of feminist meta analyses of fandom being conducted by centrumlumina are also being conducted by many other fans, in turn – thus pointing to how commonplace such acts of knowledge sharing are within feminist fandom. Secondly, Ashling's integration of centrumlumina's meta analyses into her discussion of feminist fandom, suggesting that I, in turn, examine them, once again demonstrates the reciprocal nature of feminist knowledge sharing within feminist fandom and the operation of feminist fandom as a gift economy. As Hellekson (2009, 115) notes, meta analysis is but one of many 'gifts' exchanged between fans that are incorporated into the larger fantext as 'a part of something greater'.

Feminist knowledge as subcultural capital

However, as I have argued elsewhere, the successful performance of an ability to partake in feminist knowledge sharing within feminist fandom increasingly bears 'subcultural capital' for the beholder (Hannell 2017a). Thornton (1995) describes 'subcultural capital' as a kind of 'hipness', comprised of specific artefacts and knowledge, which confers a recognized social status and distinction on its owner. Possessing subcultural capital involves being 'in the know' (11–12) about the norms of a given subculture and being able to navigate them with ease and authenticity. Being a feminist fan therefore requires the development of a particular knowledge that functions as subcultural capital within feminist fandom. As with many digital feminist spaces, a certain fluency in feminist vocabulary and principles is required to participate (Clark-Parsons 2018; Kanai 2020a). Yet, in addition to the expectation that one will be well versed in the queer and feminist subcultural vocabulary that circulates on Tumblr, one must also be well versed in popular media culture, as well as the norms and expectations of a given fan community. On Tumblr, a literacy in feminist knowledge and vocabulary forms one of many literacies expected of Tumblr users given the platform vernacular's emphasis, as detailed in Chapter 2, on 'combinatory literacies' (Kanai 2019). The ability to skilfully share one's feminist knowledge with other users can increase an individual's insider status and prestige within feminist fandom, signalling their familiarity with Tumblr's complex platform vernacular and sensibility.

Subsequently, while exchanges of feminist knowledge within feminist fandom operate as an educative tool for both identity formation and community building, they also operate as a form of distinction and exclusion. Consider, for instance, 22-year-old Lily's (#53) remark that 'I'm not sure how to properly express myself with important subjects like these', which reveals how this uncertainty limited her ability to meaningfully engage in feminist fandom.

Additionally, the processes of inclusion and exclusion produced by the subcultural capital of feminist knowledge within feminist fandom are compounded by other barriers to entry, such as the language barriers I discussed in Chapter 3 or the anxiety-laden discourses from Chapter 1 positioning adolescence as inherently 'under-informed'. The reliance on specialized queer and feminist subcultural vocabulary on Tumblr subsequently risks limiting some feminist fans' self-expression, undercutting the pedagogical potential of the space. While Tumblr can operate as a highly productive space for interest- and affinity-based peer-learning and knowledge sharing under the rubric of fandom's gift economy, it can also reproduce social inequalities in a variety of ways. Thus, while I earlier explored knowledge sharing within feminist fandom within the context of fandom's gift economy, this arguably reflects a more utopian framing of these processes of learning and knowledge sharing. It is important, in turn, to critically locate these acts of knowledge exchange within a wider context (such as that detailed in Chapter 3) and consider how they might reinforce processes of exclusion.

As Tiidenberg, Hendry, and Abidin (2021) highlight, when a Tumblr user lacks one (or more) of the many literacies required of participation in a given 'silo' on Tumblr, it can be highly disorienting and can even lead to departure from the platform. This is where the intense interest – and affinity-based nature of feminist knowledge production and knowledge sharing within feminist fandom on Tumblr, as a 'passionate affinity space' (Gee and Hayes 2011), becomes particularly important with regard to member retention, where

> [i]f, however, a user finds something that sparks their interest, they still need to put in the time and the effort to get acquainted with Tumblr's functionality, its vernacular and understand the shared sensibility. This is not obvious, and our participants do have experiences of failing in this. However, the drive to try again after failing further illustrates *the power of the affinity* we are trying to describe here.
>
> (Tiidenberg, Hendry, and Abidin 2021, 55)

Reflexive listening and un/learning in feminist fandom

The shared affects, interests, and affinities of feminist fans play an important role in motivating them to undertake this continuous, reflexive, process of learning and unlearning within feminist fandom on Tumblr. As I discussed in

Chapter 1, my participants conceived of their feminist identities as processual and emergent. They emphasized that their commitment to an *ongoing* process of learning and self-improvement was central to the processual nature of their identities as feminist fans. Moreover, I argued that their identities as feminist fans work as a form of group identity work and belonging work marked by a commitment to continuous growth and change. Indeed, feminism, and feminist identities, is often complex, processual, and emergent, and a commitment to ongoing, continual learning has long been conceived of as a central tenet of feminism. Sara Ahmed (2017, 11), for instance, writes that 'to become a feminist is to stay a student'. Likewise, the notion of 'a work in progress' is central to both fandom and the study of fandom. These understandings of both feminism and fandom as processual can thus be carried over to my participants' understandings of feminist fandom as a work in progress, once again demonstrating the reciprocal relationship between both feminism *and* fandom in theory and in practice.

From lurking to listening

Continual learning was one of the most significant aspects of the ongoing and processual nature of my participants' identities as feminist fans. Across their responses to my research survey, two interrelated modes of engaging in feminist learning emerged to which an ongoing process of critical self-reflection was central: *listening* and *learning*. Reflexivity is more broadly central to feminist pedagogies, wherein practising reflexivity takes the form of critical self-reflection and conversations with the self. Shrewsbury (1993, 8–9) highlights that this commitment to growth and renewal gives feminist pedagogy its life:

> Feminist pedagogy is engaged teaching/learning – engaged with the self in a continuing reflective process; engaged actively with the material being studied; engaged with others in a struggle to get beyond our sexism and racism and classism and homophobia and other destructive hatreds and to work together to enhance our knowledge … Fundamental to a feminist perspective is a commitment to growth, to renewal, to life. The vision itself must continue to evolve.

While many feminist fans emphasized that engaging in the kinds of feminist knowledge sharing I detailed above is a particularly meaningful mode of participation in feminist fandom, many in turn framed *listening* as equally important. Ari (#182), for example, explained that while she did try to engage in feminist knowledge sharing, through contributing to 'dialogue and discourses', she more often dedicated time to 'listening and trying to morph and extend my personal knowledge and opinions of feminist topics'. Listening attentively to the lived experiences of others emerged as an important part of the ongoing group identity work of feminist fandom, and it is something my participants took very seriously. Many of my research participants, in turn, positioned listening as an *obligation* required of them as feminists. I find Nick Couldry's (2009) understanding of the politics of listening particularly useful to consider here:

> Listening here is, first and foremost, the act of recognising what others *have to say*, recognising *that* they have something to say or, better, that they, like all human beings, have the capacity to give an account of their lives that is reflexive and continuous, an ongoing, embodied process of reflection.
>
> (579–80; original emphasis)

Couldry attends to the relationship between listening and an ongoing process of both recognition and reflection, which makes it highly compatible with feminist pedagogies. As Rinaldi (2006, 65) argues, such modes of listening produce 'sensitivity to the patterns that connect, to that which connects us to others; abandoning ourselves to the conviction that our understanding and our own being are but small parts of a broader integrated knowledge that holds the universe together'. In practice, listening is akin in many ways to the act of lurking. However, unlike the anxiety-laden descriptions of lurking that I described in Chapter 3, here the act of *lurking as listening* is framed by feminist fans in a more agentic and desirable manner, emerging as a valuable mode of participation in feminist fandom.

Consider, for example, Jessica's (#280) earlier description of lurking, learning, and shaping her views and opinions as her 'favourite thing' to do within feminist fandom on Tumblr. Additionally, laughingpinecone (#259) explicitly acknowledged the pedagogical benefits of 'lurking' in her responses to my survey, explaining how she carried forwards what she had learned while 'lurking' into her own production of feminist knowledge within feminist fandom through her contributions to the fantext:

> Lurking the ongoing talks, since long before they were called discourse, made me aware of themes and issues, which naturally ended up informing my own creative output, in the ways I portray women and men as well.

As Crawford (2011) notes, to reconceptualize lurking as listening is to reframe 'a set of behaviours once seen as vacant and empty into receptive and reciprocal practices' (527). Indeed, within fan studies, lurking has acquired negative connotations. It has been described as occupying a 'less participatory' (Bury 2018, 130), less 'influential' (Baym 2000, 144–7), less 'active' (Hills 2002, 172), and ultimately less fannish role within the fan community, and the term is often used to imply that lurkers unevenly draw upon a community 'without contributing back' in turn (Jenkins, Ford, and Green 2013, 156–9). Additionally, fan studies scholars methodologically position lurking as an ethically complicated, if not entirely problematic, position on the part of the researcher (Busse and Hellekson 2012; Phillips 2013; Zubernis and Davis 2016).

Within the context of my ethnographic data, reconceptualizing lurking as listening, however, captures how the behaviours often understood as lurking, and thus non-participatory, provide a meaningful way to engage in an active and ongoing process of informal learning within the passionate affinity space of feminist fandom. For example, Mzyraj (#217) explained that, while her shyness affected her ability to 'be out in the community discussing these things', she nevertheless remained committed to 'listen[ing] and always keep[ing] an open mind'. Here, we can see how lurking as listening allows us to capture the active, receptive, and reflexive nature of this mode of participation within feminist fandom. Similarly, Josie (#227) positioned listening as her preferred mode of participation, noting that 'I'd much rather listen to what others have to say and share that than come up with something myself', and Di (#133) explained that 'I do my best at listening to others and become more knowledgeable'. As Jenkins, Ford, and Green (2013, 158) note, many participants in online communities, especially in passionate affinity spaces, learn through '"lurking" or observing from the margins'. Lave and Wenger (1991) describe such acts of observation as a 'legitimate' mode of 'peripheral participation' that is central to the learning process. Many feminist fans thus frame listening as a transformative experience and as the agent of active and ongoing change within one's understanding and practice of myriad feminisms.

Listening across difference

Feminist fans subsequently approach their listening pedagogically, viewing listening as a means for acknowledging difference between themselves and others without 'demand[ing] that differences be bridged' (Ratcliffe 2005, 53). For many of my participants, listening emerged as a meaningful way to reflexively acknowledge their privilege, engage with other feminist fans' experiences and perspectives, and foster meaningful communication across difference. These modes of listening 'across the boundaries of difference' (Cervenak et al. 2002, 342) in order to expand one's understandings of positionalities beyond one's own are central to feminist pedagogy. They, Couldry (2016) argues, provide knowledge of the world that enables us to recognize and respond to issues and identities that we least understand and may rarely hear. We can see this in effect across my survey, interview, and observational data. For example, Elizabeth (#303), who explicitly positions herself as a 'white, heterosexual passing, physically able, mostly mentally healthy, middle-class woman', explained that her self-awareness of her privilege compelled her to 'keep my mouth shut' and, instead, 'listen to what other people have to say'. Additionally, we can see this at work in the responses of J (#90), who describes her ongoing process of reflexively engaging with questions of voice and listening as part of her commitment to her 'work in progress' identity as a feminist:

> Currently, I am involved both at work and outside of work in feminist activism. I've been working on finding my place – as a white woman, where is my voice necessary? What other work can I do, where my voice shouldn't be the loudest, to help others be heard? Where do I need to listen and continue learning? I think it's very much a work in progress, but my feminist identity and work is very important to me.
>
> (J, #90)

Feminist fans' commitment to reflexive listening (and the processes of learning it facilitates) is in part motivated by a desire to undertake the relational belonging work required of creating and maintaining their understanding of feminist fandom on Tumblr as a safe space. Note, for example, Sabrina's (#25) comments that I discussed earlier with regard to her desire to 'create safe, open platforms'. My participants' responses reveal how these processes of listening as a form of relational work are motivated by a feminist ethic of care (Preissle and Han 2012) towards others that relies on a capacity for empathy, patience, and receptiveness to the experiences of others. As Collins (2009, 281–2) notes, the feminist 'ethic of caring suggests that personal expressiveness, emotions, and empathy are central to the knowledge validation process'. Florangel (#9), for example, explained that her approach to participating in feminist fandom is 'all about listening and being listened to'. She later added that this more broadly involves 'mutual understanding on respectful grounds'. Similarly, Josie (#227) highlighted the relationship between empathy, care, and listening within feminist fandom:

At this point, I'm not sure if I can articulate what feminism means to me. It's ... encompasses more than before. For me, it involves a lot of listening. Caring about other people. Lots of empathy.

We can also see this feminist ethic of care at work in Morgan's (#322) account of reflexively listening within feminist fandom:

I engage in these issues by reading posts, reading new stories from new authors, and looking for conversations where I am going to learn something by expanding what I think and understand about the world, and the potential impacts of my ways of being on others. ... There is always something new to learn and grow about life. ... It's an ongoing discovery. I don't think there's anywhere to get to, so much as an intention to be the kind of person around whom people feel welcome, acknowledged.

(Morgan, #322)

Morgan emphasizes his commitment to personal growth and renewal, framing his experience of listening and learning within feminist fandom as an open-ended and 'ongoing discovery'. Moreover, he highlights how an ethic of care, underpinned by 'an intention to be the kind of person around whom people feel welcome, acknowledged', is at work throughout this process. Thus, the act of listening, and by extension learning, that he engages in is motivated by a self-reflexive desire to extend feelings of belonging to all members of feminist fandom who congregate on Tumblr. As I noted in Chapter 2, this ongoing feminist identity work can be understood as a form of relationally negotiated belonging work that feminist fans undertake to accomplish belonging, both for themselves and others, within feminist fandom. Furthermore, the focus of participants like Florangel (#9), Josie (#227), and Morgan (#322) on the pedagogical importance of listening to the experiential knowledge shared by others aligns with Black feminist epistemologies that position lived experience as an important 'criterion of knowing' (Omolade 1987; Collins 2009).

Listening as loving perception

Elsewhere, participants spoke highly of the affective and connective power of these processes of listening and learning across difference within feminist fandom. Spelertoneel (#36), for example, described this in some detail:

I am a feminist, and I am one because I find that feminism empowers people, and empowers and inspires kindness amongst people. It gives voices to those unheard and a way to find perspective in those areas in which you're not a minority. It makes you critical of yourself but doesn't punish you. It teaches you – if you are allowed to be educated and you listen to those who teach you, you become a kinder person. I truly believe that.

Here, spelertoneel's account of the impact of feminist listening across difference, of hearing the voices of those previously 'unheard', not only adheres to the feminist ethic of care through her emphasis on active listening as a form of kindness and empathy, but it also adheres to decolonial feminist philosopher Maria Lugones's (1990) theory of 'loving perception'. Lugones describes these moments of listening across difference as a kind of playful 'world-travelling' that speaks to 'the acquired flexibility in shifting from the mainstream construction of life to other constructions of life where [one] is more or less "at home"' (390). The forms of loving perception Lugones describes require one to reflexively 'look, and listen and check and question' (Frye 1983, 60). To travel between 'worlds', then, is to be willing to listen to different 'description[s] of experience' (Lugones 1990, 396), and be open and receptive to the experiences of others. We can see this at work in spelertoneel's (#36) description of feminism as 'a way to find perspective in those areas in which you're not a minority'. Moreover, spelertoneel's (#36) description of feminism as something which 'makes you critical of yourself but doesn't punish you', adding that it instead 'teaches you' and makes you a 'kinder person' also adheres to Lugones's (1990, 401) description of loving perception as involving 'openness to surprise, openness to being a fool, openness to self-construction or reconstruction and to construction or reconstruction of the "worlds" we inhabit'. This openness to the educative function of listening thus allows spelertoneel to construct and reconstruct her understanding of the 'worlds' she inhabits based on the process of actively listening to the perspectives, and lived experiences, of those around her.

Lugones's (1990) concept of 'loving perception' therefore speaks to feminist fans' accounts of the processes within feminist fandom that encourage active listening and self-reflection, fostering a willingness to grow and develop through reflexive forms of looking, listening, checking, and questioning. This 'loving praxis' (Cervenak et al. 2002, 352) is tied to the empathetic recognition of one another's 'complex personhood' (Gordon 2008, 5) as a meaningful source of information, education, and knowledge sharing. A willingness to *listen* thus produces a willingness to recognize and attend to the complex personhood of others, which is central, Lugones (1990, 390) argues, to an intersectional and 'pluralistic feminism'. As Cervenak et al. (2002, 353) highlight, this is hugely beneficial pedagogically:

Taking seriously 'the stories people tell about themselves' and the ways they tell them opens up multiple spaces for self-recognition, and carves out loving worlds structured by the creative and critical practice of listening and learning.

Notably, Lugones's description of world-travelling as related to one's understanding of what it means to be 'at ease in a "world"' (397) echoes Carrillo's (2005) conceptualization of 'differential belonging' that I discussed in Chapter 3, as a mode of belonging that allows for contextual movement between various modes, or 'worlds', of belonging according to one's needs. This process involves negotiating 'across such boundaries of difference to build intimate knowledge of that which lies between self and other' (Carrillo 2005, 38). Thus, the processes of listening within feminist fandom are more broadly related to the kinds of belonging one can access and inhabit.

However, Ortega (2009, 60) cautions against such utopian renditions of 'loving perception' within our understandings of feminist spaces, arguing that, in 'the relationship between some white feminists and women of colour', there are those who 'seem to have understood the need for a better way of perceiving but whose wanting leads them to continue to perceive arrogantly, to distort their objects of perception, all the while thinking they are loving perceivers'. For instance, building upon Frye's (1983) schema of 'loving perception', Ortega (2009, 61; my emphasis) questions the distinction between those 'who *look and listen*, as Frye suggests, but do not *check and question*'. Indeed, the experiences of non-belonging detailed in Chapter 3 lend credence to this more critical rendition of listening across difference. While my white feminist fans might discursively position themselves as 'intersectional feminists', this does not necessarily produce a willingness to thoroughly attend to, and thus *listen to* or *lovingly perceive*, those who occupy more marginal social locations than their own. Hence, this failure to *lovingly perceive* could be at work in the *SJW fatigue* directed towards the *anti-racist killjoy fan* that I detailed in Chapter 3. We are once again reminded of the complex and contradictory nature of the relationship between fandom and feminism.

Reflexive un/learning

Yet, in terms of Ortega's (2009) specific critique of the disjuncture between *looking and listening* and *checking and questioning*, many feminist fans nevertheless emphasized their willingness to reflexively *check* and *question* as well as *learn* and *unlearn*. For my research participants, listening was especially important precisely because it facilitates the ongoing process of learning and unlearning within feminist fandom. As Hoodfar (1992, 305) notes, 'developing the ability to listen and speak to other constituencies more effectively' not only 'makes working across differences more feasible', it also contributes to the process of 'unlearning privilege'. In order to *learn*, and thus *question* and *unlearn*, one must be willing to *listen*. Unlearning has long been a feature of discussions about feminist pedagogy, and the term is used to describe the processes by which we seek to address, reflect upon, and dismantle our own complicity within structures of power and domination. Black feminist scholar bell hooks (1989, 46), for example, writes that 'learning about other groups ... can be a way to unlearn racism, to challenge structures of dominance'. Thus, Shrewsbury's (1993; my emphasis) aforementioned description of feminist pedagogy as involving engaging with others in an ongoing 'struggle to *get beyond* our sexism and racism and classism and homophobia and other destructive hatreds and to work together to enhance our knowledge' can be understood as describing the continual process of *unlearning*. Feminist pedagogy therefore involves learning, unlearning, and relearning.

Many feminist fans emphasized how they sought to unlearn their conscious and unconscious biases, such as racism or sexism or homophobia, *through* feminist fandom. Across these accounts, the kinds of learning facilitated by feminist fandom, as detailed above, are central to the broader ongoing project of *unlearning* one's hegemonic understanding of social and cultural phenomena and, instead, crafting a more oppositional, nuanced, and empathetic understanding of a wide range of identities and issues. Consider, for example, Sahvana's (#321) earlier comments about learning to 'actively work against my own racism', which, in turn, 'opened the doors to learning to stop being bigoted in other sense: ableism, transphobia, and misogyny as well'. She described this as a 'long process of detoxing my bigotry that ended with me as a better person in general'. Likewise, ecoantics (#234) described how the process of unlearning transformed not only her world view but also her sense of self:

> Then when I joined Tumblr, I followed a lot of blogs that posted social justice content, and I started to learn about intersectionality. I unlearned a lot of unconscious biases that had been inherent in the 90% white suburban Midwest culture I grew up in. I started to unlearn white feminism and started to learn intersectional feminism. ... Social justice content online helped me start to understand the immense disadvantages, struggles, and biases that people with

disabilities, homeless people, and people below the poverty line face. I slowly unlearned a lot of internalised homophobia and realised I was bisexual with a preference for women.

The ongoing process of unlearning described by ecoantics locates feminist fandom as a conduit for reversing processes of interpellation and, instead, working towards further developing alternative and more oppositional interpretations of the 'identities, interests, and needs' (Fraser 1990, 67) of both herself and others. Thus, feminist fandom's position as a counterpublic sphere is deeply connected to the processes of learning and unlearning detailed by my participants.

Across my ethnographic data, a willingness to commit to a much broader lifelong, continual, and ongoing process of feminist learning and unlearning forms a core part of the group identity work and the belonging work required of being a feminist fan. As Shrewsbury (1993, 11) notes, feminist pedagogy 'takes seriously the goal of lifelong learning'. Subsequently, my participants highlighted their willingness and openness to engage in a lifelong process of learning and unlearning. Josie (#227), for example, whose account of the connection between feminist becoming and recognizing her positionality as a Métis person I discussed in Chapter 1, explained: 'I fully expect I will constantly have to check myself and learn/unlearn new ways of thinking'. This, she explained, was motivated by her intention 'to not become complacent'. Later, she added:

> I'll be unlearning stuff for the rest of my life. I'm embarrassed that at one point I was very much into the 'if you mess up once you're done' line of thinking, and how there wasn't room for mistakes. If you said or did something wrong, you were a bad person and there was no coming back from that. The thing is though, is that this is just so unforgiving and doesn't allow for people to learn and change and GROW. I think my early time on Tumblr was pretty bad for that. I was terrified of saying or doing something wrong. I much prefer being able to learn from mistakes. Like. I'm gonna make mistakes. But I make an effort to learn from them and make amends where possible. I also try to extend that mindset to others. People can grow. I would find it so hard to go on if I didn't believe that people could change. I have to believe that we can all be better.
>
> (Josie, #227)

Above, Josie explains how she had initially conceived of her feminism as both static and absolutist but has since come to embrace a much more fluid understanding of feminism that is committed to a vision of growth and renewal. She also explains how she extended this approach to feminist learning and unlearning to others, producing a hopeful rendition of the belief that, in her words, 'we can all be better'. This is where to be *called out*, as detailed in Chapter 3, can also work as an act of being *called back in* through this narrative of forgiveness, growth, and renewal. Additionally, this also affirms how the affectively intense, affinity- and interest-based forms of learning within feminist fandom on Tumblr encourage feminist fans to try and try again in an ongoing process of growth and renewal. Here, we can once again return to Lugones's (1990) loving praxis with regard to the developmental trajectory of feminist fandom. Josie's description of coming to embrace a feminism that is forgiving and open to continual change and growth echoes Lugones's (1990, 400; original emphasis) claim that 'we are not self-important, we are not fixed in particular constructions of ourselves, which is part of saying that we are *open to self-construction* ... we are not wedded to a particular way of doing things'. This mode of continual feminist knowledge production and knowledge sharing is thus 'not about solving a problem but about remaining open to pursue new ways of thinking' (Cervenak et al. 2002, 354), much like the process Josie describes. Moreover, the reflexive practices of growth and self-improvement that Josie describes are typical of feminist pedagogical approaches to lifelong learning (Burke and Jackson 2006).

While these feminist fans positioned themselves as agents of knowledge about feminism, as detailed previously, they also position themselves as continually in pursuit of new feminist knowledge. This is something that they described enthusiastically, positioning the pursuit of new knowledge as central to the pleasures of participating in feminist fandom. For example, drarry_fanatic (#141) excitedly explained that feminist fandom 'continues to inspire and teach me new things everyday!' Elsewhere, Lane (#63) explained, 'I love engaging in fandom and getting excited about things, but I also love everything I'm learning (and unlearning), not just about feminism but racism, classism, the world.' Feminist identity work and belonging work on Tumblr thus involve a pleasurable process of 'learning, realising, and discovering' (Byron et al. 2019, 2250).

Thus, actively engaging in an open-ended and lifelong process of reflexive feminist learning and unlearning is central to the pedagogical function of feminist fandom. Listening, which my participants self-reflexively position as lurking, is integral to this process of un/learning, operating as a means for feminist fans to reflexively acknowledge their privilege, engage with others' perspectives, and foster meaningful dialogue across difference. Such acts of active and engaged listening across difference adhere to a feminist ethic of care in their focus on listening as a form of kindness and empathy. They are therefore central to the relational belonging work required of maintaining the understanding of feminist fandom on Tumblr as a safe space. My participants accounts of pedagogical listening, I subsequently argue, adhere to Lugones's (1990) concept of loving perception through their emphasis on the importance of exercising a willingness to grow and develop through forms of looking, listening, checking, and questioning. Moreover, such willingness to continuously look, listen, check, and question lends itself to my participants' emphasis on the importance of *unlearning*, in turn. From this, we are once again reminded of the ongoing process of growth and renewal that is central to the feminist (and thus feminist-fannish) project, producing a more hopeful and generative rendition of the developmental trajectory of feminist fandom captured across my data.

Conclusion

Throughout this chapter, I returned to a number of the themes discussed throughout the preceding chapters in order to examine their pedagogical function within feminist fandom. My analysis is therefore not only informed by the preceding chapters; it also further shapes and enhances our understanding of them. For instance, throughout this chapter I explored the role of fan-created paratexts in the learning process, arguing that these fan-created texts have the capacity to function as feminist teaching moments that enable and encourage fans to develop their critical media literacies. Building upon my earlier conceptualization of feminist identities as active, ongoing, and processual, I explored feminist fans' accounts of the importance of engaging in a continuous process of feminist learning and feminist knowledge sharing through their engagements with the discourses, practices, and positionalities of feminist fandom. Additionally, for my research participants, the pleasures of engaging in feminist fandom were deeply connected to the pleasures of feminist learning and knowledge sharing and were thus central to feeling a sense of belonging within feminist fandom.

My analysis locates feminist fandom as a fruitful site for engaging in feminist learning and knowledge sharing. Across my ethnographic data, feminist learning is described as an ongoing, self-reflexive, multivalent, and ultimately transformative process. Learning, my participants emphasize, requires a willingness to listen across difference, as well as a willingness to check and question and, when necessary, engage in subsequent acts of *unlearning*. Feminist knowledge sharing is in turn described as an open-ended, reciprocal, and multigenerational process that many participants engage in out of a sense of duty and obligation towards their imagined feminist peers. These accounts reveal the intimate relationship between feminist fandom and feminist pedagogy and demonstrate the fundamental importance of informal and everyday spaces in which such acts of feminist learning and knowledge sharing may take place. Fandom subsequently plays an important role in 'bringing feminism to a wider audience and providing spaces for the multiplicity of voices therein' (Harvey 2020, 57). Within *feminist* fandom, actively and deliberately engaging in an ongoing process of informal learning and, by extension, knowledge sharing form a core practice of feminist fandom and are central to the group identity work, and belonging work, required of being a feminist fan.

Conclusion

Bringing together feminist cultural studies and fan studies, one of the primary concerns of *Feminist Fandom* has been to reveal and examine media fandom's position at the intersection of the multidirectional and co-constitutive relationship between popular feminisms, popular culture, and digital cultures. Throughout the book, I have drawn upon the insights and experiences of over three-hundred feminist fans to explicate how fannish and feminist modes of cultural consumption, production, and critique are increasingly converging, opening up informal, ordinary, and everyday spaces for young people, in particular although not exclusively, to engage with feminism. In doing so, I have emphasized that media fandom does not exist in a vacuum but is constituted by the same social, cultural, and political forces that have come to shape fourth-wave feminisms. In turn, the experiences documented throughout *Feminist Fandom* speak to the ways in which broader shifts within feminist practice, theory, and activism over the past decade have shaped and informed the social and cultural practices of feminist fandom. This book subsequently forges sustained dialogue between feminist cultural studies and fan studies methodologically, empirically, and theoretically. In concluding this book, I summarize the themes I have discussed and developed throughout and reflect upon my key findings and the implications of these findings in relation to the research questions I set out to investigate. I also consider future directions for this area of study and reiterate the importance of approaching my ethnographic data with due criticality and respect.

Reflections on fandom and feminism

Feminist Fandom contributes to an emergent body of literature examining the contours of young people's engagement with contemporary feminisms within a digital context. As I discussed in the introduction and Chapter 1, despite media fandom's established history of engaging with a feminist politics of recognition, as well as its central role within contemporary youth culture, it has remained markedly absent in scholarly accounts of young people's engagement with feminism and development of feminist identities. While feminist becoming has been a lively subject of inquiry over the last three decades, much of the literature on feminist becoming focuses on the significance of educational contexts as fertile ground for feminist identity development, for example focusing on university and high school. More recent accounts have explored the significance of the internet and digital cultures, as well as popular culture, as conduits for feminist becoming for young people. However, such perspectives have failed to account for the role of media fandom, as a 'passionate affinity space' (Gee and Hayes 2011) situated at the intersection of digital feminisms, digital cultures, and popular culture, in the development of young people's feminist identities. *Feminist Fandom* has thus been produced by a desire to remedy this gap.

Feminist Fandom can also be situated within an established body of work within fan studies examining a range of fan practices which, as Duffett (2013, 73) writes, offer 'a tool for social criticism'. Despite the dominance of these perspectives within fan studies, the feminist valences of media fandom are too often taken for granted. They have evaded sustained scholarly analysis at the level of ethnographic lived experience,[1] and are rarely contextualized within the broader cultural moment in which a range of feminisms have achieved a 'new luminosity' (Gill 2016b, 1) within popular media cultures. Additionally, many of these perspectives remain preoccupied with fannish textual productivity in ways that risk losing sight of the importance of paratextuality and the paratextual circulation of popular culture within the communities of feminist fandom.

Likewise, while feminists have long been interested in the ways in which popular cultural texts offer interpretative frameworks for what feminism *means*, they often fail to account for the ways in which these cultural texts paratextually circulate more broadly within our mediated environment. What sort of cultural work do the audiences who populate the text undertake? In turn, in Chapter 1, I adopted Gray's (2010) theorization of paratextual circulation to examine how the popular cultural texts *circulated, consumed,* and *produced* by fans are central to the process of feminist becoming. My analysis of feminist fans' self-narratives revealed how feminist identity development is organized and structured by the discourses, practices, and subject positions of media fandom. For example, the circulation of texts within the social structures of fandom on Tumblr operates as a means for establishing initial points of contact between young people and feminist discourses and practices, subsequently shaping their understandings of feminism on not only at a *textual* level (their interpretation of the fan object) but at a *paratextual* level of the fantext. For my participants, the *fantext* – encapsulating the entirety of fan-created texts, discussions, interpretations, and analyses – introduced them to feminist interpretative frameworks, concepts, and discourses through the lens of the popular cultural texts they are interested in as fans. In doing so, the circulation, consumption, and production of the fantext initiate a consciousness-raising process that enables feminist fans to both *make sense of feminism* and *make feminist sense of* popular culture.

The paratextual circulation of popular culture thus operates as a way for fans to learn about feminism, facilitating various modes of feminist knowledge production and knowledge sharing that many of my participants would seldom access elsewhere. This is something I explored in more depth in Chapter 4, where I examined the connections between feminist fandom and feminist pedagogy. A feminist politics of recognition remains central to the pedagogic impetus of feminist fandom, I argue, precisely because fans are characterized by their sustained collective proximity, or 'critical closeness' (Stein; interviewed in Morimoto 2019), to popular cultural texts. By virtue of their fannish attachments to popular culture, they are deeply concerned with questions of representation, storytelling, and meaning-making. We saw this, for example, in feminist fans' accounts of developing critical feminist and social justice-oriented media literacies through their affinity-based and interest-driven ties to media fandom. Such processes of informal learning, I noted, often corresponded to their salient identity categories, such as sexuality, gender identity, or race. Crucially, many emphasized that these processes of informal learning within feminist fandom allowed them to redress some of the constraints produced by the social, cultural, and educational norms of their local contexts, thus aligning these forms of 'out-of-school' learning with those of a 'passionate affinity space' (Gee and Hayes 2011). My analysis subsequently complicates the work of fan studies scholars who frame fandom as a *supplementary* educational space.

In turn, I positioned the production and circulation of fan-created paratexts within feminist fandom as a form of collective, public, multigenerational feminist knowledge sharing. For instance, participants emphasized that their collective production, consumption, and circulation of the fantext allowed them to share information about feminist discourses and practices and initiate educative processes of feminist consciousness-raising among their peers. This was particularly important for my participants who identified as feminists before their first encounters with feminist fandom, who reported taking up fannish modes of cultural production to engage with a feminist politics of recognition and produce their own interpretations and reworkings of popular cultural texts. My older participants also emphasized that they were particularly committed to feminist knowledge sharing, framing it as a form of inter-generational mentoring and community support on Tumblr. In Chapter 4, I situated these acts of feminist knowledge production and sharing within the context of fandom's gift economy, positioning feminist knowledge production as a 'gift' that one anticipates other fans to receive and reciprocate in turn. I subsequently locate feminist fandom as a space where fans co-produce, negotiate, and contest meanings of feminism through their production, consumption, and circulation of the fantext.

Throughout my analysis, the connections between fandom, feminist becoming, and feminist pedagogy emerged as central to the counterpublic potential of media fandom on Tumblr. My research places feminist fandom on Tumblr within an established history of online feminist counterpublics. I examined this in Chapter 2 with reference to my participants' use of spatial metaphors to describe Tumblr as their 'home'. Drawing upon theorizations of Tumblr's technological affordances and platform vernacular, I explored how Tumblr emerges as a space where feminist fans may openly discuss experiences, share interests and information, and connect with like-minded people 'without shame'. For example, a number of my participants emphasized how their engagement with feminist fandom had prompted processes of transformation in their sense of self, for example with relation to their sexuality or race. These accounts subsequently adhered to Fraser's conceptualization of counterpublics as spaces that permit members of subordinated social groups to 'invent and circulate counter-discourses, which in turn permit them to formulate oppositional interpretations of their identities, interests, and needs' (Fraser 1990, 67). Tumblr's affinity with counterpublic modes of address was central to my participants' understanding of feminist fandom on Tumblr as an imagined transnational community of 'like-minded' feminist fans.

However, my analysis also revealed that feminist fandom does not necessarily produce an unconditional or fixed sense of belonging in its bringing together of fannish and feminist practices, discourses, and positionalities. Instead, more complex and contingent accounts of belonging are detailed throughout this book. While, as I discussed in the introduction, scholars have established connections between the popularization, or mainstreaming, of fannish and feminist identities within popular media cultures, my findings complicate this picture. As I highlighted in Chapter 2, my participants were drawn to participating in feminist fandom on Tumblr in particular because its technological affordances and platform vernacular produced a culture of anonymity and privacy. This is something that not only informed my findings but also my methodological orientation to the research. For many of my participants, the culture of privacy afforded by Tumblr was central to their sense of safety and belonging on the site. They affectively experienced Tumblr as feeling *more private, more intimate*, and thus *more safe* than other social networking sites. Such an understanding of Tumblr as a 'safe space' was heightened in particular for my queer participants – especially those who were young, closeted, and rural – who use feminist fandom to undertake various forms of queer identity work and establish a sense of solidarity with an imagined queer community. For these participants, the privacy norms of Tumblr, combined with its 'queer normativity' (Tiidenberg, Hendry, and Abidin 2021), enabled them to create protective 'firewalls of visibility' (Jenkins, Ito, and boyd 2016, 57) that work to reduce their risk of exposure to harm – both on- and offline.

Additionally, the privacy norms of the platform allayed participants' fears about negative peer judgement and alignment with negative *SJW fangirl as pathology* stereotypes that bring together gendered anti-fan and anti-feminist tropes. My research thus counters recent claims within fan studies that position fandom as a normative and widely accepted cultural identity. Instead, it reaffirms Scott's (2019, 13) assertion that fan culture's shift from the 'margins to the mainstream' has (re)produced a 'structured secondariness' (5) for fangirls, fans of colour, and queer fans, and their engagement with popular culture.

As a number of fan studies, girls studies, and feminist scholars have contended, gendered modes of anti-fandom often rely on a disavowal of fandom as *too feminine* and *too emotional*, as an excess of affect. Concurrently, as I argued in Chapter 2, feminist fandom is deeply affective, marked by the 'intensities of feeling' (Thrift 2004) produced by fannish and feminist positionalities (also see Shetty 2022). Indeed, one of the most significant modes of belonging that my participants articulated relied upon a deeply affective imagined community of feminist fans on Tumblr. Drawing upon perspectives from both fan studies and feminist theory on the affective intensities of both fannish and feminist identities, I argued that the imagined community of feminist fandom is primarily constituted by a sense of *shared feeling*, weaving together the affective and the relational. The affective intensities of feminist fans' fannish investments in popular culture are structured, organized, and reproduced by their feminism, and vice versa, as shared feminist frameworks operate as a way for feminist fans to organize their affective investments in particular texts. Here my analysis makes visible the connections between feminist fandom and the impassioned modes of feminist popular culture critique associated with contemporary fourth-wave feminisms that I initially discussed in the introduction. However, the affective intensities of feminist fandom are also implicated in my participants' desire to have a safe and private space to collectively express their thoughts and *feelings* about both fandom and feminism, resulting in the emergence of the *SJW fangirl as pathology* discourse I discussed in Chapters 2 and 3. Future research on feminist fandom may subsequently wish to further consider how the gendered contours of contemporary anti-fandom that drive feminist fans to engage with media fandom in private or semi-private digital spaces align with emergent forms of popular misogyny and anti-feminism that manifest in digital contexts.

Feminist fandom as a work in progress

Throughout *Feminist Fandom*, I have argued that feminist fandom is a space in which fans engage in an ongoing process of negotiation and contestation over meanings of feminism/s. In turn, my analysis positions feminist fandom as a fruitful site for feminist identity work, both collectively and individually. We can see this, for instance, in the processes of feminist transference I described in Chapter 1, where feminist fans use the discourses and practices of fandom to work through their positionalities. The identity work of feminist fandom also emerged in Chapter 4 through participants' emphasis on feminist knowledge production and knowledge sharing as an ongoing collective responsibility central to meaningful participation in feminist fandom. Likewise, participants' descriptions of feminist fandom on Tumblr as a safe space in Chapter 2 centred an implicit understanding of the collective relational work and belonging work required of maintaining the safety of the space. However, feminist fandom's emphasis on process and emergence positions it as a fruitful site for continuous engagement in various forms of feminist identity work.

This book has presented a digital ethnographic examination of the relationship between media fandom and young people's engagements with digital feminism. It is deeply informed by my personal history within feminist fandom, and my data was collected and analysed not as an outsider, but through active and prolonged participation within the feminist fan community on Tumblr for well over a decade. While I remain deeply committed to a localized production of my ethical stance in line with my participants' wishes and expectations (see Whiteman 2012) and have endeavoured to achieve 'an authentic presentation of the people under inquiry' (Shkedi 2004, 93), in committing my analysis to the page I inadvertently present a fixed and linear narrative that contradicts my participants' understanding of their identities as emergent, fluid, and in process. Feminist fan communities bring together fannish and feminist discourses, practices, and positionalities in ways that are constantly evolving in terms of form, content, and intent. Attempting to capture this in all of its complexity and unfixity has not been an easy undertaking.

In Chapter 1, I drew attention to the commonalities between scholarly understandings of fandom as a work in progress, as well as understandings of feminist identities, and feminism, as complex, processual, and emergent. Throughout my data collection, participants emphasized that feminist fandom has provided them with opportunities to continually discuss and refine their understandings of multiple feminisms, both in theory and in practice. They subsequently positioned themselves as open to new concepts, discourses, and practices. Many of these accounts drew upon discursive themes of youth and adolescence, positioning youth as a time of formation, renewal, and exploration of the self.

I returned to these themes in Chapter 4, when I explored participants' participation in a continual process of reflexive *listening* and *(un)learning*, once again reaffirming the connections between feminist fandom and feminist pedagogy. Building upon Couldry's (2009) understanding of the politics of listening, I examined my participants' accounts of *lurking as listening* in order to interrogate normative fan studies framings of lurking that position it as non-participatory, passive, and ultimately less legitimate. Instead, I positioned *lurking as listening* as an active, receptive, critical, and reflexive mode of participation within feminist fandom aligned with feminist pedagogies of listening across difference. I later explored the connections between the process of listening and the process of (un)learning. The unlearning of hegemonic and normative understandings of the social world, I highlighted, has an established history within feminist pedagogy, and, in feminist fans' accounts, unlearning is intrinsically connected to the ongoing processes of self-reflection, learning, and discovery prompted by listening. A commitment to a lifelong, continual, and ongoing process of feminist listening, learning, and unlearning forms a core part of the group identity work and belonging work required of *being* a feminist fan and *belonging* to feminist fandom. As I conclude this book, this identity work continues beyond the confines of my analysis.

My ethnographic analysis of feminist fandom on Tumblr has subsequently enabled me to examine the lived experience of a transitory and ephemeral moment in the site's history. The experiences captured throughout my data in many cases refer to what Watercutter (2019) describes as Tumblr's 'halcyon days', the 'three or four years around 2013'. This is something my participants also acknowledged throughout their responses to my survey in particular, which notably situates their most intense and sustained engagement with feminist fandom in the period leading up to the emergence of popular feminism around 2014. Future work may give due consideration to the possibility that young people's participation in media fandom may have facilitated the heightened visibility of feminism within both popular and digital culture at a time when fannish and feminist modes of cultural consumption, production, and critique are increasingly ubiquitous.

Complexities and contradictions

Since I formally began this research in 2016, Tumblr's user base and activity has steadily declined. Many feminist fans, for example, reported that, as they moved into higher education or full-time employment, they now have less time to dedicate to feminist fandom on the platform (and elsewhere) and are subsequently engaging with feminist fandom on a more intermittent basis. Like Tiidenberg, Hendry, and Abidin (2021) and Cavalcante's (2019) research participants, feminist fans also report difficulties sustaining the affective intensities of feminist fandom on Tumblr and the SJW fatigue they produce for long periods of time, instead preferring periods of embrace and retreat. Others emphasized that they have more recently moved their fannish and feminist online activity elsewhere, including Twitter and TikTok, as new platforms with alternative affordances and vernaculars have grown in popularity. Shetty (2022), in her doctoral research, for example, suggests that fannish podcasting could be one such site at which these discourses and identities come together in highly insightful and productive ways. However, for my own participants, their nostalgia towards an imagined past of Tumblr nevertheless persists.

Tumblr's wavering popularity and declining market value, as detailed in the introduction, were exacerbated by two key events that occurred towards the end of my data collection. Firstly, in mid-2018 investigative news reports revealed that a significant number of Tumblr accounts posing as Black Lives Matter activists were connected to a Russian state-sponsored disinformation campaign operating throughout the 2016 US presidential election (see Sommerlad 2018). The news came as a surprise to many Tumblr users who had become accustomed to the sense of spatial belonging afforded by the platform. Tumblr's implication in the proliferation of disinformation campaigns circulating through online networks (see Bennett and Livingston 2018) thus risks destabilizing vernacular understandings of Tumblr as a safe space for those wishing to engage in counterpublic modes of address.

Secondly, as noted in the introduction, in December 2018, in response to various corporate, commercial, and legal imperatives governing the platform, Tumblr made a much-critiqued decision to ban adult content on users' blogs (Bronstein 2020; Pilipets and Paasonen 2022). Many were quick to express their concern about the impact of this decision on the platform's LGBT users who found in Tumblr a space to undertake queer identity work with regard to gender, sexuality, and sex and relationships. For example, writing for *The Guardian*, Ho (2018) expressed her concern about the impact that these changes would have on 'the marginalised communities who have found, within Tumblr's more tolerant stance toward legal adult material, a safe haven to explore and establish their sexual and gender identities'. Tumblr, in turn, reportedly lost up to 20 per cent of its users following this decision (Romano 2018; Liao 2019). However, in late 2022, Tumblr announced a revision of their community guidelines to once again permit nudity, mature subject matter, and sexual themes (tumblr staff 2022). This announcement, at the time of writing, ushered in a resurgent popular Tumblr nostalgia. Writing for *Vogue*, Jones (2022) connects nostalgic discussions about the possibility of a 'Tumblr revival' to concerns about the future of Twitter following its controversial acquisition by tech billionaire Elon Musk. Tumblr's uncertain future subsequently forms part of an wider unpredictable social media landscape, where the 'societal perceptions and perceived value' of a platform previously characterized by discourses of decline 'can change dramatically in response to contemporary discourses' (Miltner and Gerrard 2022, 50) like those, at the time of writing, currently surrounding Twitter.

Moreover, Tumblr has become increasingly embroiled in the US culture wars over the past decade, exemplified most clearly by right-wing anti-feminist discourses about 'social justice warriors' (Nagle 2017). The links between Tumblr, digital feminism, and media fandom are by no means uncomplicated or straightforward, and in some contexts feminist fans themselves mobilize anti-SJW discourses in an expression of what I term 'SJW fatigue'. It is hard to say, then, with any certainty what the future of the platform and its role within the popular imaginary and social media landscape holds.

To turn away from Tumblr, I will now reflect on other sites of contradiction within my research. In my introduction to *Feminist Fandom*, I discussed my methodological orientation to this research and, later in Chapter 3, emphasized the necessity of feminist researchers to proceed with due compassion *and* due criticality towards research about young people's feminisms. Thus, while my analysis has explored the potential of media fandom to operate as a feminist pedagogical space that facilitates feminist identity development, consciousness-raising, community building, knowledge production, and knowledge sharing, it is also important, especially as I conclude this book, to question and, where necessary, interrogate the gaps and silences in many feminist fans' accounts. One of the most significant outcomes of this methodological orientation to my data analysis was its insight into the ways in which feminist fans' narratives, while rich and varied, at times contradicted one another. In doing so, they revealed the powerful processes of inclusion and exclusion at work within feminist fandom, as well as digital feminist spaces more broadly.

Most significantly, across Chapters 2 and 3, I distinguished between two divergent understandings of feminist fandom that circulate within the fannish imaginary on Tumblr. The first, I argued, represented a normative celebratory understanding of fandom as inherently progressive or resistant – one that circulates within fan studies, fandom, and Tumblr 'metafandom' (Tiidenberg, Hendry, and Abidin 2021). Alternatively, the second understanding instead of feminist fandom foregrounded the structuring force of whiteness within both fannish and feminist spaces, revealing how access to belonging within feminist fandom is differentially distributed in ways that necessitate more precarious and contingent modes of 'differential belonging' (Carrillo 2005). Many of my participants of colour expressed their frustration with feminist fandom's elevation of white characters, as well as the failure, if not refusal, of many feminist fans to address whiteness 'as a racialised identity' (Pande 2018a, 82).

This often positions the feminist fan of colour as an *anti-racist killjoy fan*, whose refusal to engage in a joyful, celebratory, fannish affect towards both the fantext and fandom itself is read by other (white) fans as sabotaging (white) fans' happiness and ability to 'escape' within feminist fandom. Underpinning this logic, I argued, is an assumption that fannish affect should supersede one's social location. The anti-racist killjoy fan is at increased risk of online trolling and abuse on Tumblr as they are subject to the defensive moves of white fragility. The experiences of white fragility reported by feminist fans of colour should be considered in contrast to, or perhaps more fittingly in conjunction with, participants' narratives detailed in Chapter 1 marked by a performative disavowal of 'white feminism' in favour of a supposedly 'intersectional' feminist identity. This performative process of disavowal, I argued, is central to the identity work undertaken by many feminist fans and is configured through anxiety-laden discourses about regulating, disciplining, and improving the feminist (and fannish) self. However, as Kanai (2020a) and others have noted, a disavowal of complicity with white feminism in pursuit of a supposedly intersectional feminist identity often obscures the reinvigoration of a whiteness centred on individual self-monitoring and self-discipline. My findings in relation to whiteness and non-belonging can be situated alongside an emergent body of literature within fan studies examining race and fandom.

Notably, other forms of exclusion also emerged throughout my analysis, for example with regard to language, nationality, and cultural barriers. For instance, I discussed the responses of participants from the Global South who expressed their discomfort towards the myopic focus of much feminist fandom on the Anglophone North American and European context, thus extending the forces of neocolonialization and neo-imperialism within a digital context. In Chapter 4, I also suggested that feminist knowledge within feminist fandom can be understood as a form of subcultural capital. The successful performance of an ability to participate in feminist knowledge sharing within feminist fandom thus risks reinforcing hierarchical processes of exclusion as, like many digital feminist spaces, a certain fluency in feminist vocabulary and principles is required to participate. The complexities of these experiences cannot be neatly interpreted within normative celebratory theories of fannish resistance within fan studies.

The accounts I have examined throughout *Feminist Fandom* therefore make visible the multiplicitous, complex, and often contradictory meanings of feminism and feminist practice that are circulated, negotiated, and contested within fannish spaces, reminding us that there is no singular or fixed 'feminism' implicated in feminist fandom or contemporary feminism more broadly. However, they also undoubtedly affirm Banet-Weiser's (2018) assertion that some feminisms are afforded more popularity than others within the 'economy of visibility' (18) that characterizes our contemporary cultural moment. In turn, the accounts of non-belonging within feminist fandom articulated by participants of colour can be contextualized with regard to the ways in which whiteness pervades the feminisms that are afforded the most visibility within popular and digital cultures, subsequently effacing more dynamic and intersectional feminist iterations and practices. Nevertheless, a number of my participants did position feminist fandom as a space in which they had engaged with less-visible intersectional, queer, and indigenous feminisms. Like popular feminisms, fannish feminisms are multiplicitous and multivalent. They exist along a continuum.

Simultaneously, the dominant understandings of feminist fandom, articulated both within my ethnographic data and within scholarly theorizations of fandom, call for the necessity of a sharper understanding of the complex and contradictory ways in which difference is simultaneously levelled out and heightened within fannish spaces. While my analysis reveals the role of social media platforms like Tumblr in facilitating the relationship between media fandom and young people's engagements with digital feminism, we must also remain mindful of its complex role in the re-entrenchment of structural inequalities both in its architecture and in its use. Digital spaces are not disembodied but instead extend and reproduce offline inequalities and power imbalances. Just as they can become key spaces for feminist education and activism, they can also become aggregators of online misogyny and bring other forms of structural inequality into stark relief. As Rivers (2017, 115) notes, 'the relationship between feminism and social media is as fraught as it is productive'. Likewise, we need to think together the rise of popular feminism and new forms of feminist practice and activism, as typified by feminist fandom, alongside, and in tandem with, intensified misogyny and the resurgence of the far-right.[2]

In concluding *Feminist Fandom*, I do not want to present a reductive or overly deterministic account of feminist fandom, yet I also do not wish to foreclose due critique. In turn, our understandings of feminist fandom, and the relationship of media fandom to digital feminisms more broadly, should be open to change in line with its emergent nature. This also adheres to understandings of youth as a time of process and continual recalibration. The processual nature of fannish feminisms, as well as feminist fans' commitment to continuous growth and change, hopefully implies that there is ultimately room for movement and progress. This calls for a flexible approach to the observations and findings detailed throughout this book. *Feminist Fandom* is not an uncritical celebration of the relationship between media fandom and digital feminisms. It should instead be understood as an attempt to bring together some of the complex, ambivalent, and contradictory ways in which feminist fandom remains entangled with digital and popular cultures which at once challenge, and yet continue to be shaped by, relations of power and domination.

Notes

Introduction

1 This is to ensure compliance with Tumblr's Terms of Service, which at the time of writing stipulates that users must be aged 13 and above to use the platform.

2 Following the work of Henry Jenkins (2006a), I understand the term 'production' to refer not only to the creation of digital products but also to the interactive and dynamic processes of cultural consumption that is embedded in production. My understanding of cultural production recognizes that young people often 'take up or consume popular images, and combine, critique, adapt, or incorporate them in their own media productions' (Weber and Mitchell 2007, 27).

3 Indeed, many fan studies scholars rely upon the visibility of fannish modes of consumption and production in their research (Bury 2005; Booth 2010; Stein 2015).

4 For a detailed breakdown of the affordances of Tumblr compared to social networking sites such as Facebook, see Renninger (2015) and Tiidenberg, Hendry, and Abidin (2021). Also see Chapter 2.

5 However, Tiidenberg, Hendry, and Abidin (2021, 131–3) do offer an interesting discussion of the platform's top-down embrace of social justice and civic engagement.

6 Yet, as a relative newcomer to fandom, not particularly well versed in the fannish norms and expectations of LiveJournal, I often struggled to access the closed LiveJournal communities where much fannish activity occurred at the time (see Chin 2018).

7 This approach largely adhered to the editorial philosophy of the *Journal of Transformative Works and Cultures* (2020), whose guidelines on the protection of fan sources stipulate that researchers should obtain permission from the creator of any fanworks cited in a piece of research.

Chapter 1

1 Similarly, in *By Any Media Necessary,* Jenkins and Shresthova (2016) conceptualize popular culture as a 'civic pathway'. They claim that fandom represents one of many

possible spaces where people come together around their shared passions and interests, which can in turn act as 'springboards for civic and political participation' (271) (also see Hannell 2021).

2   Hills's notion of fandom-as-transformative should not be conflated with Busse's (2013) typology of *transformative* versus *affirmational* fandom (drawing upon obsession_inc 2009). Their respective uses of 'transformative' are very distinct. Hills uses the term to describe a genre of self-narratives about identity development, while Busse uses the term to refer to modes of fandom, fan practices, and fan communities.

3   Similarly, Fiske (1987) and Jenkins (1992) have referred to this as a communal fan-produced 'meta text' that is larger, richer, and more complex than the original (also see Hellekson 2009). This is something I have discussed with regard to feminist fandom elsewhere (see Hannell 2017b).

4   In Canada, Métis are people of mixed European and Indigenous ancestry.

Chapter 2

1   Affect theory has been widely adopted within Euro-American cultural studies and beyond, yet the concept remains somewhat open-ended and has been taken up by scholars in a number of ways. While some distinguish between affect and emotion (Grossberg 1992b; Probyn 2005; Pedwell and Whitehead 2012), many others use the terms interchangeably (Ngai 2005). Affect is ultimately concerned with the way *feeling* resonates and is negotiated and experienced. For affect theorists such as Grossberg (1992a, b) and Hillis, Paasonen, and Petit (2015), affect concerns both the *quantity* and *quality*, or rather *intensity*, of feeling.

2   The *Supernatural* fandom has received a notable, perhaps disproportionate, amount of scholarly attention within fan studies. See, for example, Zubernis and Larsen (2012). At the time of writing, a literature search for the term 'Supernatural' on the *Transformative Works and Cultures* database, as a 'flagship publication' (Morimoto and Chin 2017, 187) within fan studies, returns over 125 individual results.

3   For a more detailed discussion of the alternative contexts in which the term 'social justice warrior' is mobilized, often in more celebratory terms by Tumblr users themselves, see Tiidenberg, Hendry, and Abidin (2021, 140–5).

4   We see elements of *SJW Fangirl as Pathology* at work, for instance, in one of the responses Barker, Smith, and Attwood (2021, 129) received to their international survey of more than 10,000 *Game of Thrones* audience members. One of their respondents laments encountering 'SJWs [bullshit] about the "sexual exploitation" on the show', which we could interpret as an allusion to the well-documented

critique of sexual violence in cultural texts like *Game of Thrones* within feminist
fandom (Ferreday 2015; Hannell 2017a). This can be positioned within a wider
cultural and industrial context charted by Suzanne Scott (2019), whereby
normative (read: male, cisgender, heterosexual, white) fans mobilize around a
collective disdain towards fans who occupy more marginal identities, especially
along gendered lines.

5   As Sharp and Shannon (2020) highlight, the *r* in safe*r* spaces acknowledges that no
space is ever universally safe. This becomes abundantly clear within the context of
my own ethnographic data in Chapter 3.

Chapter 3

1   Skeggs (1997) has similarly noted the conceptual duality of the relationship
between identity and non-identity, highlighting the importance of non-
identification in the process of locating identities and feelings of belongingness.

2   This is something that Pande's (2018a, 54–5) participants also discussed.

Chapter 4

1   Also see Sharp and Shannon (2020); Robards et al. (2020).

2   AO3 stands for Archive of Our Own. Run by the Organisation for Transformative
Works and Cultures, Archive of Our Own is a non-profit open-source
repository, or archive, of fan fiction and fanworks contributed by users.
See https://archiveofourown.org/.

3   This is contrast to the media industries' selective co-optation of the fannish gift
economy detailed by Suzanne Scott (2019).

4   One of the few exceptions to this was a response written by 64-year-old Wendy
(#118), one of my oldest respondents, who expressed her concern that 'younger
people tend to feel that we don't have anything relevant to contribute'. Unlike some
of my other findings with regard to multi-generationality, Wendy's remark aligns
more closely with Neta Yodovich's (2022) findings on age and exclusion within
feminist fandom.

5   Notably, many fans cross-post their fanworks across AO3 and Tumblr. For
example, a fanfiction author may upload their fanfiction to the repository of
fanworks on AO3 and subsequently post to Tumblr to alert their followers that
they have done so.

6   These responses notably include the Tumblr blog *diversehighfantasy*, which
     I discussed in Chapter 1 in relation to Grace's (#264) experience of coming to
     understand feminism within the context of race and ethnicity.

Conclusion

1   With the exception of Neta Yodovich's (2022) recent work on *science fiction*, rather
     than *media,* fandom.
2   This is something Scott (2019) charts with fascinating insight with regard to the
     relationship between the culture wars and the uneven mainstreaming of fandom in
     North America.

References

Affuso, Elizabeth. 2018. 'Everyday Costume: Feminized Fandom, Retail, and Beauty Culture'. In *The Routledge Companion to Media Fandom*, edited by Melissa A. Click and Suzanne Scott, 184–92. Oxon: Routledge.

Agosto, Denise E., June Abbas, and Robin Naughton. 2012. 'Relationships and Social Rules: Teens' Social Network and Other ICT Selection Practices'. *Journal of the American Society for Information Science and Technology* 63 (6):1108–24. doi: 10.1002/asi.22612.

Ahmed, Sara. 2004a. 'Affective Economies'. *Social Text* 22 (2):117–39.

Ahmed, Sara. 2004b. *The Cultural Politics of Emotion*. Edinburgh: Edinburgh University Press.

Ahmed, Sara. 2004c. 'Declarations of Whiteness: The Non-performativity of Anti-racism'. *Borderlands E-Journal* 3 (2).

Ahmed, Sara. 2006. 'Orientations: Toward a Queer Phenomenology'. *GLQ: A Journal of Lesbian and Gay Studies* 12 (4):543–74.

Ahmed, Sara. 2010. *The Promise of Happiness*. Durham, NC: Duke University Press.

Ahmed, Sara. 2012. *On Being Included: Racism and Diversity in Institutional Life*. London: Duke University Press.

Ahmed, Sara. 2017. *Living a Feminist Life*. London: Duke University Press.

Aikau, Hokulani, Karla Erickson, and Jennifer Pierce. 2007. *Feminist Waves, Feminist Generations: Life Stories from the Academy*. Minneapolis, MN: University of Minnesota Press.

Akyel, Esma. 2014. '#Direnkahkaha (Resist Laughter): "Laughter Is a Revolutionary Action"'. *Feminist Media Studies* 14 (6):1093–4. doi: 10.1080/14680777.2014.975437.

Altınay, Rüstem Ertuğ. 2014. '"There Is a Massacre of Women": Violence against Women, Feminist Activism, and Hashtags in Turkey'. *Feminist Media Studies* 14 (6):1102–3. doi: 10.1080/14680777.2014.975445.

Anderson, Ben. 2009. 'Affective Atmospheres'. *Emotion, Space and Society* 2 (2):77–81. doi: https://doi.org/10.1016/j.emospa.2009.08.005.

Anderson, Benedict. 1983. *Imagined Communities: Reflections on the Origin and Spread of Nationalism*. London: Verso.

Anderson, Kristin J. 2015. *Modern Misogyny: Anti-feminism in a Post-feminist Era*. New York, NY: Oxford University Press.

Anselmo, Diana W. 2018. 'Gender and Queer Fan Labor on Tumblr'. *Feminist Media Histories* 4 (1):84–114. doi: 10.1525/fmh.2018.4.1.84.

Anthias, Floya. 2002. 'Where Do I Belong? Narrating Collective Identity and Translocational Positionality'. *Ethnicities* 2 (4):451–514.

Anthias, Floya. 2015. 'Interconnecting Boundaries of Identity and Belonging and Hierarchy-Making within Transnational Mobility Studies: Framing Inequalities'. *Current Sociology* 62 (4):172–90.

Applebaum, Barbara. 2010. *Being White, Being Good: White Complicity, White Moral Responsibility, and Social Justice Pedagogy*. Lanham, MA: Lexington Books.

Aziz, Razia. 1992. 'Feminism and the Challenge of Racism: Deviance or Difference?' In *Knowing Women: Feminism and Knowledge*, edited by Helen Crowley and Susan Himmelweit, 291–305. Cambridge: Polity.

Bacon-Smith, Camille. 1992. *Enterprising Women: Television Fandom and the Creation of Popular Myth*. Philadelphia, PA: University of Pennsylvania Press.

Bamberg, Michael, Anna De Fina, and Deborah Schiffrin. 2011. 'Discourse and Identity Construction'. In *Handbook of Identity Theory and Research*, edited by Seth J. Schwartz, Koen Luyckx, and Vivian L. Vignoles, 177–99. New York, NY: Springer.

Banet-Weiser, Sarah. 2015a. 'Popular Misogyny: A Zeitgeist'. Culture Digitally, accessed 23 January 2020. http://culturedigitally.org/2015/01/popular-misogyny-a-zeitgeist/.

Banet-Weiser, Sarah. 2015b. 'Whom Are We Empowering? Popular Feminism and the Work of Empowerment'. Console-ing Passions International Conference on Television, Video, Audio, New Media and Feminism, Dublin, June 19.

Banet-Weiser, Sarah. 2018. *Empowered: Popular Feminism and Popular Misogyny*. London: Duke University Press.

Banet-Weiser, Sarah, and Kate M. Miltner. 2015. '#MasculinitySoFragile: Culture, Structure, and Networked Misogyny'. *Feminist Media Studies* 16 (1):171–4. doi: 10.1080/14680777.2016.1120490.

Banet-Weiser, Sarah, and Laura Portwood-Stacer. 2017. 'The Traffic in Feminism: An Introduction to the Commentary and Criticism on Popular Feminism'. *Feminist Media Studies* 17 (5):884–8. doi: 10.1080/14680777.2017.1350517.

Barker, Martin, Clarissa Smith, and Feona Attwood. 2021. *Watching Game of Thrones: How Audiences Engage with Dark Television*. Manchester: University of Manchester Press.

Bartky, Sandra Lee. 1975. 'Toward a Phenomenology of Feminist Consciousness'. *Social Theory and Practice* 3 (4):425–39.

Baym, Nancy. 2000. *Tune in, Log on: Soaps, Fandom, and Online Community*. London: Sage.

Baym, Nancy. 2015. *Personal Connections in the Digital Age*. Cambridge: Polity.

Beck, Ulrich. 1992. *Risk Society: Towards a New Modernity*. London: Sage.

Beltran, Mary. 2010. 'Meaningful Diversity: Exploring Questions of Equitable Representation in Ensemble Cast Shows'. *Flow* 12:(7).

Bennett, Andy. 2004. 'Virtual Subculture? Youth, Identity and the Internet'. In *After Subculture: Critical Studies in Contemporary Youth Culture*, edited by Andy Bennett and Keith Kahn-Harris, 162–72. Basingstoke: Palgrave Macmillan.

Bennett, Andy, and Brady Robards. 2014. *Mediated Youth Cultures: The Internet, Belonging and New Cultural Configurations*. Basingstoke: Palgrave Macmillan.

Bennett, Lance W., and Steven Livingston. 2018. 'The Disinformation Order: Disruptive Communication and the Decline of Democratic Institutions'. *European Journal of Communication* 33 (2):122–39. doi: 10.1177/0267323118760317.

Berlant, Lauren. 2008. *The Female Complaint: The Unfinished Business of Sentimentality in American Culture.* Durham, NC: Duke University Press.

Berlant, Lauren. 2011. *Cruel Optimism.* Durham, NC: Duke University Press.

Berlant, Lauren, and Michael Warner. 1995. 'What Does Queer Theory Teach Us about X?' *PMLA* 110 (3):343–9.

Best, Amy. 2011. 'Youth Identity Formation: Contemporary Identity Work'. *Sociology Compass* 5 (10):908–22. doi: 10.1111/j.1751-9020.2011.00411.x.

Bettie, Julie. 2014. *Women without Class: Girls, Race, and Identity.* Oakland, CA: University of California Press.

Bolin, Göran. 2016. 'Passion and Nostalgia in Generational Media Experiences'. *European Journal of Cultural Studies* 19 (3):250–64.

Bondi, L. I. Z., and Damaris Rose. 2003. 'Constructing Gender, Constructing the Urban: A Review of Anglo-American Feminist Urban Geography'. *Gender, Place & Culture* 10 (3):229–45. doi: 10.1080/0966369032000114000.

Booth, Paul. 2010. *Digital Fandom.* New York, NY: Peter Lang.

Booth, Paul. 2015. 'Fandom: The Classroom of the Future'. *Transformative Works and Cultures* 19.

Booth, Paul. 2017. *Digital Fandom 2.0.* 2nd edn. New York, NY: Peter Lang.

Booth, Paul, and Peter Kelly. 2013. 'The Changing Faces of Doctor Who Fandom: New Fans, New Technologies, Old Practices?' *Participations* 10 (1):56–72.

boyd, danah. 2007. 'Why Youth (Heart) Social Network Sites: The Role of Networked Publics in Teenage Social Life'. In *Youth, Identity, and Digital Media*, edited by David Buckingham, 119–42. Cambridge, MA: MIT Press.

boyd, danah. 2011. 'Social Network Sites as Networked Publics: Affordances, Dynamics, and Implication'. In *A Networked Self: Identity, Community, and Culture on Social Network Sites*, edited by Zizi Papacharissi, 39–58. London: Routledge.

boyd, danah. 2012. 'The Politics of "Real Names"'. *Communications of the ACM* 55 (8):29. doi: 10.1145/2240236.2240247.

boyd, danah. 2014. *It's Complicated: The Social Lives of Networked Teens.* New Haven, CT: Yale University Press.

Braidotti, Rosi. 2011. *Nomadic Subjects: Embodiment and Sexual Difference in Contemporary Feminist Theory.* 2nd edn. New York, NY: Columbia University Press.

Brett, Ingrid, and Sarah Maslen. 2021. 'Stage Whispering: Tumblr Hashtags beyond Categorization'. *Social Media + Society* 7 (3):20563051211032138. doi: 10.1177/20563051211032138.

Bronstein, Carolyn. 2020. 'Pornography, Trans Visibility, and the Demise of Tumblr'. *TSQ: Transgender Studies Quarterly* 7 (2):240–54. doi: 10.1215/23289252-8143407.

Brunsdon, Charlotte. 1997. *Screen Tastes: Soap Opera to Satellite Dishes*. London: Routledge.

Budgeon, Shelley. 2001. 'Emergent Feminist(?) Identities: Young Women and the Practice of Micropolitics'. *European Journal of Women's Studies* 8 (1):7–28. doi: 10.1177/135050680100800102.

Burke, Penny Jane, and Sue Jackson. 2006. *Reconceptualising Lifelong Learning: Feminist Interventions*. London: Routledge.

Burton, Julian. 2020. 'Screaming into the Void: Reconceptualising Privacy, the Personal, and the Public through the Perspectives of Young Tumblr Users'. In *a Tumblr Book: Platform and Cultures*, edited by Allison McCracken, Alexander Cho, Louisa Stein, and Indira Neill Hoch, 103–13. Ann Arbor, MI: University of Michigan Press.

Bury, Rhiannon. 2005. *Cyberspaces of Their Own: Female Fandoms Online*. New York, NY: Peter Lang.

Bury, Rhiannon. 2016. 'Technology, Fandom and Community in the Second Media Age'. *Convergence* 23 (6):627–42. doi: 10.1177/1354856516648084.

Bury, Rhiannon. 2018. '"We're Not There": Fans, Fan Studies, and the Participatory Continuum'. In *The Routledge Companion to Media Fandom*, edited by Melissa A. Click and Suzanne Scott, 123–31. Oxon: Routledge.

Busse, Kristina. 2013. 'Geek Hierarchies, Boundary Policing, and the Gendering of the Good Fan'. *Participations* 10 (1):73–91.

Busse, Kristina. 2017. *Framing Fan Fiction: Literary and Social Practices in Fan Fiction Communities*. Iowa City, IA: University of Iowa Press.

Busse, Kristina, and Karen Hellekson. 2012. 'Identity, Ethics and Fan Privacy'. In *Fan Culture: Theory/Practice*, edited by Lynn Zubernis and Katherine Larsen, 38–56. Newcastle-upon-Tyne: Cambridge Scholars.

Bussoletti, Arianna. 2022. '"Tumblr Is Dominated by America": A Study of Linguistic and Cultural Differences in Tumblr Transnational Fandom'. *The Communication Review*:1–18. doi: 10.1080/10714421.2022.2126589.

Butcher, Helen, Ros Coward, Marcella Evaristi, Jenny Garber, Rachel Harris, and Janice Winship. 1974. *Images of Women in the Media*. Birmingham: Centre for Contemporary Cultural Studies.

Byron, Paul, Brady Robards, Benjamin Hanckel, Son Vivienne, and Brendan Churchill. 2019. '"Hey, I'm Having These Experiences": Tumblr Use and Young People's Queer (Dis)connections'. *International Journal of Communication* 13:2239–59.

Carbin, Maria, and Sara Edenheim. 2013. 'The Intersectional Turn in Feminist Theory: A Dream of a Common Language?' *European Journal of Women's Studies* 20 (3):233–48. doi: 10.1177/1350506813484723.

Carrillo, Aimee Rowe. 2005. 'Be Longing: Toward a Feminist Politics of Relation'. *NWSA Journal* 17 (2):15–46.

Castleberry, Garret. 2015. 'Game(s) of Fandom: The Hyperlink Labyrinths That Paratextualize Game of Thrones Fandom'. In *Television, Social Media and Fandom,* edited by Alison F. Slade, Amber J. Narro, and Dedria Givens-Carroll, 127–45. London: Lexington Books.

Cattien, Jana. 2019. 'When "Feminism" Becomes a Genre: Alias Grace and "Feminist" Television'. *Feminist Theory* 20 (3):321–39. doi: 10.1177/1464700119842564.

Cavalcante, Andre. 2019. 'Tumbling into Queer Utopias and Vortexes: Experiences of LGBTQ Social Media Users on Tumblr'. *Journal of Homosexuality* 66 (12):1715–35. doi: 10.1080/00918369.2018.1511131.

centrumlumina. 2016a. 'But!: A Response to Responses'. Tumblr, Last Modified 18 August 2016, accessed 09 January 2020. https://centrumlumina.tumblr.com/post/148893785870/fandoms-race-problem-and-the-ao3-ship-stats.

centrumlumina. 2016b. 'Fandom's Race Problem and the AO3 Ship Stats'. Tumblr, Last Modified 13 August 2016, accessed 08 January 2020. https://centrumlumina.tumblr.com/post/148893785870/fandoms-race-problem-and-the-ao3-ship-stats.

Cervenak, Sarah J., Karina L. Cespedes, Caridad Souza, and Andrea Straub. 2002. 'Imagining Differently: The Politics of Listening in a Feminist Classroom'. In *This Bridge We Call Home: Radical Visions for Transformation*, edited by Gloria Anzaldúa and AnaLouise Keating. New York, NY: Routledge.

Chayka, Kyle. 2022. 'How Tumblr Become Popular for Being Obsolete'. *The New Yorker*, accessed 11 January 2023. https://www.newyorker.com/culture/infinite-scroll/how-tumblr-became-popular-for-being-obsolete.

Chidgey, Red. 2021. 'Postfeminism™: Celebrity Feminism, Branding and the Performance of Activist Capital'. *Feminist Media Studies* 21 (7):1055–71. doi: 10.1080/14680777.2020.1804431.

Chin, Bertha. 2018. 'It's about Who You Know: Social Capital, Hierarchies and Fandom'. In *A Companion to Media Fandom and Fan Studies*, edited by Paul Booth, 325–41. Oxford: Wiley-Blackwell.

Cho, Alexander. 2015. 'Queer Reverb: Tumblr, Affect, Time'. In *Networked Affect*, edited by Susanna Paasonen and Ken Hillis, 43–57. Cambridge, MA: MIT Press.

Christensen, Ann-Dorte. 2017. 'Belonging and Unbelonging from an Intersectional Perspective'. *Gender, Technology and Development* 13 (1):21–41. doi: 10.1177/097185240901300102.

Clark, Meredith. 2020. 'DRAG THEM: A Brief Etymology of So-Called "Cancel Culture"'. *Communication and the Public* 5 (3–4):88–92. doi: 10.1177/2057047320961562.

Clark, Rosemary. 2016. '"Hope in a Hashtag": The Discursive Activism of #WhyIStayed'. *Feminist Media Studies* 16 (5):788–804. doi: 10.1080/14680777.2016.1138235.

Clark-Parsons, Rosemary. 2018. 'Building a Digital Girl Army: The Cultivation of Feminist Safe Spaces Online'. *New Media & Society* 20 (6):2125–44. doi: 10.1177/1461444817731919.

Cochrane, Kira. 2013. 'The Fourth Wave of Feminism: Meet the Rebel Women'. *The Guardian*, accessed 11 April 2021. https://www.theguardian.com/world/2013/dec/10/fourth-wave-feminism-rebel-women.

Cohen, Anthony. 1985. *The Symbolic Construction of Community*. Abingdon: Routledge.

Collins, Patricia Hill. 2009. *Black Feminist Thought: Knowledge, Consciousness, and the Politics of Empowerment*. 2nd edn. New York, NY: Routledge.

Coppa, Francesca. 2006. 'Writing Bodies in Space: Media Fan Fiction as Theatrical Performance'. In *Fan Fiction and Fan Communities in the Age of the Internet*, edited by Karen Hellekson and Kristina Busse, 225–44. Jefferson, NC: McFarland.

Coppa, Francesca. 2014. 'Fuck Yeah, Fandom Is Beautiful'. *Journal of Fandom Studies* 2 (1):73–82. doi: 10.1386/jfs.2.1.73_1.

Couldry, Nick. 2009. 'Rethinking the Politics of Voice'. *Continuum* 23 (4):579–82. doi: 10.1080/10304310903026594.

Couldry, Nick. 2016. *Listening beyond the Echoes: Media, Ethics, and Agency in an Uncertain World*. London: Routledge.

Cover, Rob. 2019. 'Competing Contestations of the Norm: Emerging Sexualities and Digital Identities'. *Continuum (Mount Lawley, W.A.)* 33 (5):602–13. doi: 10.1080/10304312.2019.1641583.

Crawford, Kate. 2011. 'Listening, Not Lurking: The Neglected Form of Participation'. In *Cultures of Participation*, edited by Hajo Greif, Larissa Hjorth, and Amparo Lasén, 63–74. Berlin, Germany: Peter Lang.

Cristofari, Cécile, and Matthieu Guitton. 2017. 'Aca-fans and Fan Communities: An Operative Framework'. *Journal of Consumer Culture* 17 (3):713–31. doi: 10.1177/1469540515623608.

Currie, Dawn, Deirdre Kelly, and Shauna Pomerantz. 2007. '"The Power to Squash People": Understanding Girls' Relational Aggression'. *British Journal of Sociology of Education* 28 (1):23–37. doi: 10.1080/01425690600995974.

Currie, Dawn, Deirdre Kelly, and Shauna Pomerantz. 2009. *'Girl Power:' Girls Reinventing Girlhood*. New York, NY: Peter Lang.

Cvetkovich, Ann. 2003. *An Archive of Feelings: Trauma, Sexuality, and Lesbian Public Cultures*. Durham, NC: Duke University Press.

Dame, Avery. 2016. 'Making a Name for Yourself: Tagging as Transgender Ontological Practice on Tumblr'. *Critical Studies in Media Communication* 33 (1):23–37. doi: 10.1080/15295036.2015.1130846.

Daniels, Jessie. 2009. *Cyber Racism: White Supremacy Online and the New Attack on Civil Rights*. Lanham, MD: Rowman & Littlefield Publishers.

Daniels, Jessie. 2016. 'The Trouble with White Feminism: Whiteness, Digital Feminism, and the Intersectional Internet'. In *The Intersectional Internet: Race, Sex, Class, and Culture Online*, edited by Safiya Umoja Noble and Brendesha M. Tynes, 41–60. New York, NY: Peter Lang.

Dare-Edwards, Helena Louise. 2015. 'Interrogating Tweendom Online: "Fangirl as Pathology", Gender/Age, and iCarly Fandom'. Doctor of Philosophy, School of Film, Television and Media Studies, University of East Anglia.

De Kosnik, Abigail. 2016. *Rogue Archives: Digital Cultural Memory and Media Fandom*. Cambridge, MA: MIT Press.

Dean, Jonathan. 2010. 'Feminism in the Papers'. *Feminist Media Studies* 10 (4):391–407. doi: 10.1080/14680777.2010.514112.

DiAngelo, Robin. 2011. 'White Fragility'. *International Journal of Critical Pedagogy* 3 (2):54–70.

DiAngelo, Robin. 2018. *White Fragility: Why It's So Hard for White People to Talk about Racism*. Boston, MA: Beacon Press.

DiAngelo, Robin. 2021. *Nice Racism: How Progressive White People Perpetuate Racial Harm*. Dublin: Random House.

Dow, Bonnie. 1996. *Prime-Time Feminism: Television, Media Culture, and the Women's Movement since 1970*. Philadelphia, PA: University of Pennsylvania Press.

Downing, Nancy, and Kristin Roush. 1985. 'From Passive Acceptance to Active Commitment: A Model of Feminist Identity Development for Women'. *The Counseling Psychologist* 13 (4):695–709. doi: 10.1177/0011000085134013.

Duffett, Mark. 2013. *Understanding Fandom*. London: Bloomsbury.

Durham, Meenakshi Gigi. 2021. *MeToo: The Impact of Rape Culture in the Media*. Cambridge: Polity.

Dyer, Richard. 1997. *White*. Oxon: Routledge.

Eckert, Stine, and Linda Steiner. 2016. 'Feminist Uses of Social Media: Facebook, Twitter, Tumblr, Pinterest, and Instagram'. In *Defining Identity and the Changing Scope of Culture in the Digital Age*, edited by Alison Novak, 210–29. Hershey, PA: Information Science Reference.

Enli, Gunn, and Nancy Thumim. 2012. 'Socializing and Self-Representation Online: Exploring Facebook'. *Observatorio Journal* 6 (1):87–105.

Fathallah, Judith. 2015. 'Statements and Silence: Fanfic Paratexts for ASOIAF/Game of Thrones'. *Continuum* 30 (1):75–88. doi: 10.1080/10304312.2015.1099150.

Felski, Rita. 2002. 'Introduction'. *New Literary History* 33 (4):607–22.

Fenstermaker, Sarah, and Candace West. 2002. *Doing Gender, Doing Difference: Inequality, Power, and Institutional Change*. London: Routledge.

Ferreday, Debra. 2003. 'Unspeakable Bodies: Erasure, Embodiment and the Pro-Ana Community'. *International Journal of Cultural Studies* 6 (3):277–95. doi: 10.1177/13678779030063003.

Ferreday, Debra. 2011. *Online Belongings: Fantasy, Affect and Web Communities*. Bern, Switzerland: Peter Lang.

Ferreday, Debra. 2015. 'Game of Thrones, Rape Culture and Feminist Fandom'. *Australian Feminist Studies* 30 (83):21–36. doi: 10.1080/08164649.2014.998453.

Ferreday, Debra, and Geraldine Harris. 2017. 'Investigating "Fame-inism": The Politics of Popular Culture'. *Feminist Theory* 18 (3):239–43. doi: 10.1177/1464700117721876.

Filipovic, Jill. 2007. 'Blogging While Female: How Internet Misogyny Parallels "Real-World" Harassment'. *Yale Journal of Law and Feminism* 19 (1):295–303.

Fischer, Mia. 2016. '#Free_CeCe: The Material Convergence of Social Media Activism'. *Feminist Media Studies* 16 (5):755–71. doi: 10.1080/14680777.2016.1140668.

Fiske, John. 1987. *Television Culture*. New York, NY: Routledge.

Fiske, John. 1992. 'The Cultural Economy of Fandom'. In *The Adoring Audience: Fan Culture and Popular Media*, edited by Lisa Lewis, 30–49. London: Routledge.

Flagg, Barbara J. 2005. 'Whiteness as Metaprivilege'. *Washington University Journal of Law and Policy* 18:1–11.

Flood, Michelle. 2019. 'Intersectionality and Celebrity Culture'. *Women's Studies in Communication* 42 (4):422–6. doi: 10.1080/07491409.2019.1682917.

Frankenberg, Ruth. 1993. *White Women, Race Matters: The Social Construction of Whiteness*. London: Routledge.

Fraser, Nancy. 1990. 'Rethinking the Public Sphere: A Contribution to the Critique of Actually Existing Democracy'. *Social Text* (25/26):56–80. doi: 10.2307/466240.

Fraser, Nancy. 1997. *Justice Interruptus: Critical Reflections on 'Postsocialist' Condition*. London: Routledge.

Fraser, Nancy. 2013. *Fortunes of Feminism: From State-Managed Capitalism to Neoliberal Crisis*. London: Verso.

Friedan, Betty. 1963. *The Feminine Mystique*. New York, NY: Norton.

Frye, Marilyn. 1983. *The Politics of Reality: Essays in Feminist Theory*. Freedom, CA: Crossing Press.

García-Rapp, Florencia. 2018. 'Trivial and Normative? Online Fieldwork within YouTube's Beauty Community'. *Journal of Contemporary Ethnography* 48 (5):619–44. doi: 10.1177/0891241618806974.

Gauntlett, David. 2000. 'Web Studies: A User's Guide'. In *Web Studies*, edited by David Gauntlett, 2–18. London: Arnold.

Gee, James Paul. 2005. 'Semiotic Social Spaces and Affinity Spaces: From the Age of Mythology to Today's School'. In *Beyond Communities of Practice: Language, Power and Social Context*, edited by David Barton and Karin Tusting, 214–32. Cambridge: Cambridge University Press.

Gee, James Paul, and Elisabeth Hayes. 2011. *Language and Learning in the Digital Age*. Edited by Elisabeth Hayes. 1st edn. Abingdon: Routledge.

Gee, James Paul, and Elizabeth Hayes. 2010. *Women and Gaming: The Sims and 21st Century Learning*. New York, NY: Palgrave Macmillan.

Geertz, Clifford. 1973. *The Interpretation of Cultures*. New York, NY: Basic Books.

Genette, Gérard. 1997. *Paratexts: Thresholds of Interpretation*. Cambridge: Cambridge University Press.

Geraghty, Lincoln. 2015a. 'Introduction: Fans and Paratexts'. In *Popular Media Cultures: Fans, Audiences and Paratexts*, edited by Lincoln Geraghty, 1–14. London: Palgrave Macmillan.

Geraghty, Lincoln. 2015b. *Popular Media Cultures: Fans, Audiences and Paratexts*. London: Palgrave Macmillan.

Gibbs, Martin, James Meese, Michael Arnold, Bjorn Nansen, and Marcus
　　Carter. 2015. '#Funeral and Instagram: Death, Social Media, and Platform
　　Vernacular'. *Information, Communication & Society* 18 (3):255–68.
　　doi: 10.1080/1369118x.2014.987152.

Giddens, Anthony. 1991. *Modernity and Self-Identity: Self and Society in the Late
　　Modern Age.* Cambridge: Polity.

Gill, Rosalind. 2007a. 'Critical Respect: The Difficulties and Dilemmas of Agency and
　　"Choice" for Feminism'. *European Journal of Women's Studies* 14 (1):69–80.

Gill, Rosalind. 2007b. *Gender and the Media.* Cambridge: Polity.

Gill, Rosalind. 2007c. 'Postfeminist Media Culture: Elements of a Sensibility'. *European
　　Journal of Cultural Studies* 10 (2):147–66. doi: 10.1177/1367549407075898.

Gill, Rosalind. 2016a. 'Post-Postfeminism?: New Feminist Visibilities in Postfeminist
　　Times'. *Feminist Media Studies* 16 (4):610–30. doi: 10.1080/14680777.2016.1193293.

Gill, Rosalind. 2016b. 'Postfeminism and the New Cultural Life of Feminism'.
　　Diffractions (6):1–8.

Gill, Rosalind, and Christina Scharff. 2011. *New Femininities: Postfeminism, Identity and
　　Neoliberalism.* Basingstoke: Palgrave Macmillan.

Gillespie, Tarleton. 2018. *Custodians of the Internet.* New Haven, CT: Yale University
　　Press.

Ging, Debbie, and Eugenia Siapera. 2019. *Gender Hate Online: Understanding the New
　　Anti-feminism.* Cham, Switzerland: Springer International.

Gordon, Avery. 2008. *Ghostly Matters: Haunting and the Sociological Imagination.*
　　Minneapolis, MN: University of Minnesota Press.

Gordon, Hava Rachel. 2010. *We Fight to Win: Inequality and the Politics of Youth
　　Activism.* New Brunswick, NJ: Rutgers University Press.

Gorton, Kristyn. 2007. 'Theorizing Emotion and Affect: Feminist Engagements'.
　　Feminist Theory 8 (3):333–48. doi: 10.1177/1464700107082369.

Gray, Jonathan. 2003. 'New Audiences, New Textualities: Anti-fans and Non-fans'.
　　International Journal of Cultural Studies 6 (1):64–81.

Gray, Jonathan. 2010. *Show Sold Separately: Promos, Spoilers, and Other Media
　　Paratexts.* New York, NY: New York University Press.

Gray, Jonathan, Cornel Sandvoss, and C. Lee Harrington. 2007. *Fandom: Identities and
　　Communities in a Mediated World.* 1st edn. London: New York University Press.

Gray, Kishonna. 2012. 'Intersecting Oppressions and Online Communities'. *Information,
　　Communication & Society* 15 (3):411–28. doi: 10.1080/1369118x.2011.642401.

Gray, Mary. 2009. *Out in the Country: Youth, Media and Visibility in Rural America.*
　　New York, NY: New York University Press.

Gray, Mary. 2014. 'Negotiating Identities/Queering Desires: Coming out Online and
　　the Remediation of the Coming-out Story'. In *Identity Technologies: Constructing
　　the Self Online,* edited by Anna Poletti and Julie Rak, 167–97. London: University of
　　Wisconsin Press.

Grossberg, Lawrence. 1992a. 'Is There a Fan in the House?: The Affective Sensibility of Fandom'. In *The Adoring Audience: Fan Culture and Popular Media*, edited by Lisa Lewis, 50–68.

Grossberg, Lawrence. 1992b. *We Gotta Get out of This Place: Popular Conservatism and Postmodern Culture*. New York, NY: Routledge.

Grosz, Elisabeth. 1999. *Becomings: Explorations in Time, Memory and Futures*. Ithaca, NY: Cornell University Press.

Guerrero-Pico, Mar, Maria-Jose Establés, and Rafael Ventura. 2018. 'Killing off Lexa: "Dead Lesbian Syndrome" and Intra-fandom Management of Toxic Fan Practices in an Online Queer Community'. *Participations* 15 (1):311–33.

Guillard, Julianne. 2016. 'Is Feminism Trending? Pedagogical Approaches to Countering (Sl)activism'. *Gender and Education* 28 (5):609–26. doi: 10.1080/09540253.2015.1123227.

Habib, Sadia, and Michael Ward. 2019. 'Conclusion: Young People Negotiating Belonging in Changing Times'. In *Identities, Youth and Belonging: International Perspectives*, edited by Sadia Habib and Michael Ward, 195–212. London: Palgrave Macmillan.

Halberstam, Jack. 2005. *In a Queer Time and Place: Transgender Bodies, Subcultural Lives*. New York, NY: New York University Press.

Hall, Stuart. [1981] 2016. 'Notes on Deconstructing "the Popular"'. In *People's History and Socialist Theory*, edited by Raphael Samuel, 227–40. Oxon: Routledge.

Hamad, Hannah, and Anthea Taylor. 2015. 'Introduction: Feminism and Contemporary Celebrity Culture'. *Celebrity Studies* 6 (1):124–7. doi: 10.1080/19392397.2015.1005382.

Hannell, Briony. 2017a. '"Game of Thrones" War on Women': Fandom and Feminist Discourse on Tumblr', Fan Studies Network Conference, University of Huddersfield, 25 June 2017.

Hannell, Briony. 2017b. 'Restoring the Balance: Feminist Meta-Texts and the Productivity of Tumblr's Game of Thrones Fans'. In *Fan Phenomena: Game of Thrones*, edited by Kavita Mudan Finn, 70–81. Bristol: Intellect Books.

Hannell, Briony. 2020a. 'Fan Girls'. In *The International Encyclopedia of Gender, Media, and Communication*, edited by Karen Ross, 1–5. Hoboken, NJ: Wiley-Blackwell.

Hannell, Briony. 2020b. 'Fan Studies and/as Feminist Methodology'. *Transformative Works and Cultures* 33. doi: https://doi.org/10.3983/twc.2020.1689.

Hannell, Briony. 2021. 'Muslim Girlhood, Skam Fandom, and DIY Citizenship'. *Girlhood Studies* 14 (2):46–62.

Harrington, C. Lee, and Denise D. Bielby. 1995. *Soap Fans: Pursuing Pleasure and Making Meaning in Everyday Life*. Philadelphia, PA: Temple University Press.

Harrington, C. Lee, and Denise D. Bielby. 2010. 'Autobiographical Reasoning in Long-Term Fandom'. *Transformative Works and Cultures* 5.

Harris, Anita. 2008a. *Next Wave Cultures: Feminism, Subcultures, Activism*. New York, NY: Routledge.

Harris, Anita. 2008b. 'Young Women, Late Modern Politics, and The Participatory Possibilities of Online Cultures'. *Journal of Youth Studies* 11 (5):481–95. doi: 10.1080/13676260802282950.

Harris, Anita. 2010. 'Mind the Gap: Attitudes and Emergent Feminist Politics since the Third Wave'. *Australian Feminist Studies* 25 (66):475–84. doi: 10.1080/08164649.2010.520684.

Harris, Anita. 2012. 'Online Cultures and Future Girl Citizens'. In *Feminist Media: Participatory Spaces, Networks and Cultural Citizenship*, edited by Elke Zobl and Ricarda Drüeke, 213–25. Bielefeld, Germany: Transcript.

Harvey, Alison. 2020. *Feminist Media Studies*. Cambridge: Polity.

Hellekson, Karen. 2009. 'A Fannish Field of Value: Online Fan Gift Culture'. *Cinema Journal* 48 (4):113–18. doi: 10.1353/cj.0.0140.

Hellekson, Karen, and Kristina Busse. 2006. *Fan Fiction and Fan Communities in the Age of the Internet*. Jefferson, NC: McFarland.

Hellekson, Karen, and Kristina Busse. 2014. *The Fan Fiction Studies Reader*. Iowa City, IA: University of Iowa Press.

Hemmings, Clare. 2011. *Why Stories Matter: The Political Grammar of Feminist Theory*. London: Duke University Press.

Hemmings, Clare. 2012. 'Affective Solidarity: Feminist Reflexivity and Political Transformation'. *Feminist Theory* 13 (2):147–61. doi: 10.1177/1464700112442643.

Hendry, Natalie Ann. 2020a. 'New Ways of Seeing: Tumblr, Young People, and Mental Illness'. In *A Tumblr Book: Platform and Cultures*, edited by Allison McCracken, Alexander Cho, Louisa Stein, and Indira Neill Hoch, 315–25. Ann Arbor, MI: University of Michigan Press.

Hendry, Natalie Ann. 2020b. 'Young Women's Mental Illness and (In-)visible Social Media Practices of Control and Emotional Recognition'. *Social Media + Society* 6 (4):205630512096383. doi: 10.1177/2056305120963832.

Hercus, Cheryl. 2005. *Stepping out of Line: Becoming and Being a Feminist*. New York, NY: Routledge.

Herring, Scott. 2010. *Another Country: Queer Anti-urbanism*. New York: New York University Press.

Hillis, Ken, Susanna Paasonen, and Michael Petit. 2015. 'Introduction: Networks of Transmission: Intensity, Sensation, Value'. In *Networked Affect*, edited by Ken Hillis, Susanna Paasonen, and Michael Petit, 1–24. Cambridge, MA: MIT Press.

Hillman, Serena, Jason Procyk, and Carman Neustaedter. 2014a. '"alksjdf;Lksfd": Tumblr and the Fandom User Experience'. 2014 Conference on Designing Interactive Systems, New York, NY, June 21–5.

Hillman, Serena, Jason Procyk, and Carman Neustaedter. 2014b. '"It's More the Real Me": The Appropriations of Tumblr by Fandoms'. The Grace Hopper Celebration of Women in Computing, Phoenix, AZ, October 8–10.

Hillman, Serena, Jason Procyk, and Carman Neustaedter. 2014c. 'Tumblr Fandoms, Community & Culture'. 17th ACM Conference on Computer Supported Cooperative Work & Social Computing, Baltimore, MD, February 15–19.

Hills, Matt. 2002. *Fan Cultures*. London: Routledge.

Hills, Matt. 2014. 'Returning to "Becoming-a-Fan" Stories: Theorising Transformational Objects and the Emergence/Extension of Fandom'. In *The Ashgate Research Companion to Fan Cultures*, edited by Linda Duits, Koos Zwaan, and Stijn Reijnders. Farnham: Ashgate.

Hinck, Ashley. 2019. *Politics for the Love of Fandom: Fan-Based Citizenship in the Digital Age*. Baton Rouge, LA: Louisiana State University Press.

Hine, Christine. 2015. *Ethnography for the Internet: Embedded, Embodied and Everyday*. London: Bloomsbury.

Ho, Vivian. 2018. "Tumblr's Adult Content Ban Dismays Some Users: "It Was a Space Space"'. *The Guardian*, Last Modified 4 December 2018, accessed 15 June 2020. https://www.theguardian.com/technology/2018/dec/03/tumblr-adult-content-ban-lgbt-community-gender.

Hobson, Janell. 2008. 'Digital Whiteness, Primitive Blackness'. *Feminist Media Studies* 8 (2):111–26. doi: 10.1080/00220380801980467.

Hollows, Joanne, and Rachel Moseley. 2006. *Feminism in Popular Culture*. Oxford: Berg.

Hoodfar, Homa. 1992. "Feminist Anthropology and Critical Pedagogy: The Anthropology of Classrooms' Excluded Voices". *Canadian Journal of Education* 17 (3):303–20.

hooks, bell. 1989. *Talking Back: Thinking Feminist, Thinking Black*. Cambridge, MA: South End Press.

hooks, bell. 1994a. *Ain't I a Woman?* London: Pluto Press.

hooks, bell. 1994b. *Teaching to Transgress: Education as the Practice of Freedom*. New York, NY: Routledge.

hooks, bell. 1996. *Reel to Real: Race, Sex, and Class at the Movies*. New York, NY: Routledge.

hooks, bell. 2003. *Teaching Community: A Pedagogy of Hope*. New York: Routledge.

hooks, bell. 2009. *Belonging: A Culture of Place*. New York, NY: Routledge.

hooks, bell. 2014. *Feminist Theory: From Margin to Center*. London: Routledge.

Hornsby, Elizabeth R. 2020. 'A Case for Critical Methods Sense Making, Race, and Fandom'. In *Fandom, Now in Color*, edited by Rukmini Pande, 17–28. Iowa City, IA: University of Iowa Press.

Ignatieff, Michael. 2001. *Human Rights as Politics and Idolatry*. Princeton, NJ: Princeton University Press.

Ito, Mizuko, Heather Horst, Matteo Bittanti, danah boyd, Becky Herr Stephenson, Patricia Lange, C. J. Pascoe, and Laura Robinson. 2009. *Living and Learning with New Media: Summary of Findings from the Digital Youth Project*. Cambridge, MA: MIT Press.

Jackson, Sue. 2018. 'Young Feminists, Feminism and Digital Media'. *Feminism & Psychology* 28 (1):32–49. doi: 10.1177/0959353517716952.

Jackson, Sue. 2020. '"A Very Basic View of Feminism": Feminist Girls and Meanings of (celebrity) Feminism'. *Feminist Media Studies*:1–19. doi: 10.1080/14680777.2020.1762236.

James, Allison, Chris Jenks, and Alan Prout. 1998. *Theorizing Childhood*. Oxford: Polity.

Jenkins, Henry. 1992. *Textual Poachers: Television Fans and Participatory Culture*. London: Routledge.

Jenkins, Henry. 2006a. *Convergence Culture*. London: New York University Press.

Jenkins, Henry. 2006b. *Fans, Bloggers and Gamers: Exploring Participatory Culture*. London: New York University Press.

Jenkins, Henry. 2007. 'Afterword: The Future of Fandom'. In *Fandom: Identities and Communities in a Mediated World*, edited by Jonathan Gray, Cornel Sandvoss, and C. Lee Harrington, 357–64. New York, NY: New York University Press.

Jenkins, Henry, Sam Ford, and Joshua Green. 2013. *Spreadable Media: Creating Value and Meaning in a Networked Culture*. New York, NY: New York University Press.

Jenkins, Henry, Mizuko Ito, and danah boyd. 2016. *Participatory Culture in a Networked Era: A Conversation on Youth, Learning, Commerce, and Politics*. Cambridge: Polity.

Jenkins, Henry, Gabriel Peters-Lazaro, and Sangita Shresthova. 2020. 'Popular Culture and the Civic Imagination: Foundations'. In *Popular Culture and the Civic Imagination*, edited by Henry Jenkins, Gabriel Peters-Lazaro, and Sangita Shresthova, 1–30. New York, NY: New York University Press.

Jenkins, Henry, and Sangita Shresthova. 2016. '"It's Called Giving a Shit!": What Counts as "Politics?"'. In *By Any Media Necessary: The New Youth Activism*, edited by Henry Jenkins, Sangita Shresthova, Liana Gamber-Thompson, Neta Kligler-Vilenchik, and Arely M Zimmerman, 253–89. New York, NY: New York University Press.

Jenkins, Henry, Sangita Shresthova, Liana Gamber-Thompson, Neta Kligler-Vilenchik, and Arely Zimmerman. 2016. *By Any Media Necessary: The New Youth Activism*. New York, NY: New York University Press.

Jenner, Mareike. 2017. 'Binge-Watching: Video-on-Demand, Quality TV and Mainstreaming Fandom'. *International Journal of Cultural Studies* 20 (3):304–20. doi: 10.1177/1367877915606485.

Jensen, Joli. 1992. 'Fandom as Pathology: The Consequences of Characterization'. In *The Adoring Audience: Fan Culture and Popular Media*, edited by Lisa A. Lewis, 9–29. London: Routledge.

Jiménez, Ileana. 2016. '#SayHerName Loudly: How Black Girls Are Leading #BlackLivesMatter'. *Radical Teacher* 106. doi: 10.5195/rt.2016.310.

Johnson, Derek. 2017. 'Fantagonism: Factions, Institutions, and Constitutive Hegemonies of Fandom'. In *Fandom: Identities and Communities in a Mediated World*, edited by Jonathan Gray, C. Lee Harrington, and Cornel Sandvoss, 369–86. New York: New York University Press.

Johnson, Derek. 2018. 'Fantagonism, Franchising, and Industry Management of Fan Privilege'. In *The Routledge Companion to Media Fandom*, edited by Melissa A. Click and Suzanne Scott. London: Routledge.

Johnson, Merri Lisa. 2003. 'Jane Hocus, Jane Focus: An Introduction'. In *Jane Sexes It Up: True Confessions of Feminist Desire*, edited by Merri Lisa Johnson. New York, NY: Four Walls Eight Windows.

Jones, Daisy. 2022. 'Is Tumblr about to Make a Comeback?'. *Vogue*, accessed 21 December 2022. https://www.vogue.co.uk/arts-and-lifestyle/article/tumblr-renaissance.

Jun, Li. 2021. 'In the Name of #RiceBunny: Legacy, Strategy, and Efficacy of the Chinese #MeToo Movement'. In *The Routledge Handbook of the Politics of the #MeToo Movement*, edited by Giti Chandra and Irma Erlingsdóttir, 343–59. Oxon: Routledge.

Kanai, Akane. 2017. 'Girlfriendship and Sameness: Affective Belonging in a Digital Intimate Public'. *Journal of Gender Studies* 26 (3):293–306. doi: 10.1080/09589236.2017.1281108.

Kanai, Akane. 2019. *Gender and Relatability in Digital Culture: Managing Affect, Intimacy and Value*. Cham, Switzerland: Palgrave Macmillan.

Kanai, Akane. 2020a. 'Between the Perfect and the Problematic: Everyday Femininities, Popular Feminism, and the Negotiation of Intersectionality'. *Cultural Studies* 34 (1):25–48. doi: 10.1080/09502386.2018.1559869.

Kanai, Akane. 2020b. 'Between the Perfect and the Problematic: Everyday Femininities, Popular Feminism, and the Negotiation of Intersectionality'. *Cultural Studies*:1–24. doi: 10.1080/09502386.2018.1559869.

Kanai, Akane, and Caitlin McGrane. 2020. 'Feminist Filter Bubbles: Ambivalence, Vigilance and Labour'. *Information, Communication & Society*:1–16. doi: 10.1080/1369118X.2020.1760916.

Kaplan, Ann E. 2003. 'Feminist Futures: Trauma, the Post-9/11 World and a Fourth Feminism?' *Journal of International Women's Studies* 4 (2):46–59.

Keller, Jessalynn. 2012a. '"It's a Hard Job Being an Indian Feminist:" Mapping Girls' "Close Encounters" on the Feminist Blogosphere'. In *Feminist Media: Participatory Spaces, Networks, and Cultural Citizenship* edited by Elke Zobl and Ricarda Drüeke, 136–45. Bielefeld, Germany: Transcript.

Keller, Jessalynn. 2012b. 'Virtual Feminisms: Girls' Blogging Communities, Feminist Activism, and Participatory Politics'. *Information, Communication & Society* 15 (3):429–47. doi: 10.1080/1369118X.2011.642890.

Keller, Jessalynn. 2015. 'Girl Power's Last Chance? Tavi Gevinson, Feminism, and Popular Media Culture'. *Continuum* 29 (2):274–85. doi: 10.1080/10304312.2015.1022947.

Keller, Jessalynn. 2016a. *Girls' Feminist Blogging in a Postfeminist Age*. London: Routledge.

Keller, Jessalynn. 2016b. 'Making Activism Accessible: Exploring Girls' Blogs as Sites of Contemporary Feminist Activism'. In *Girlhood and the Politics of Place*, edited by Claudia Mitchell and Carrie Rentschler, 261–78. Oxford: Berghahn Books.

Keller, Jessalynn. 2019. '"Oh, She's a Tumblr Feminist": Exploring the Platform Vernacular of Girls' Social Media Feminisms'. *Social Media + Society* 5 (3):2056305119867442. doi: 10.1177/2056305119867442.

Keller, Jessalynn. 2020. 'A Politics of Snap: Teen Vogue's Public Feminism'. *Signs* 45 (4):817–43. doi: 10.1086/707797.

Keller, Jessalynn, Kaitlynn Mendes, and Jessica Ringrose. 2016. 'Speaking "Unspeakable Things": Documenting Digital Feminist Responses to Rape Culture'. *Journal of Gender Studies*:1–15. doi: 10.1080/09589236.2016.1211511.

Keller, Jessalynn, and Jessica Ringrose. 2015. '"But Then Feminism Goes out the Window!": Exploring Teenage Girls' Critical Response to Celebrity Feminism'. *Celebrity Studies* 6 (1):132–5. doi: 10.1080/19392397.2015.1005402.

Keller, Jessalynn, and Maureen Ryan. 2015. 'Call for Chapters: Emergent Feminisms and the Challenge to Postfeminist Media Culture', accessed 31 March 2017. http://arcyp. ca/archives/4244.

Keller, Jessalynn, and Maureen Ryan. 2018. *Emergent Feminisms: Complicating a Postfeminist Media Culture*. London: Routledge.

Kellner, Douglas, and Jeff Share. 2007. 'Critical Media Literacy, Democracy, and the Reconstruction of Education'. In *Media Literacy: A Reader*, edited by Donaldo Macedo and Shirley R. Steinbeirg, 3–23. New York, NY: Peter Lang.

Kelly, Liz, Sheila Burton, and Linda Regan. 1994. 'Researching Women's Lives or Studying Women's Oppression? Reflections on What Constitutes Feminist Research'. In *Researching Women's Lives from a Feminist Perspective*, edited by Mary Maynard and June Purvis, 27–48. Oxon: Routledge.

Kennedy, Tracy. 2007. 'The Personal Is Political: Feminist Blogging and Virtual Consciousness Raising'. *The Scholar and Feminist Online* 5:(2).

Kenney, Moria. 2001. *Mapping Gay L.A.: The Intersection of Place and Politics*. Philadelphia, PA: Temple University Press.

Kim, Crystal, and Jessica Ringrose. 2018. '"Stumbling upon Feminism": Teenage Girls' Forays into Digital and School-Based Feminisms'. *Girlhood Studies* 11 (2):46–62. doi: 10.3167/ghs.2018.110205.

Kim, Jinsook. 2017. '#iamafeminist as the "Mother Tag": Feminist Identification and Activism against Misogyny on Twitter in South Korea'. *Feminist Media Studies*:1–17. doi: 10.1080/14680777.2017.1283343.

Kohnen, Melanie. 2018. 'Tumblr Pedagogies'. In *A Companion to Media Fandom and Fan Studies*, edited by Paul Booth, 456–77. Oxford: Wiley-Blackwell.

Kolko, Beth. 2000. 'Erasing @race: Going White in the (Inter)face'. In *Race in Cyberspace*, edited by Beth E. Kolko, Lisa Nakamura, and Gilbert B. Rodman, 213–32. New York, NY: Routledge.

Korobkova, Ksenia. 2014. Schooling the Directioners: Connected Learning and Identity-Making in the One Direction Fandom. In *The Digital Media and Learning Research Hub Reports on Connected Learning*. Irvine, CA: Digital Media and Learning Research Hub.

Kuntsman, Adi. 2012. 'Introduction: Affective Fabrics of Digital Cultures'. In *Digital Cultures and the Politics of Emotion: Feelings, Affect and Technological Change*, edited by Athina Karatzogianni and Adi Kuntsman. London: Palgrave Macmillan.

Kuurne, Kaisa, and Atte Vieno. 2022. 'Developing the Concept of Belonging Work for Social Research'. *Sociology (Oxford)* 56 (2):280–96. doi: 10.1177/00380385211037867.

Lähdesmäki, Tuuli, Tuija Saresma, Kaisa Hiltunen, Saara Jäntti, Nina Sääskilahti, Antti Vallius, and Kaisa Ahvenjärvi. 2016. 'Fluidity and Flexibility of "Belonging"'. *Acta Sociologica* 59 (3):233–47. doi: 10.1177/0001699316633099.

Lamerichs, Nicolle. 2018. *Productive Fandom: Intermediality and Affective Reception in Fan Cultures*. Amsterdam: Amsterdam University Press.

Larson, Kyle Ross. 2016. 'Counterpublic Intellectualism: Feminist Consciousness-Raising Rhetorics on Tumblr'. Master of Arts, Department of English, Miami University.

Latina, Daniela, and Stevie Docherty. 2014. 'Trending Participation, Trending Exclusion?' *Feminist Media Studies* 14 (6):1103–5. doi: 10.1080/14680777.2014.975449.

Lave, Jean, and Etienne Wenger. 1991. *Situated Learning: Legitimate Peripheral Participation*. Cambridge: Cambridge University Press.

Lawrence, Emilie, and Jessica Ringrose. 2018. '@NoToFeminism, #FeministsAreUgly and Misandry Memes: How Social Media Feminist Humour Is Calling out Anti-feminism'. In *Emergent Feminisms: Complicating a Postfeminist Media Culture*, edited by Jessalynn Keller and Gery W. Ryan, 211–32. London: Routledge.

Leavenworth, Maria Lindgren. 2015. 'The Paratext of Fan Fiction'. *Narrative* 23 (1):40–60. doi: 10.1353/nar.2015.0004.

Lenhart, Amanda. 2015. Teens, Social Media & Technology Overview 2015. In *Pew Internet and American Life Project*. Washington, DC: Pew Research Center.

Lesko, Nancy. 1996. 'Denaturalizing Adolescence: The Politics of Contemporary Representations'. *Youth & Society* 28 (2):139–61.

Lewis, Lisa. 1992. *The Adoring Audience: Fan Culture and Popular Media*. London: Routledge.

Lewis, Ruth, and Susan Marine. 2015. 'Weaving a Tapestry, Compassionately: Toward an Understanding of Young Women's Feminisms'. *Feminist Formations* 27 (1):118–40.

Lewis, Ruth, Susan Marine, and Kathryn Kenney. 2016. '"I Get Together with My Friends and Try to Change It". Young Feminist Students Resist "Laddism", "Rape Culture" and "Everyday Sexism"'. *Journal of Gender Studies*: 1–17. doi: 10.1080/09589236.2016.1175925.

Liao, Shannon. 2019. 'After the Porn Ban, Tumblr Users Have Ditched the Platform as Promised'. Last Modified 14 March 2019, accessed 15 June. https://www.theverge.com/2019/3/14/18266013/tumblr-porn-ban-lost-users-down-traffic.

Lincoln, Siân. 2014. 'Young People and Mediated Private Space'. In *Mediated Youth Cultures: The Internet, Belonging and New Cultural Configurations*, edited by Andy Bennett and Brady Robards, 42–58. Basingstoke: Palgrave Macmillan.

Livingstone, Sonia, and Julian Sefton-Green. 2016. *The Class: Living and Learning in a Digital Age*. New York, NY: New York University Press.

Lorde, Audre. 1984. *Sister Outsider: Essays and Speeches*. Trumansburg, NY: Crossing Press.

Losh, Elizabeth. 2014. 'Hashtag Feminism and Twitter Activism in India'. *Social Epistemology Review and Reply Collective* 3 (3):11–22.

Lothian, Alexis, Kristina Busse, and Robin Anne Reid. 2007. '"Yearning Void and Infinite Potential": Online Slash Fandom as Queer Female Space'. *English Language Notes* 45 (2):103–11.

Loza, Susana. 2014. 'Hashtag Feminism, #SolidarityIsForWhiteWomen, and the Other #FemFuture'. *Ada: A Journal of Gender, New Media, and Technology* (5).

Lugones, Maria. 1990. 'Playfulness, "World"-Travelling, and Loving Perception'. In *Making Face, Making Soul: Haciendo Caras: Creative and Critical Perspectives by Feminists of Color*, edited by Gloria Anzaldúa, 390–402. San Francisco, CA: Aunt Lute Books.

Madden, Emma. 2019. 'How Tumblr Helped Queer Mainstream Pop'. Pitchfork, accessed 06 November 2019. https://pitchfork.com/features/article/2010s-how-tumblr-culture-legitimized-queer-fandom-frank-ocean-troye-sivan-one-direction/.

Madden, Mary, Amanda Lenhart, Sandra Cortesi, Urs Gasser, Maeve Duggan, Aaron Smith, and Meredith Beaton. 2013. Teens, Social Media, and Privacy. In *Pew Internet and American Life Project*. Washington, DC: Pew Research Center.

Marine, Susan, and Ruth Lewis. 2014. '"I'm in This for Real": Revisiting Young Women's Feminist Becoming'. *Women's Studies International Forum* 47:11–22. doi: 10.1016/j.wsif.2014.06.008.

Marinucci, Mimi. 2010. *Feminism Is Queer*. London: Zed Books.

Marwick, Alice, and danah boyd. 2010. 'I Tweet Honestly, I Tweet Passionately: Twitter Users, Context Collapse, and the Imagined Audience'. *New Media & Society* 13 (1):114–33. doi: 10.1177/1461444810365313.

Marwick, Alice, and danah boyd. 2014. 'Networked Privacy: How Teenagers Negotiate Context in Social Media'. *New Media & Society* 16 (7):1–17. doi: 10.1177/1461444814543995.

Marwick, Alice, and Robyn Caplan. 2018. 'Drinking Male Tears: Language, the Manosphere, and Networked Harassment'. *Feminist Media Studies* 18 (4):543–59. doi: 10.1080/14680777.2018.1450568.

Massanari, Adrienne. 2017. '#Gamergate and the Fappening: How Reddit's Algorithm, Governance, and Culture Support Toxic Technocultures'. *New Media & Society* 19 (3):329–46. doi: 10.1177/1461444815608807.

Massanari, Adrienne, and Shira Chess. 2018. 'Attack of the 50-foot Social Justice Warrior: The Discursive Construction of SJW Memes as the Monstrous Feminine'. *Feminist Media Studies* 18 (4):525–42. doi: 10.1080/14680777.2018.1447333.

Maxfield, Mary. 2016. 'History Retweeting Itself: Imperial Feminist Appropriations of "Bring Back Our Girls"'. *Feminist Media Studies* 16 (5):886–900. doi: 10.1080/14680777.2015.1116018.

May, Vanessa. 2011. 'Self, Belonging and Social Change'. *Sociology* 45 (3):363–78. doi: 10.1177/0038038511399624.

May, Vanessa. 2013. *Connecting Self to Society: Belonging in a Changing World.* Basingstoke: Palgrave Macmillan.

Mazzarella, Sharon, and Norma Pecora. 2007. 'Revisiting Girls' Studies'. *Journal of Children and Media* 1 (2):105–25. doi: 10.1080/17482790701339118.

McAdams, Dan. 2011. 'Narrative Identity'. In *Handbook of Identity Theory and Research*, edited by Seth Schwartz, Koen Luyckx, and Vivian Vignoles, 99–115. New York, NY: Springer.

McAdams, Dan, Ruthellen Josselson, and Amia Lieblich. 2006. *Identity and Story: Creating Self in Narrative.* Washington, DC: American Psychological Association.

McCracken, Allison. 2017. 'Tumblr Youth Subcultures and Media Engagement'. *Cinema Journal* 57 (1):151–61. doi: 10.1353/cj.2017.0061.

McCracken, Allison, Alexander Cho, Louisa Stein, and Indira Neill Hoch. 2020. *A Tumblr Book: Platform and Cultures.* Ann Arbor, MI: University of Michigan Press.

McIntosh, Peggy. 1989. 'White Privilege: Unpacking the Invisible Knapsack'. *Peace and Freedom* July/August:10–12.

McLaughlin, Caitlin, and Jessica Vitak. 2011. 'Norm Evolution and Violation on Facebook'. *New Media & Society* 14 (2):299–315. doi: 10.1177/1461444811412712.

McRobbie, Angela. 2009. *The Aftermath of Feminism.* Thousand Oaks, CA: Sage.

McRobbie, Angela. 2015. 'Notes on the Perfect'. *Australian Feminist Studies* 30 (83):3. doi: 10.1080/08164649.2015.1011485.

Megarry, Jessica. 2014. 'Online Incivility or Sexual Harassment? Conceptualising Women's Experiences in the Digital Age'. *Women's Studies International Forum* 47:46–55. doi: 10.1016/j.wsif.2014.07.012.

Mendes, Kaitlynn. 2015. *SlutWalk: Feminism, Activism and Media.* Basingstoke: Palgrave Macmillan.

Mendes, Kaitlynn, Jessalynn Keller, and Jessica Ringrose. 2019. *Digital Feminist Activism: Girls and Women Fight Back against Rape Culture.* Oxford: Oxford University Press.

Meraz, Sharon, and Zizi Papacharissi. 2013. 'Networked Gatekeeping and Networked Framing on #Egypt'. *The International Journal of Press/Politics* 18 (2):138–66. doi: 10.1177/1940161212474472.

Merrick, Helen. 2009. *The Secret Feminist Cabal: A Cultural History of Science Fiction Feminisms.* Seattle, WA: Aqueduct Press.

Miller, Linn. 2003. 'Belonging to Country – a Philosophical Anthropology'. *Journal of Australian Studies* 27 (76):215–23. doi: 10.1080/14443050309387839.

Miltner, Kate M., and Ysabel Gerrard. 2022. "'Tom Had Us All Doing Front-End Web Development": A Nostalgic (Re)imagining of Myspace'. *Internet Histories* 6 (1–2):48–67. doi: 10.1080/24701475.2021.1985836.

Min, Wonjung, Dal Yong Jin, and Benjamin Han. 2018. 'Transcultural Fandom of the Korean Wave in Latin America: Through the Lens of Cultural Intimacy and Affinity Space'. *Media, Culture & Society* 41 (5):604–19. doi: 10.1177/0163443718799403.

Mitchell, Claudia, and Jacqueline Reid-Walsh. 2004. 'Girls' Websites: A Virtual "Room of One's Own"?' In *All About the Girl: Culture, Power, and Identity*, edited by Anita Harris, 173–82. London: Routledge.

Monaghan, Whitney. 2022. 'Feminism at the Movies: Sex, Gender, and Identity in Contemporary American Teen Cinema'. *Feminist Media Studies*:1–16. doi: 10.1080/14680777.2022.2108481.

Moon, Dreama. 1999. 'White Enculturation and Bourgeois Ideology: The Discursive Production of "Good (White) Girls"'. In *Whiteness: The Communication of Social Identity*, edited by T. K. Nakayama and Judith Martin, 177–97. London: Sage.

Morimoto, Lori. 2018. 'Ontological Security and the Politics of Transcultural Fandom'. In *A Companion to Media Fandom and Fan Studies*, edited by Paul Booth, 342–64. Oxford: Wiley-Blackwell.

Morimoto, Lori. 2019. It's a Thing! Podcast. In *Episode 5: Louisa Stein*.

Morimoto, Lori, and Bertha Chin. 2017. 'Reimagining the Imagined Community: Online Media Fandoms in the Age of Global Convergence'. In *Fandom: Identities and Communities in a Mediated World*, edited by Jonathan Gray, Cornel Sandvoss, and C. Lee Harrington, 174–88. New York, NY: New York University Press.

Mulvey, Laura. 1975. 'Visual Pleasure and Narrative Cinema'. *Screen* 16:6–18.

Murphy, Mark. 2011. 'The Ties That Bind: Distinction, Recognition and the Relational'. *International Journal of Interdisciplinary Social Sciences* 5 (10):103–16.

Nadkarni, Ashwini, and Stefan Hofmann. 2012. 'Why Do People Use Facebook?' *Personality and Individual Differences* 52 (3):243–49. doi: https://doi.org/10.1016/j.paid.2011.11.007.

Nagle, Angela. 2017. *Kill All Normies: Online Culture Wars from 4chan and Tumblr to Trump and the Alt-Right*. Winchester: Zero Books.

Nakamura, Lisa. 2002. *Cybertypes: Race, Ethnicity, and Identity on the Internet*. London: Routledge.

Nakamura, Lisa. 2015. 'The Unwanted Labour of Social Media: Women of Colour Call Out Culture as Venture Community Management'. *New Formations* 86 (86):106–12. doi: 10.3898/NEWF.86.06.2015.

Naples, Nancy. 2013. 'Sustaining Democracy: Localization, Globalization, and Feminist Praxis'. *Sociological Forum* 28 (4):657–81. doi: 10.1111/socf.12054.

Narai, Ria. 2017. 'Female-Centered Fan Fiction as Homoaffection in Fan Communities'. *Transformative Works and Cultures* (24). doi: 10.3983/twc.2017.1014.

Nash, Jennifer. 2019. *Black Feminism Reimagined: After Intersectionality*. Durham, NC: Duke University Press.

Naylor, Alex. 2016. "'My Skin Has Turned to Porcelain, to Ivory, to Steel": Feminist Fan Discourses, Game of Thrones, and the Problem of Sansa'. In *The Woman Fantastic in Contemporary American Media Culture*, edited by Elyce Rae Helford, Shiloh Carroll, Sarah Gray, and Michael R. Howard, 39–60. Jackson, MI: University Press of Mississippi.

Negra, Diane. 2004. "'Quality Postfeminism?": Sex and the Single Girl on HBO'. *Genders* (39).

Negra, Diane. 2014. 'Claiming Feminism: Commentary, Autobiography and Advice Literature for Women in the Recession'. *Journal of Gender Studies* 23 (3):275–86. doi: 10.1080/09589236.2014.913977.

Ng, Eve. 2017. 'Between Text, Paratext, and Context: Queerbaiting and the Contemporary Media Landscape'. *Transformative Works and Cultures* (24).

Ngai, Sianne. 2005. *Ugly Feelings*. Cambridge, MA: Harvard University Press.

Nikunen, Kaarina. 2007. 'The Intermedial Practises of Fandom'. *Nordicom Review* 28 (2):111–28.

Nissenbaum, Helen. 2010. *Privacy in Context: Technology, Policy, and the Integrity of Social Life*. Stanford, CA: Stanford University Press.

Noble, Safiya Umoja, and Brendesha Tynes. 2016. *The Intersectional Internet: Race, Sex, Class, and Culture Online*. New York, NY: Peter Lang.

obsession_inc. 2009. 'Affirmational Fandom vs. Transformational Fandom'. Dreamwidth, Last Modified 1 June 2009, accessed 17 April 2017. https://obsession-inc.dreamwidth.org/82589.html.

Olufemi, Lola. 2020. *Feminism Interrupted: Disrupting Power*. London: Pluto Press.

Omolade, Barbara. 1987. 'A Black Feminist Pedagogy'. *Women's Studies Quarterly* 15 (3/4):32–9.

Ortega, Mariana. 2009. 'Being Lovingly, Knowingly Ignorant: White Feminism and Women of Colour'. *Hypatia* 21 (3):56–74.

Pande, Rukmini. 2018a. *Squee from the Margins: Fandom and Race*. Iowa City, IA: University of Iowa Press.

Pande, Rukmini. 2018b. 'Who Do You Mean by "Fan?" Decolonizing Media Fandom Identity'. In *A Companion to Media Fandom and Fan Studies*, edited by Paul Booth, 417–34. Oxford: Wiley-Blackwell.

Pande, Rukmini. 2020a. *Fandom, Now in Color: A Collection of Voices*. Iowa City, IA: Iowa University Press.

Pande, Rukmini. 2020b. 'Introduction'. In *Fandom, Now in Color*, edited by Rukmini Pande, 1–14. Iowa City, IA: University of Iowa Press.

Papacharissi, Zizi. 2014. *Affective Publics: Sentiment, Technology, and Politics*. New York, NY: Oxford University Press.

Patai, Daphne. 2014. 'Feminist Pedagogy Reconsidered'. In *Handbook of Feminist Research: Theory and Praxis*, edited by Sharlene Nagy Hesse-Biber, 557–82. Thousand Oaks, CA: Sage.

Pedwell, Carolyn, and Anne Whitehead. 2012. 'Affecting Feminism: Questions of Feeling in Feminist Theory'. *Feminist Theory* 13 (2):115–29. doi: 10.1177/1464700112442635.

Penley, Constance. 1997. *NASA/Trek: Popular Science and Sex in America*. London: Verso.

Phelan, Sean. 2019. 'Neoliberalism, the Far Right, and the Disparaging of "Social Justice Warriors"'. *Communication, Culture & Critique* 12 (4):455–75. doi: 10.1093/ccc/tcz040.

Phillips, Tom. 2013. 'Fandom and Beyond: Community, Culture and Kevin Smith Fandom'. Doctor of Philosophy, School of Film, Television and Media Studies, University of East Anglia.

Phipps, Alison. 2020. *Me, Not You: The Trouble with Mainstream Feminism*. Manchester: Manchester University Press.

Phipps, Alison, Jessica Ringrose, Emma Renold, and Carolyn Jackson. 2017. 'Rape Culture, Lad Culture and Everyday Sexism: Researching, Conceptualizing and Politicizing New Mediations of Gender and Sexual Violence'. *Journal of Gender Studies*:1–8. doi: 10.1080/09589236.2016.1266792.

Piepmeier, Alison. 2009. *Girl Zines: Making Media, Doing Feminism*. New York, NY: New York University Press.

Pilipets, Elena, and Susanna Paasonen. 2022. 'Nipples, Memes, and Algorithmic Failure: NSFW Critique of Tumblr Censorship'. *New Media & Society* 24 (6):1459–80. doi: 10.1177/1461444820979280.

Podmore, Julie A., and Alison L. Bain. 2021. 'Whither Queer Suburbanisms? Beyond Heterosuburbia and Queer Metronormativities'. *Progress in Human Geography* 45 (5):1254–77. doi: 10.1177/0309132520979744.

Pomerantz, Shauna. 2008. *Girls, Style, and School Identities: Dressing the Part*. New York, NY: Palgrave Macmillan.

Popova, Milena. 2020. 'How Tumblr's Temporal Functions Shape Community Memory and Knowledge'. In *A Tumblr Book: Platform and Cultures*, edited by Allison McCracken, Alexander Cho, Louisa Stein, and Indira Neill Hoch, 81–90. Ann Arbor, MI: University of Michigan Press.

Portwood-Stacer, Laura. 2012. 'Media Refusal and Conspicuous Non-consumption: The Performative and Political Dimensions of Facebook Abstention'. *New Media & Society* 15 (7):1041–57. doi: 10.1177/1461444812465139.

Preece, Jenny, Blair Nonnecke, and Dorine Andrews. 2004. 'The Top Five Reasons for Lurking: Improving Community Experiences for Everyone'. *Computers in Human Behavior* 20 (2):201–23. doi: 10.1016/j.chb.2003.10.015.

Preissle, Judith, and Yuri Han. 2012. 'Feminist Research Ethics'. In *Handbook of Feminist Research: Theory and Praxis*, edited by Sharlene Nagy Hesse-Biber, 583–605. Thousand Oaks, CA: Sage.

Price, L. 2019. 'Fandom, Folksonomies and Creativity: The Case of the Archive of Our Own'. In *The Human Position in an Artificial World: Creativity, Ethics and AI in Knowledge Organization*, 11–37. Germany: Ergon Verlag. doi: 10.5771/9783956505508-11.

Prins, Annelot. 2017. 'Who Run the World? Feminism and Commodification in Beyonce's Star Text'. *Digressions* 2 (2):29–44.

Probyn, Elspeth. 1996. *Outside Belongings: Disciplines, Nations and the Place of Sex*. London: Routledge.

Probyn, Elspeth. 2005. *Blush: Faces of Shame*. Minneapolis, MN: University of Minnesota Press.

Puwar, Nirmal. 2004. *Space Invaders: Race, Gender and Bodies Out of Place*. Oxford: Berg.

Quinn, Rebecca Dakin. 1997. 'An Open Letter to Institutional Mothers'. In *Generations: Academic Feminists in Dialogue*, edited by Devoney Looser and Ann E. Kaplan, 174–82. Minneapolis, MN: University of Minnesota Press.

Ratcliffe, Krista. 2005. *Rhetorical Listening: Identification, Gender, Whiteness*. Carbondale, SI: Southern Illinois University Press.

Rattansi, Ali, and Ann Phoenix. 2005. 'Rethinking Youth Identities: Modernist and Postmodernist Frameworks'. *Identity* 5 (2):97–123. doi: 10.1207/s1532706xid0502_2.

Reilly, Maura. 2018. *Curatorial Activism: Towards an Ethics of Curating*. New York, NY: Thames & Hudson.

Reinhard, CarrieLynn. 2018. *Fractured Fandoms: Contentious Communications in Fan Communities*. London: Lexington Books.

Renninger, Bryce. 2015. '"Where I Can Be Myself … Where I Can Speak My Mind": Networked Counterpublics in a Polymedia Environment'. *New Media & Society* 17 (9):1513–29. doi: 10.1177/1461444814530095.

Rentschler, Carrie. 2014. 'Rape Culture and the Feminist Politics of Social Media'. *Girlhood Studies* 7 (1):65–82.

Rentschler, Carrie, and Samantha Thrift. 2015. 'Doing Feminism in the Network: Networked Laughter and the "Binders Full of Women" Meme'. *Feminist Theory* 16 (3):329–59. doi: 10.1177/1464700115604136.

Retallack, Hanna, Jessica Ringrose, and Emilie Lawrence. 2016. '"Fuck Your Body Image": Teen Girls' Twitter and Instagram Feminism in and around School'. In *Learning Bodies*, edited by Julia Coffey, Shelley Budgeon, and Helen Cahill, 85–103. Singapore: Springer.

Riddel, Kathleen. 2021. '"My Whole World Shifted": Identity and Transformation in Becoming-a-Fan Narratives'. *Journal of Fandom Studies* 9 (3):195–211.

Rinaldi, Carlina. 2006. *In Dialogue with Reggio Emilia: Listening, Researching and Learning*. London: Routledge.

Ringrose, Jessica, and Emma Renold. 2016. 'Teen Feminist Killjoys? Mapping Girls' Affective Encounters with Femininity, Sexuality, and Feminism at School'.

In *Girlhood and the Politics of Place*, edited by Claudia Mitchell and Carrie Rentschler, 104–21. Oxford: Berghahn Books.

Rivers, Nicola. 2017. *Postfeminism(s) and the Arrival of the Fourth Wave:* Turning Tides: Palgrave Macmillan.

Robards, Brady, Paul Byron, Brendan Churchill, Benjamin Hanckel, and Son Vivienne. 2020. 'Tumblr as a Space of Learning, Connecting, and Identity Formation for LGBTIQ+ Young People'. In *A Tumblr Book: Platform and Cultures*, edited by Allison McCracken, Alexander Cho, Louisa Stein, and Indira Neill Hoch, 281–92. Ann Arbor, MI: University of Michigan Press.

Romano, Aja. 2014. 'Untitled Blog Post'. dailydot.tumblr.com, accessed 17 June. https://dailydot.tumblr.com/post/106237217070/feminism-isnt-a-fandom-equality-is-not-the.

Romano, Aja. 2018. 'Tumblr Is Banning Adult Content. It's about So Much More than Porn', Last Modified 17 December 2018, accessed 15 June 2020. https://www.vox.com/2018/12/4/18124120/tumblr-porn-adult-content-ban-user-backlash.

Rottenberg, Catherine. 2018. *The Rise of Neoliberal Feminism*. New York, NY: Oxford University Press.

Rowley, Christina. 2010. 'An Intertextual Analysis of Vietnam War Films and US Presidential Speeches'. Doctor of Education, School of Sociology, Politics and International Studies, School of Experimental Psychology, University of Bristol.

Russo, Julie, and Eve Ng. 2017. 'Envisioning Queer Female Fandom'. *Transformative Works and Cultures* (24). doi: 10.3983/twc.2017.1168.

Safronova, Valeriya. 2014. 'Millennials and the Age of Tumblr Activism'. *The New York Times*, accessed 30 June 2020. https://www.nytimes.com/2014/12/21/style/millennials-and-the-age-of-tumblr-activism.html.

Salter, Michael. 2013. 'Justice and Revenge in Online Counter-Publics: Emerging Responses to Sexual Violence in the Age of Social Media'. *Crime, Media, Culture* 9 (3):225–242.

Sandvoss, Cornel. 2005. *Fans: The Mirror of Consumption*. Oxford: Polity.

Savage, Michael, Gaynor Bagnall, and Brian Longhurst. 2005. *Globalization and Belonging*. London: Sage.

Scharff, Christina. 2012. *Repudiating Feminism: Young Women in a Neoliberal World*. London: Routledge.

Scharff, Christina. 2016. 'The Psychic Life of Neoliberalism: Mapping the Contours of Entrepreneurial Subjectivity'. *Theory, Culture & Society* 33 (6):107–22. doi: 10.1177/0263276415590164.

Schilt, Kristen, and Jenifer Bratter. 2015. 'From Multiracial to Transgender?: Assessing Attitudes toward Expanding Gender Options on the US Census'. *TSQ: Transgender Studies Quarterly* 2 (1):77–100. doi: 10.1215/23289252-2848895.

Scott, Suzanne. 2019. *Fake Geek Girls: Fandom, Gender, and the Convergence Culture Industry*. New York, NY: New York University Press.

Sedgwick, Eve. 1990. *Epistemology of the Closet*. Berkeley, CA: University of California Press.

Sharp, Megan, and Barrie Shannon. 2020. 'Becoming Non-binary: An Exploration of Gender Work in Tumblr'. In *Gender, Sexuality and Race in the Digital Age*, edited by D. Nicole Farris, D'Lane R. Compton, and Andrea P. Herrera, 137–50. Cham: Springer International Publishing.

Shetty, Parinita. 2022. 'Marginally Fannish: Fan Podcasts as Sites of Public Pedagogy and Intersectional Education'. Doctor of Philosophy, School of Education, University of Leeds.

Shkedi, Asher. 2004. 'Narrative Survey: A Methodology for Studying Multiple Populations'. *Narrative Inquiry* 14 (1):87–111. doi: https://doi.org/10.1075/ni.14.1.05shk.

Shorey, Samantha. 2015. 'Fragmentary Girls: Selective Expression on the Tumblr Platform'. Master of Arts, Department of Communication, University of Massachusetts.

Shrewsbury, Carolyn. 1993. 'What Is Feminist Pedagogy?' *Women's Studies Quarterly* 21 (3/4):8–16.

Sills, Sophie, Chelsea Pickens, Karishma Beach, Lloyd Jones, Octavia Calder-Dawe, Paulette Benton-Greig, and Nicola Gavey. 2016. 'Rape Culture and Social Media: Young Critics and a Feminist Counterpublic'. *Feminist Media Studies* 16 (6):935–51. doi: 10.1080/14680777.2015.1137962.

Skeggs, Beverley. 1997. *Formations of Class and Gender*. London: Sage.

Skeggs, Beverley. 2019. 'The Forces that Shape Us: The Entangled Vine of Gender, Race and Class'. *The Sociological Review* 67 (1):28–35. doi: 10.1177/0038026118821334.

Smith-Prei, Carrie, and Maria Stehle. 2016. *Awkward Politics: Technologies of Popfeminist Activism*. London: McGill-Queen's University Press.

Smith, Stacy, Marc Choueiti, Katherine Pieper, Traci Gillig, Carmen Lee, and Dylan DeLuca. 2015. Inequality in 700 Popular Films: Examining Portrayals of Gender, Race, & LGBT Status from 2007 to 2014. In *Media, Diversity & Social Change Initiative*. Los Angeles, CA: USC Annenberg, School for Communication and Journalism.

Sobande, Francesca, Akane Kanai, and Natasha Zeng. 2022. 'The Hypervisibility and Discourses of "Wokeness" in Digital Culture'. *Media, Culture & Society*: 01634437221117490. doi: 10.1177/01634437221117490.

Solomon, Deborah. 2009. 'Fourth-Wave Feminism'. *The New York Times*, accessed 21 February 2017. http://www.nytimes.com/2009/11/15/magazine/15fob-q4-t.html.

Sommerlad, Joe. 2018. 'Russian Hackers Used Tumblr to Spread "Fake News" during US Election, Company Reveals'. *The Independent*, Last Modified 26 March 2018, accessed 15 June 2020. https://www.independent.co.uk/life-style/gadgets-and-tech/news/tumblr-russian-hacking-us-presidential-election-fake-news-internet-research-agency-propaganda-bots-a8274321.html.

Stanley, Liz, and Sue Wise. 1993. *Breaking out Again: Feminist Ontology and Epistemology*. 2nd edn. London: Routledge.

Stein, Louisa. 2015. *Millennial Fandom: Television Audiences in the Transmedia Age*. Iowa, IA: University of Iowa Press.

Stein, Louisa. 2017. '"Fandom/Resistance" Keynote'. Fan Studies Network Conference, University of Huddersfield, 24 June 2017.

Stein, Louisa. 2018. 'Tumblr Fan Aesthetics'. In *The Routledge Companion to Media Fandom*, edited by Melissa A. Click and Suzanne Scott, 86–97. Oxon: Routledge.

Stein, Louisa. 2019. 'Dissatisfaction and Glee: On Emotional Range in Fandom and Feels Culture'. In *Anti-fandom: Dislike and Hate in the Digital Age*, edited by Melissa A. Click, 81–101. New York: New York University Press.

Suler, John. 2004. 'The Online Disinhibition Effect'. *CyberPsychology & Behavior* 7 (3):321–26.

Taft, Jessica. 2011. *Rebel Girls: Youth Activism and Social Change across the Americas*. New York, NY: New York University Press.

Taft, Jessica. 2017. 'Teenage Girls' Narratives of Becoming Activists'. *Contemporary Social Science* 12 (1–2):27–39. doi: 10.1080/21582041.2017.1324173.

Taylor, Anthea. 2016. *Celebrity and the Feminist Blockbuster*. Basingstoke: Palgrave Macmillan.

Taylor, Lisa, and Jasmin Zine. 2014. 'Introduction: The Contested Imaginaries of Reading Muslim Women and Muslim Women Reading Back'. In *Muslim Women, Transnational Feminism and the Ethics of Pedagogy: Contested Imaginaries in Post-9/11 Cultural Practice*, edited by Lisa K. Taylor and Jasmin Zine, 1–22. London: Routledge.

Tennent, Emma, and Sue Jackson. 2017. '"Exciting" and "Borderline Offensive": Bloggers, Binaries, and Celebrity Feminism'. *Feminist Media Studies*:1–14. doi: 10.1080/14680777.2017.1391858.

The Roestone Collective. 2014. 'Safe Space: Towards a Reconceptualization'. *Antipode* 46 (5):1346–65. doi: 10.1111/anti.12089.

Thelandersson, Fredrika. 2013. 'Tumblr Feminism: Third-Wave Subjectivities in Practice'. MA Media, Culture, and Communication, Department of Media, Culture, and Communication, New York University.

Thelandersson, Fredrika. 2014. 'A Less Toxic Feminism: Can the Internet Solve the Age Old Question of How to Put Intersectional Theory into Practice?' *Feminist Media Studies* 14 (3):527–30. doi: 10.1080/14680777.2014.909169.

Thornham, Sue. 2007. *Women, Feminism and Media*. Edinburgh: Edinburgh University Press.

Thornton, Sarah 1995. *Club Cultures: Music, Media and Subcultural Capital*. Cambridge: Polity.

Thrift, Nigel. 2004. 'Intensities of Feeling: Towards a Spatial Politics of Affect'. *Geografiska Annaler: Series B, Human Geography* 86 (1):57–78. doi: 10.1111/j.0435-3684.2004.00154.x.

Thrift, Samantha. 2014. '#YesAllWomen as Feminist Meme Event'. *Feminist Media Studies* 14 (6):1090–2. doi: 10.1080/14680777.2014.975421.

Tiidenberg, Katrin, Natalie Ann Hendry, and Crystal Abidin. 2021. *tumblr*. Cambridge: Polity.

Transformative Works and Cultures. 2020. 'Submission Preparation Checklist', accessed 01 April 2020. https://journal.transformativeworks.org/index.php/twc/about/submissions.

Tuchman, Gaye. 1979. 'Women's Depiction by the Mass Media'. *Signs* 4 (3):528–42.

Tuck, Eve, and K. Wayne Yang. 2013. *Youth Resistance Research and Theories of Change*. Edited by Eve Tuck and K. Wayne Yang. London: Routledge.

tumblr staff. 2022. 'This Is Not a Drill. Our New Community Guidelines Are Here'. Last Modified 01 November 2022, accessed 07 December 2022. https://www.tumblr.com/staff/699744158019190784/this-is-not-a-drill-our-new-community-guidelines.

Turk, Tisha. 2014. 'Fan Work: Labor, Worth, and Participation in Fandom's Gift Economy'. *Transformative Works and Cultures* (15). doi: 10.3983/twc.2014.0518.

Valenti, Jessica. 2009. 'The Fourth Wave(s) of Feminism'. accessed 14 November 2017. http://jessicavalenti.com/2009/11/14/the-fourth-waves-of-feminism/.

Valenti, Jessica. 2014. 'When Everyone Is a Feminist, Is Anyone?', accessed 30 March 2017. https://www.theguardian.com/commentisfree/2014/nov/24/when-everyone-is-a-feminist.

van Dijck, José. 2013. '"You Have One Identity": Performing the Self on Facebook and LinkedIn'. *Media, Culture & Society* 35 (2):199–215. doi: 10.1177/0163443712468605.

van Zoonen, Liesbet. 1992. 'The Women's Movement and the Media: Constructing a Public Identity'. *European Journal of Communication* 7:453–76.

van Zoonen, Liesbet. 1994. *Feminist Media Studies*. London: Sage.

Vander Wal, Thomas. 2007. 'Folksonomy Coinage and Definition', accessed 20 August 2022. http://vanderwal.net/folksonomy.html.

Varghese, Neema, and Navin Kumar. 2020. 'Feminism in Advertising: Irony or Revolution? A Critical Review of Femvertising'. *Feminist Media Studies*:1–19. doi: 10.1080/14680777.2020.1825510.

Villesèche, Florence, Sara Louise Muhr, and Martyna Śliwa. 2018. 'From Radical Black Feminism to Postfeminist Hashtags: Re-claiming Intersectionality'. *Emphemera: Theory & Politics in Organization* 18 (1):1–16.

Wånggren, Lena. 2016. 'Our Stories Matter: Storytelling and Social Justice in the Hollaback! Movement'. *Gender and Education* 28 (3):401–15. doi: 10.1080/09540253.2016.1169251.

Warfield, Katie. 2016. '"Reblogging Someone's Selfie Is Seen as a Really Nice Thing to Do:" Spatiality and Emplacement within a Non-dominant Platform Vernacular on Tumblr', Association of Internet Researchers Conference, Berlin, Germany, October 5–8.

Warner, Kristen. 2015. 'ABC's Scandal and Black Women's Fandom'. In *Cupcakes, Pinterest, and Ladyporn: Feminized Popular Culture in the Early Twenty-First Century*, edited by Elana Levine, 32–50. Urbana, IL: University of Illinois Press.

Warner, Kristen. 2018. '(Black Female) Fans Strike Back: The Emergence of the Iris West Defense Squad'. In *The Routledge Companion to Media Fandom*, edited by Melissa A. Click and Suzanne Scott, 253–61. Oxon: Routledge.

Watercutter, Angela. 2019. 'The Internet Needs Tumblr More Than Ever'. *Wired*, accessed 06 November 2019. https://www.wired.com/story/tumblr-reinvigorated/.

Weber, Sandra, and Claudia Mitchell. 2007. 'Imagining, Keyboarding, and Posting Identities: Young People and New Media Technologies'. In *Youth, Identity, and Digital Media*, edited by David Buckingham, 25–48. Cambridge, MA: MIT Press.

Wekker, Gloria. 2016. *White Innocence: Paradoxes of Colonialism and Race*. Durham, NC: Duke University Press.

Wetherell, Margaret. 2012. *Affect and Emotion: A New Social Science Understanding*. London: Sage.

Wexler, Philip. 1992. *Becoming Somebody: Toward a Social Psychology of School*. London: Falmer Press.

Whannel, Garry. 2010. 'News, Celebrity, and Vortextuality: A Study of the Media Coverage of the Michael Jackson Verdict'. *Cultural Politics* 6 (1):65–84. doi: 10.2752/175174310X12549254318782.

Whiteman, Natasha. 2012. *Undoing Ethics: Rethinking Practice in Online Research*. New York, NY: Springer.

Williams, Bronwyn, and Amy Zenger. 2012. *New Media Literacies and Participatory Popular Culture across Borders*. New York, NY: Routledge.

Wills, Emily Regan. 2013. 'Fannish Discourse Communities and the Construction of Gender in the X-Files'. *Transformative Works and Cultures* 14. doi: 10.3983/twc.2013.0410.

Winch, Alison. 2012. 'The Girlfriend Gaze'. *Soundings* (52):21–32.

Winch, Alison. 2013. *Girlfriends and Postfeminist Sisterhood*. Basingstoke: Palgrave Macmillan.

Woo, Benjamin. 2018. 'The Invisible Bag of Holding: Whiteness and Media Fandom'. In *The Routledge Companion to Media Fandom*, edited by Melissa A. Click and Suzanne Scott, 245–52. Oxon: Routledge.

Wyn, Johanna, and Rob White. 1997. *Rethinking Youth*. London: Sage.

Yancy, George. 2012. *Look, a White!: Philosophical Essays on Whiteness*. Philadelphia, PA: Temple University Press.

Yancy, George. 2017. *Black Bodies, White Gazes: The Continuing Significance of Race in America*. 2nd edn. Lanham, MD: Rowman & Littlefield.

Yodovich, Neta. 2021. 'Defining Conditional Belonging: The Case of Female Science Fiction Fans'. *Sociology (Oxford)* 55 (5):871–87. doi: 10.1177/0038038520949848.

Yodovich, Neta. 2022. *Women Negotiating Feminism and Science Fiction Fandom: The Case of the 'Good' Fan.* Cham, Switzerland: Palgrave Macmillan.

Yuval-Davis, Nira. 2006. 'Belonging and the Politics of Belonging'. *Patterns of Prejudice* 40 (3):197–214.

Zaslow, Emilie. 2009. *Feminism, INC.: Coming of Age in Girl Power Media Culture.* New York, NY: Palgrave Macmillan.

Zobl, Elke, and Ricarda Drüeke. 2012. *Feminist Media: Participatory Spaces, Networks and Cultural Citizenship.* Bielefeld, Germany: Transcript.

Zubernis, Lynn, and Katherine Larsen. 2012. *Fandom at the Crossroads: Celebration, Shame and Fan/Producer Relationships.* Newcastle upon-Tyne: Cambridge Scholars.

Zubernis, Lynn, and Kelsey Davis. 2016. 'Growing Pains: The Changing Ethical Landscape of Fan Studies'. *Journal of Fandom Studies* 4 (3):301–206.

Index